SUPERVISOR TRAINING

Guide to Supervision Series
Published and distributed by Karnac Books

Other titles in the Series

A Different Wisdom: Reflections on Supervision Practice
Penny Henderson

Orders

Tel: +44 (0)20 7431 1075; Fax: +44 (0)20 7435 9076

E-mail: shop@karnacbooks.com

www.karnac books.com

SUPERVISOR TRAINING
Issues and Approaches

edited by

Penny Henderson

KARNAC

First published in 2009 by
Karnac Books Ltd
118 Finchley Road, London NW3 5HT

British Library Cataloguing in Publication Data

A C.I.P. for this book is available from the British Library

ISBN 978 1 85575 402 7

Edited, designed and produced by The Studio Publishing Services Ltd
www.publishingservicesuk.co.uk
e-mail: studio@publishingservicesuk.co.uk

Printed in Great Britain

www.karnacbooks.com

CONTENTS

ACKNOWLEDGEMENTS

Many colleagues have contributed to the book. First, and most profoundly, thanks go to the authors of the chapters who have engaged full heartedly in the project, and tolerated my requests for re-writes and even cuts with generosity.

Second, thanks to colleagues who have read my contributions, most particularly Caro Bailey, Brigid Proctor, Hazel Johns, and Anthea Millar. You have sustained me in the moments of difficulty as author and editor, and encouraged and advised me in ways only you know.

Members of my supervision development group, and of the Cambridge Supervision Training (CST) staff team, and current and past students on the courses, have been and are hugely influential. Thank you.

Acknowledgement is also due for permission to reproduce illustrations as follows.

To TMS Development International, for permission to reproduce Figures 3.1 and 3.2, and Table 3.1.

To Sue Wheeler for permission to reproduce Figure 9.1.

ABOUT THE EDITOR AND CONTRIBUTORS

Caro Bailey is a British Association for Counselling and Psychotherapy (BACP) accredited counsellor and supervisor. She has worked for over thirty years as a counsellor, supervisor, and trainer. She works in private practice in Bristol and with colleagues on the CASCADE Training Supervision course.

Valerie Batts, PhD, is Executive Director and co-founder of VISIONS Inc., a consulting organization that helps individuals and groups effectively to recognize, understand, and appreciate differences (www.visions-inc.org). She leads the consultation and training components of the company. Author of *Modern Racism: New Melody for the Same Old Tune,* she is the originator of the VISIONS training model and experiential workshops. As a licensed clinical psychologist, she provides training to human service providers, clinicians, educators, and managers, nationally and internationally, to develop and maintain environments that support, respect, and appreciate differences.

Rose Battye is a counsellor and psychotherapist, registered with BACP and UKCP. Having worked for eighteen years in the NHS, subsequently she has worked as an independent practitioner. She has co-tutored, with Anna Gilchrist, supervision courses in the person-centred approach to supervision since 1998, and over the years has worked as a trainer in various subjects, including supervision, with other counselling and psychotherapy institutions.

Roger Casemore is Senior Teaching Fellow and Director of Counselling and Psychotherapy Courses at the University of Warwick. He has been in private practice as a person-centred therapist for over forty years and as a supervisor for over thirty years. He is a Chartered Fellow of the Chartered Institute of Personnel and Development, a Fellow and past Chair of BACP, and is currently a member of the Professional Ethics and Practice Committee.

Suzanne Dennis, BA, MSc, CQSW, is a chartered counselling psychologist and BACP accredited supervisor of individuals and groups. As senior trainer and supervisor at the Psychosynthesis and Education Trust, she developed and co-tutored the Trust's supervision course. She has set up and delivered workplace counselling services for two local authorities, and has over ten years' experience as a manager in a large organization. She has trained in a range of approaches to therapeutic work, and has been working with individuals, couples, and groups for over twenty-five years. She has a private practice in counselling, psychotherapy, and supervision in South Devon and in London.

Christine Driver is a Professional Member of the SAP (Society of Analytical Psychology) and a training therapist of FPC (Foundation for Psychotherapy and Counselling). She is Director of Training and Clinical Services at WPF Therapy, and previously ran their supervision trainings. She is also in private practice. She has written and co-edited (with E. Martin) two books on supervision: *Supervising Psychotherapy* (Sage, 2002), and *Supervision and the Analytic Attitude* (Whurr, 2005) and was Chair of BAPPS (British Association for Psychoanalytic and Psychodynamic Supervision).

Anna Gilchrist is a BACP registered counsellor and psychotherapist. She has had an independent private practice for twenty years as a counsellor, supervisor, and trainer. Since 1998, she has co-designed and tutored a supervision course with Rose Battye.

Alec Grant is a British Association for Behavioural and Cognitive Therapies (BABCP) accredited supervisor, trainer, and practitioner. He is the course leader for the PGDip/MSc in Cognitive Therapy and the Increased Access to Psychological Therapies (IAPT) PGDip in Cognitive Behavioural Therapy at the University of Brighton. His doctoral research focused on the organisational mediation and uptake of clinical supervision and he is an advocate of real time-equivalent (DVDs, audio- and video-based) forms of clinical supervision.

Penny Henderson is a BACP accredited counsellor, supervisor, and Fellow. After twenty-seven years as a counsellor, trainer, and supervisor, she is still involved in supervision, supervision training, writing, and research. She has published books, chapters, and articles about adult learning, training group workers, exam stress, counselling in primary care, medical education, and supervision.

Julie Hewson, BA (Hons), PGCE, Dip. SW, CQSW, TSTA, CTA, is Director of the Iron Mill Institute, a BACP registered supervisor, registered with UKCP, and a trainer and supervisor for the European Association of Supervision. She is a painter, photographer, and writer of short stories, and a trained mediator, coach, and coaching trainer. With colleagues, she set up the Czech Institute of Supervision, and worked in Prague. The Iron Mill Institute runs both national and European accredited courses in psychotherapy, counselling, supervision, coaching and management. This reflects the range of her application of psychological and other areas of expertise, including conflict resolution, mediation, supervision, consultancy, and teaching.

Francesca Inskipp has been involved in the counselling field since 1970 as trainer, supervisor, counsellor, writer, and broadcaster. With Brigid Proctor, she started CASCADE training for supervisors. She still maintains a small practice of supervision and counselling, and runs occasional supervision workshops with Brigid. She has been an active member of BACP since its beginning as an organization, and is an accredited supervisor and Fellow.

Anthea Millar, MA, is a counsellor, supervisor, and counselling/supervision educator. As a BACP accredited counsellor, she works in independent practice, and is also director of a four-year counselling training in Cambridge. With Penny Henderson, she co-founded Cambridge Supervision Training, which runs assessed supervision training and continuing professional development workshops for supervisors. She also regularly offers training in other parts of Europe, more recently in Latvia, Greece, and Hungary.

Antonia Murphy is a CPC Registered Member and Supervisor Member, is UKCP registered and BACP senior accredited. She graduated from WPF psychodynamic counselling, counselled in primary care, then became Co-ordinator of the Southern Derbyshire Managed Counselling Service. She is involved in the national delivery of counselling and psychotherapy in primary care as Director of Professional Standards for CPC (the Association of Counsellors and Psychotherapists in Primary Care). She is course director of CPC's specialist supervision training programme, and continues to work clinically alongside her strategic roles. She is the author of several papers on aspects of psychotherapeutic practice in primary care and the wider NHS. She was formerly editor of the *Journal for the Foundation of Psychotherapy and Counselling*, and is currently an editorial board member of the *Journal of Psychodynamic Practice* and editor of the *CPC Review*. She is co-author of *Psychological Therapies in Primary Care: Setting up a Managed Service* (Karnac, 2004).

Brigid Proctor, formerly Director of Counselling Courses at South West London College, has worked as trainer, supervisor, supervisor trainer, external assessor, consultant, and writer since retirement. She was active in the development of BACP and its various committees and is a Fellow of BACP. With Francesca Inskipp, she has co-created Open Learning Materials for supervisors and supervisees, while initiating Cascade Training Associates. She has long been driven by a desire for integrative counselling and psychotherapy that could be focused on working appropriately with the wide variety of clients, rather than counsellor preference. In 1978, she wrote/edited *Counselling Shop* (Burnett Books), in which she interviewed ten practitioners seeking wider integrative frameworks in their different theoretical and practice bases. She has contributed to many books on supervision and supervision training, and the second edition *of Group Supervision: A Guide to Creative Practice* was published by Sage in 2008.

Charlotte Sills is a UKCP registered integrative psychotherapist and BACP accredited supervisor in private practice. She is also a teaching and supervising transactional analyst, the former Head of the Transactional Analysis Department at Metanoia Institute and a Visiting Professor at Middlesex University. She is the author or co-author of several books and articles in the field of counselling and therapy, including, with Helena Hargaden, the EBMA award winning *Transactional Analysis: A Relational Perspective* (Routledge, 2002).

Michael Townend is a Reader in Cognitive Behavioural Psychotherapy and a BABCP accredited therapist, BABCP accredited supervisor, BABCP accredited trainer, and Fellow of the Higher Education Academy. He is a programme leader at the University of Derby.

Carole Waskett After many years of primary care counselling, being supervised and supervising, she now teaches, coaches, and works with NHS staff teams, within an NHS Trust and as a private practitioner. Once a psychodynamic therapist, she has made a complete shift to a solution-focused approach. She is always moving towards simplicity, pragmatism, and humour, both in and outside work.

Wendy Wood is a Senior Lecturer in Counselling and Psychotherapy and programme leader at the University of Derby.

Introduction

This book aims to create a lively and readable resource that will be informative and inspirational for those planning training for supervisors of counsellors, or who create, teach on, or apply for supervisor training. It is intended to be consciously forward looking in a period of rapid development, and is designed to highlight *differences* between providers as well as the approaches and ideas they share. It is the work of eighteen authors, all of whom are, or have been, involved in supervisor training in the UK.

Supervision courses are designed to meet and respond to the needs of senior practitioners. This entails support for them to engage with real dilemmas, and encouragement to work out their own solutions. Courses must be connected to whatever the current political and professional developments require.

Considering how much experience there now is in providing supervisor training in the UK, relatively little has been written about it. Some published details of course design and curricula created by UK trainers are referred to in Chapter One. A shared value among these authors is that supervision is a practical activity; thus, that experience, including observed practice with feedback, is crucial. Participants need courses whose structure and process mirrors what is to be learnt by way of values, skills, and approaches.

The book might well also be of interest to colleagues involved in training supervisors in other contexts and allied professions: social work, medical and nursing professions, coaching, and teaching. The chapters span a range of theoretical approaches to supervisor training, and authors thus inevitably write from quite different basic assumptions about supervision. They call on a huge range of published resources, many only available in journal articles within their particular modality that have not entered the mainstream. One great gift, thus, is the lists of references for each chapter.

Considering difference

The following questions may be a prompt to reflect on the contribution each chapter makes to the development of supervision training in general.

1. How do the ideas of each chapter develop supervision training *in general*? How do they fit with your own particular interests and approach?
2. What are the implicit and explicit assumptions about supervision within the models and approaches being described?
3. What would be different, easy, or difficult in these ideas for a supervisee from the theoretical modality within which you work?
4. Are the ideas applicable to your practice or a course you teach?
5. How many of the references they offer have you read?

Some bases for understanding about supervision

A definition of supervision now widely used was provided by Inskipp & Proctor (2001), and used as a basis for a research review by Wheeler (2003):

> A working alliance between the supervisor and counsellor in which the counsellor can offer an account or recording of her work, reflect on it, receive feedback and, where appropriate, guidance. The object of this alliance is to enable the counsellor to gain in ethical competence, confidence, compassion and creativity in order to give of her best possible service to her client. [p. 8]

There is a distinction between the functions and purposes of supervision. The primary purposes are to "ensure the welfare of clients and enhance the development of the supervisee in relation to professional practice". Different orientations and practitioners emphasize these two foci differently. Some assert that, barring live supervision, it is impossible to "ensure" the welfare of a client whom the supervisor has never met. For many, the focus is on the development and support of the supervisee, with the intention that the supervision will support and enable the supervisee's practice in the ways detailed in the Inskipp and Proctor extract.

To achieve this purpose, three main functions are commonly identified.

Educative function. This focuses on encouraging the development of supervisees' skills, abilities, understanding, personal awareness, and academic knowledge.

*Supportive and creative function.*This encourages supervisees to acknowledge and explore how personal issues, their own life events, and responses to clients affect their work. Supervisors need to be aware of elements that might be affecting supervisees' capacity to fulfil their roles and duties while not overstepping a boundary between supervision and therapy. More positively, this function supports creativity and liveliness in the work.

Managerial function. This involves supporting, appraising and assessing a supervisee's work against the norms and standards of the profession, society, or context by referring to ethical codes or organizational or legal requirements. This function may dominate when supervising trainee practitioners, where there may also be a formal or informal assessment role, and be particularly salient within organizational work where audit is a high priority, but it is also an essential element for all supervisory contracts.

In practice, supervision commonly intertwines these functions. The needs of supervisees and the stage of their career may determine which one takes precedence. It also varies with the interests and competency of supervisors and their interpretation and understanding of their responsibilities in providing supervision and the purpose it serves.

Good practice in supervision

Supervisors generally agree on the importance of an effective working alliance with supervisees. Safety in the relationship may support openness to reflection and maximum disclosure of difficulties and matters affecting fitness to practise. A safe relationship is enhanced by:

- clear negotiated contracts about expectations, aims, and functions;
- discussion of responsibilities and accountability, especially concerning welfare of clients, and relationships with employer or training organizations;
- development of a non-threatening atmosphere to facilitate an honest working alliance;
- supervisor and supervisee both being open to learning and respectful of differing learning styles;
- needs of the supervisee normally, though not exclusively, taking precedence over those of the supervisor;
- process and quality of supervision itself being reviewed regularly.

Research information about supervision and supervision training

The systematic scoping research reviews by Wheeler (2003), and Wheeler and Richards (2007) aimed to provide baselines for future UK-based research about supervision and outcomes of supervision. Wheeler (2003) identified 388 research sources, eleven of which were conducted in the UK, and only six about experienced practitioners. Of the twenty-eight that were about supervision training, none was directly about UK courses.

In a second review, of research on the impact of supervision (Wheeler & Richards, 2007), two items met their inclusion criteria for good methodology, and none relates to supervisor training. As in the previous review, most studies were from the USA, and about supervision of trainee counsellors. They found two studies that indicated that *self-awareness* is enhanced through supervision, five that provided evidence of *skill development* as a product of supervision, five that examined supervision and *self-efficacy*, two that considered the relevance of *timing* of supervision, two that explored *theoretical orientation*, one that reviewed *support and challenge* in supervision, and three that tried *to assess client outcomes*. Unsatisfactory though some of the methodologies might be, these indicative resources suggest topics for further research, and for designers of supervisor training courses to bear in mind. If supervisors and supervisees believe supervision to be useful, it is important to find and share research methodologies to test these beliefs, and capitalize on reflective practice for evidence that researchers can accept as valid.

BACP undertook a mapping exercise carried out by Docchar (2007) (internal document) to identify details about supervisor training courses. Initial results suggest there were more than eighty supervisor training courses within further and higher education and private institutions, 75% at diploma level or above. She could not identify obvious equivalence between similar qualifications.

Stevens, Goodyear, and Robertson (1997), in the USA, concluded that experience and supervision training *together* and not length of experience *alone* was associated with more supportive, less critical, and less dogmatic supervisory thoughts (quoted in Wheeler, 2003, p. 47). This is a potentially productive finding, worthy of further exploration in the UK to identify if it applies here. If supervisor training does improve on straightforward length of experience, what elements of it enable more encouraging frames of thought? Miller, Hubble, and Duncan (2008) identified the importance for highly effective *therapists* of working harder to improve performance by reaching for objectives just beyond one's level of proficiency and checking outcomes. That is, combining intentional practice with direct feedback that is specific about the next developmental step.

Accreditation expectations

Criteria for individuals to be accredited/registered are variable, and currently much in flux and development. In September 2008, the accredited supervisors from UK professional organizations totalled close to five hundred (BACP, 310; CPC, 82; BABCP, 46; EATA/ITAA, 107) plus the 198 registered BAPPS supervisors. Thus, five hundred accredited supervisors serve a population of many tens of thousands of accredited counsellors, non-accredited counsellors, trainees, and others wanting supervision. The majority of supervisors are neither accredited nor trained on an assessed course.

BACP currently does not, in 2008, have a scheme to recognize training courses for supervisors, and has yet to undertake the work that would lead to this, although Counselling and Psychotherapy in Scotland (COSCA) has gone down this path. The British Association for Psychoanalytic and Psychodynamic Supervision (BAPPS) was originally set up by people involved with one course, and registered members are expected to have had some training in supervision or considerable experience, and be registered or accredited as a counsellor or psychotherapist by one of a number of professional bodies. Sills, in this volume, describes how transactional analysis has created integrated structures within national and international TA Associations (EATA/ITAA).

Regulation and supervision competences

Predictions in Autumn 2008 are that regulation of counsellors by the Health Professions Council will be in place by 2011. The Increased Access to Psychological Therapies (IAPT) initiative has developed some initial competences for supervisors as a part of another governmental initiative. For details consult the University College London, website: http://www.ucl.ac.uk/clinical-psychology/CORE/competence_frameworks.htm or the IAPT website: www.iapt.nhs.uk/2008/02/supervision_competences_framework, or http://www.iapt.nhs.uk/2008/12/iapt-supervision-guidance/

There will be implications for training supervisors if the professional bodies lean primarily on the competences model for supervisor accreditation or research. Competences strip out assessment of knowledge in favour of "abilities", i.e., observable performance, often stated generally. There is little reference to creativity or a restorative function. The analysis is functional rather than relational. Yet, this book reveals fundamentally differing assumptions about supervision among senior practitioners that are obscured by the competences' disinterest in knowledge and assumptions. A benefit might be that competences connect to National Occupational

Standards and thus could support development of supervision across the professions.

The impact of the process of regulation, driven by governmental imperatives, has been and will be considerable. There is a current culture, exacerbated by government-funded initiatives, for services designed to follow manuals and be protocol based, and these are anathema to many counselling and supervisory approaches. There are risks that supervision will be squeezed out from highly pressured jobs within organizations without a culture that values reflective practice. Until there is a firmer evidence base, this is a particular risk for experienced practitioners.

Trainers of supervisors can contribute to the development of our professional organization's grasp, and representation, of supervision in these interesting times. I hope this book will contribute, too.

Penny Henderson
April 2009

References

Docchar, C. (2007). Mapping of UK Supervision Courses for counsellors and psychotherapists (BACP internal document).

Inskipp, F., & Proctor, B. (2001). *The Art, Craft and Tasks of Counselling Supervision, Part 1: Making the Most of Supervision* (2nd edn). Twickenham: Cascade.

Miller, S., Hubble, M., & Duncan, B. (2008). Supershrinks. *Therapy Today, 19*(3): 4–9.

Stevens, D. T., Goodyear, R. K., & Robertson, P. (1997). Supervisor development: an exploratory study in changes in stance and emphasis. *Clinical Supervisor, 16*(2): 72–88.

Supervision competences frameworks accessed at:

www.ucl.ac.uk/clinicalpsychology/CORE/supervision_framework

www.iapt.nhs.uk/2008/02/supervision_competences_framework

Wheeler, S. (2003). *Research on Supervision of Counsellors and Therapists: A Systematic Scoping Search.* Lutterworth: BACP.

Wheeler, S., & Richards, K. (2007). *The Impact of Clinical Supervision on Counsellors and Therapists, Their Practice and Their Clients. A Systematic Review of the Literature.* Lutterworth: BACP.

PART I

ISSUES

CHAPTER ONE

Training supervisors

Penny Henderson

This chapter provides a platform for the book by condensing many publications that signal the development of some British ideas in the last twenty years. It covers curriculum development and content, the creation of congruent values between the process of supervision being studied and the curriculum and methodology of the course, the aims of a course, and underlying principles. Consensus between authors is striking around the need to embody core values about supervision in the processes of the training.

Although there is no single acknowledged and generally agreed core curriculum for supervisor training, the ideas of Inskipp and Proctor (1993, 1995), Hawkins and Shohet (2006), and Page and Wosket (2001) are particularly influential. With no agreement in professional bodies or between course providers about appropriate length and style of courses for different levels of supervisory qualification, Docchar's research (2007) could not assess the depth at which elements are addressed or identify equivalence between them. Applicants find it difficult to know from course advertisements which course might best suit their needs.

Up to the1980s, many counsellors took on the supervisor role as a natural developmental step, as if this role demanded no more than experience as a counsellor and as a supervisee. Some became supervisors after many years of practice, others during or soon after completing counsellor training, largely because of their prior or other roles and experience in youth work, social work, and education or health settings. Few training courses were available for supervisors, so a minority undertook significant training. Little theory about supervision was widely available until the 1990s. An apprenticeship model was the norm, and for many people it is still the preferred route to becoming a supervisor. Stewart (2006) describes this as learning through "the crucible of experience". Even in the early years of writing about supervisor training, there were authors who wanted to encourage readers not to assume that there is a natural career progression from counselling to supervision. Rather, they assert, these are different activities, requiring distinct skills, qualities, frames of mind, and theoretical approaches (Clarkson & Gilbert, 1991).

Specifically, supervisors have to combine relevant ideas and material with finely-tuned intuition and awareness of sensory clues within the supervisory relationship. They benefit from clarity about roles and tasks, and the potential choices of focus within supervision. They must develop ethical problem-solving skills, and specific supervisory skills. Supervisors and supervisor trainers also need flexibility to engage with people whose learning styles differ from their own, particularly when these people have had prior bad experiences at school.

The therapy and supervision professions are changing rapidly. A degree level qualification will be required for therapists when regulation is implemented. Many people are training as counsellors at a younger age, some in their twenties as a first career. Some people apply to train as a supervisor after three years experience or less following initial qualification as a counsellor, even when they have undertaken counsellor training relatively early in life. This is not considered unusual among other colleagues, such as clinical and counselling psychologists, who often find themselves supervising older and more experienced colleagues because of their role or status. Some who advertise themselves as "experienced" supervisors might not have done more than a few years of supervision and might have little or no formal training in it (Henderson, 2006).

Identifying training needs

Hawkins and Shohet (2006) propose that new supervisors carry out a self-appraisal and assessment of their learning needs under the following headings:

- knowledge: the purpose and boundaries of supervision, the types of supervision;
- supervision management skills: explaining the purpose of supervision, negotiating a contract, maintaining boundaries;
- supervision intervention skills: they frame these in terms of Heron's (1975) six-category intervention analysis;
- traits or qualities, including having commitment, using authority appropriately, being sensitive and adaptable, having a sense of humour, and ethical maturity;
- commitment to own ongoing development, including supervision, commitment to professional and personal development, recognizing limitations, and getting feedback.

They emphasize the importance of exploring the concept of empathy, and of working out its expression in the supervisory relationship (*ibid.*, p. 131). Reflecting the increase in training opportunities since 2000, they propose five distinct foci for supervisor training courses. These convey the complexities of supervision, and thus the impossibility of dealing adequately with these issues within one short course or at an initial stage.

1. Core supervision course for new supervisors.
2, Core supervision for student and practice supervisors.
3. Courses in group and team supervision for those who supervise in team or group settings.
4. Therapeutic supervision courses for those who supervise in-depth counselling or psychotherapy or other therapeutic work.
5. Advanced supervision courses for those who have to supervise across teams and organizations or teach supervisors or want to become advanced practitioners.

Decisions to attend Certificate, or "core", courses may be made pragmatically, determined by time available to study, or as a "toe in the water" process to find out if supervision is a desired next career step. Participants might have extensive experience of supervision *as a supervisee,* and sometimes from having practised as a supervisor. They will be used to reflection. A course with a pragmatic practice base is valuable for those practitioners who are unwilling to put time and money aside to study for another degree, but who want some frameworks for thought, feedback on observed practice, or reassurance that their practice is sound, over and above what is available from attending a conference session or day workshop.

Course requirements and assessment

Course requirements specify criteria for application, attendance, and assignments. The Quality Assurance Agency for Higher Education (QAA) *academic* levels (2001) provide a resource for course designers to create course outcomes or propose specific learning aims in terms of Doctorates, Masters, Honours, Intermediate, and Certificate levels. However, supervision courses do not fit neatly with this academic hierarchy until they are offered at Masters level, because Certificate and Diploma courses that are primarily focused on professional development are not necessarily related to, or integrated with, academic standards.

Supervision courses might serve some participants who have prior degrees or higher education experiences and many who do not. Participants' professional experience could mean they are, or can become, capable of "critical analysis", "originality of application", or "creative syntheses of ideas", which, in QAA terms, fits at Masters level. The course *assessment criteria,* however, might not require this of all who qualify. This leaves some course designers at Certificate and Diploma levels uncertain about appropriate standards when the course is not recognized by a university or accrediting body. Some groups of practitioners or private training institutions offer short supervision courses, and have to invent their own standards as well as their curriculum topics. If the professional bodies do not wish to recognize or register Supervision Diploma training courses, perhaps most courses should be encouraged to register with one of the awarding institutions, such as ABC, or the Counselling and Psychotherapy Central Awarding Body (CPCAB), or with a university. However, this increases course costs substantially.

Courses that are registered have to ensure that written assignments (process analyses, reflective practice reports, essays, or portfolios) are linked to the aims of the course and to explicit criteria that have an obvious relationship with the theoretical orientation and academic level of the course. Professional Practice assessment can be done live, or through recorded materials with written reflections, and assessed by observation and reflection by the participant, by peers, and by the trainers. Masters level courses, because of their university locations and resources, provide more opportunities to study at the forefront of related academic disciplines. Critical analysis of texts and capacity to understand, use, and undertake research is supported and expected, and assessment has to be geared to this academic level.

It is useful to separate the requirements for the completion of a course from those necessary to complete a qualification. The latter might require practice hours, supervision hours, and external reports or references about the trainee supervisor's practice. For Increased Access to Psychological Therapies (IAPT), supervisor qualification might some day be linked to competences such as those identified by CORE (2008) or National Occupational Standards (NOS, 2008) or accreditation processes used by professional bodies. There is, as yet, little consensus on what constitutes a "qualified" or "experienced" supervisor (Henderson, 2006).

Core values and course philosophy

Clarkson and Gilbert (1991, pp. 143–169) noted some necessary shifts in frames of reference for counsellors who are training as supervisors. These arise from the change in role, and include a different sort of responsibility for clients they will never meet, and the need for more and different skills. Their summary of core concepts, below, is informed by values many counsellors and supervisors can still be expected to share almost twenty years later.

- To foster the creative drive of human beings to learn and develop.
- To respect individual differences and delight in them. Staffing contributes to this by including role models who are different.
- To convey a valuing of individual responsibility for behaviour, and responsibility towards others.
- To have a congruent value system underlying the materials to be taught.

- To embrace the paradox of valuing tradition while also being willing to change, and to learn by discovery and reflection and self direction. To foster the creative drive of human beings to learn and develop.

Weston (2004) describes how developing a training for couple supervisors in Scotland challenged their working party to clarify what they really believed in about life, as well as supervision and counselling. Their bedrock principles were that the training process needed to offer the freedom to be vulnerable and admit ignorance and mistakes, the valuing of widely different personalities and skills, and an egalitarian culture that minimized the abuse of power. They began with first principles to consider what couple counselling services needed from supervision, why they were offering a supervision course, what kind of course, what level was appropriate, and so on. There was also a focus on specific skills of supervising couple counsellors. Thus, the course developed from their assessment of training needs for an organization, and their wish to convey and embody the qualities of a good supervisory relationship. The philosophical focus was on relationships, integrity, power, and human potential. The practical implications were that "The way we taught was almost more important than what we taught".

Their decision to co-tutor emerged from the team development process. They wished to model different but complementary styles of supervising, and to demonstrate in their own relationship the egalitarian principles they wanted to inculcate. "Our differences kept us balanced."

Pocknell (2001) was an early advocate of focus on difference and equality, and providing a space to explore attitudes and prejudices within a safe learning environment. Her core curriculum included what she described as the essential elements of supervision, and common factors independent of theoretical orientation: establishing clear contracts, building an effective supervisory relationship, and holding appropriate authority in the role of supervisor.

Curriculum and syllabus

Page and Wosket (2001) and Hawkins and Shohet (2006) clarified aims for detailed content in the curriculum. They agree on the need to develop a knowledge base, to develop a supervisory style and some specific skills, and to sustain a commitment to professional and personal development.

Page and Wosket (2001) refer to the British Association for Counselling and Psychotherapy (BACP) guidelines for accreditation of supervisors for their recommendations for the design and content of supervisor training. They recommend completing a training course if supervisors intend to offer supervision beyond their own core model of counselling. Their supervisor training course has *five broad aims* (pp. 255–263):

- to gain an understanding of various theories, models and approaches;
- to develop and practise a range of interventions and feedback skills relevant to the functions of supervision. This entails creating the opportunity to experiment, make mistakes, test out a style and take risks;
- to increase awareness of personal and professional strengths and areas for development;
- to enable the supervisor to develop their own informed style and approach to supervision, integrating theory and practice;
- to develop awareness of ethical and professional practice issues to enhance the professional identity of the supervisor and instil good standards and practice.

Development of personal awareness becomes salient for supervisors to build the relationship and understand parallel process. (Parallel process includes various forms of unconscious communication enacted between counsellor and supervisor.) The supervisor might be willing to make their internal struggles and sensations explicit to a supervisee in service of explorations of parallel process, and ask for the supervisee's reactions in understanding the relevance of this.

Hawkins and Shohet (2006) recommend *principles* to design supervisor training.

- Start with a focus on self-awareness, developed through experiential learning processes.
- Develop the individual's "authority, presence and impact" through high degrees of feedback in small groups where trainees undertake supervising with their peers.

- Teach basic skills and techniques in the most lively way possible, using demonstrations, illustrations, stories, engagement, and trainees' reflecting on experiences from their lives. Provide plenty of opportunity to practise and receive feedback.
- Teach theory only when experiential learning is already under way.
- "Just-in-time" learning: learning is most effective when the learner has already recognized the need for that piece of learning, and can apply the learning close to receiving it.
- "Real-time" learning: learning is greatly enhanced by the learners addressing real issues that are current and unresolved, rather than case studies from the past. They refer to this as "real play" rather than "role play".

After the initial training period, they argue, learners need a prolonged period of supervised practice before they return to create their own integration between self-awareness, skills, theory, and their experience of practice.

They note the crucial skill of giving feedback. They encourage readers to use Heron's (1975) six categories of intervention to identify preferred and avoided ways of relating. These are: prescriptive, informative, confrontative, cathartic, catalytic, supportive. They encourage trainees to use learning about skills or theoretical maps as an *action research tool* to find out more about their own supervision.

For their advanced supervision course, they recommend less structure, and more reflection on knowledge and skills already identified, plus use of interpersonal process recall (IPR), video, trigger tapes, work on ethical dilemmas, development of trans-cultural competence, issues dealing with appraisal, evaluation, and accreditation, and reflections on case material involving inter-agency dynamics. They observe that supervision training can never be a substitute for having good supervision oneself.

Publishing ten years apart, Clarkson and Gilbert (1991) and Wheeler (2001) concur on the ethical and contractual base for supervision, but otherwise reveal how choices within courses by well-established providers differ (Table 1).

Practising ethical decision-making is essential to both a counsellor and their supervisor. Each needs to be familiar with an ethical framework. Carroll (1996, pp. 159–165) describes a four-step process that begins with creating ethical sensitivity and formulating

Table 1.1. Curriculum comparison: Clarkson and Gilbert (1991) and Wheeler (2001).

Clarkson and Gilbert (1991) Generic curriculum content	Wheeler (2001) Generic curriculum content
The nature and varieties of relationship	*Comprehensive understanding of the ethical framework*
The importance and use of individual styles	*Ethical decision making*
Contracts and contracting	Clarity about lines of responsibility and accountability
Conceptual models	*Contracts with supervisees and with placement agencies*
Educational methods, means, and media	Risk assessment
Developmental stages of learning	Managing mistakes and complaints
Intervention strategies and techniques	Balancing support and confrontation
Timing and rhythm	*Organizational dynamics*
Selecting priorities and sequences	The dynamics of power and authority and its use
Transference, countertransference, and parallel process	Balancing supervision and psychotherapy
Values and ethics	Managing cultural diversity in supervision
Organizational or contextual factors	Equal opportunities issues that affect clients, supervisees, and organizations
Group dynamics, group development and group management: methods and goals	Recognizing limits of supervisory competence
Evaluation of process and outcome	Working with theoretical diversity
Special preparation for examination or assessment procedures	Assessing trainees
Self care and modelling of personal and professional development	Supervision modality: peer, group, telephone

a moral course of action, continues by implementing an ethical decision, and concludes with emphasis on the requirement to live with the ambiguities of an ethical decision. Several authors in Wheeler and King (2001) explore the dilemmas of supervisory responsibility in relation to supervisees. A number of extremely thorough and useful BACP information sheets emphasize the legal base, and the processes of ethical decision-making (BACP Information Sheets DG1, E6, G1, G2, P4, P11, P12, P14).

Gorell Barnes, Down, and McCann (2000) evaluate the practical and theoretical issues involved in implementing effective supervisory training within a family therapy practice, and examine the relationship between supervisor and trainee, and the implications for training, in terms of power, gender, ethnicity, and sexuality.

Tudor and Worrall (2007) describe a person-centred approach to learning and deconstruct the notion of a syllabus.

Current challenges in course focus

There are some key professional development issues to be addressed in supervision training. The first is sensitization to issues of difference and equality, to working trans-culturally as a supervisor, to noticing and taking account of the many differences of learning style, life style, race, class, age, gender, sexual identity, disability, and the related value-laden issues pertinent to supervisor or supervisee. This is crucial to practice in a post-industrial society operating within a global economy. Encouraging trainee supervisors to be interested in difference and how to explore it creates a base for a safe supervisory alliance (Henderson, 2009).

Another issue is development of a capacity to talk about the supervisory relationship itself, to review it regularly, to commit to speaking when there are uncomfortable feelings about it. Scaife (2009, p. 325) invites supervisors to take responsibility for their part of a difficulty in a working alliance: "Since the difficulty is being identified by the supervisor, it is the supervisor who is experiencing the problem and inviting the assistance of the supervisee in its solution". She offers a number of useful strategies to pursue this.

Most important of all, training can offer tools to encourage an atmosphere of safety and enable intentional "play" in supervision, so that the supervisee's concerns are non-judgementally explored, stuck feelings are released, and necessary issues are addressed.

This chapter charts considerable consensus about the value base of supervisor training and how it is to be conducted. The range of topics that are considered essential in training of differing theoretical orientations vary, as Part II of this book indicates, and it is clear that even the essentials cannot be explored in depth in most of the Certificate and Diploma training courses currently available. For the sake of applicants to courses, and any future recognition by regulatory authorities, more work on equivalence for basic training through a core curriculum, and options for post qualifying provision, is desirable.

Acknowledgement

Thanks to Keith Tudor for ideas incorporated here.

References

British Association for Counselling and Psychotherapy (2003). *Making Notes of Counselling and Psychotherapy Sessions*. Information Sheet P12.

British Association for Counselling and Psychotherapy (2005). *The Ethical Framework for Good Practice in Counselling and Psychotherapy within the NHS*. Information Sheet DG10.

British Association for Counselling and Psychotherapy (2009). *Confidential Guidelines for Reporting Child Abuse*. Information Sheet E6 (updated March 2009).

British Association for Counselling and Psychotherapy (2009). *Access to Counsellor Records*. Information Sheet G1 (updated March 2009).

British Association for Counselling and Psychotherapy (2009). *Confidentiality, Counselling and the Law*. Information Sheet G2 (updated March 2009).

British Association for Counselling and Psychotherapy (2009). *Guidance for Ethical Decision Making: A Suggested Model for Practitioners*. Information Sheet P4 (updated March 2009).

British Association for Counselling and Psychotherapy (2009). *Making a Contract for Counselling and Psychotherapy*. Information Sheet P11 (updated March 2009).

British Association for Counselling and Psychotherapy (2009). *Contingency Plans if Personal Crises Impact on Independent Practice*. Information Sheet P14 (updated March 2009).

Carroll, M. (1996). *Counselling Supervision: Theory, Skills and Practice*. London: Cassells.

Carroll, M. (1999). Training in the tasks of supervision. In: E. Holloway & M. Carroll (Eds.), *Training Counselling Supervisors* (pp. 44–66). London: Sage.

Clarkson, P., & Gilbert, M. (1991). The training of counsellor trainers and supervisors. In: W. Dryden & B. Thorne (Eds.), *Training and Supervision for Counselling in Action* (pp. 143–169). London: Sage.

Docchar, C. (2007). Mapping of UK Supervision Courses for counsellors and psychotherapists (BACP internal document).

Gorell Barnes, G., Down, G., & McCann, D. (2000). *Systemic Supervision: A Portable Guide for Supervisory Training*. London: Jessica Kingsley.

Hawkins, P., & Shohet, R. (2006). *Supervision in the Helping Professions*. Maidenhead: McGraw Hill.

Henderson, P. (2006). What is a qualified supervisor? *Therapy Today, 17*(10): 51–52.

Henderson, P. (2009). *A Different Wisdom: Reflections on Supervision Practice*. London: Karnac (in press).

Heron, J. (1975). *Six Category Intervention Analysis*. Guildford: University of Surrey Press.

IAPT Supervision Competences framework (2008). http://www.iapt.nhs.uk/2008/02/supervision-competences-framework (February) and www.ucl.ac.uk/clinicalpsychology/CORE/supervision_framework.

Inskipp, F., & Proctor, B. (1993 1st edn, 2001 2nd edn). *The Art, Craft and Tasks of Counselling Supervision, Part 1: Making the Most of Supervision*. Twickenham: Cascade.

Inskipp, F., & Proctor, B. (1995 1st edn, 2001 2nd edn). *The Art, Craft and Tasks of Counselling Supervision, Part 2 Becoming a Supervisor*. Twickenham: Cascade.

National Occupational Standards: http://www.ukstandards.org/Admin/DB/0049/GEN35.pdf

Page, S., & Wosket, V. (2001). *Supervising the Counsellor: A Cyclical Model*. London: Routledge.

Pocknell, C. (2001). Tutoring on a supervision training course. *Counselling and Psychotherapy Journal, 12*(4): 32–33.

Quality Assurance Agency for Higher Education (2001). *The Framework for Higher Education Qualifications in England, Wales and Northern Ireland*. Document available online at: http://www.qaa.ac.uk/academicinfrastructure/FHEQ/EWNI/default.asp or on the Karnac website: www.karnacbooks.com.

Scaife, J. (2009). *Supervision in Clinical Practice: A Practitioner's Guide*. London: Routledge.

Stewart, N. (2006). Training standards for supervisors in primary care. In: D. Hooper & P. Weitz (Eds.), *Psychological Therapies in Primary Care: Training and Training Standards* (pp. 112–141). London: Karnac.

Tudor, K., & Worrall, M. (2007). Training supervisors. In: K. Tudor & M. Worrall (Eds.), *Freedom to Practise II: Developing Person-Centred Approaches to Supervision* (pp. 211–219). Ross-on-Wye: PCCS Books.

Weston, H. (2004). Developing a supervision training course—the practicalities. *Therapy Today, 15*(10): 39–41.

Wheeler, S. (2001). Are supervisors born or trained? *Counselling and Psychotherapy Journal, 12*(10): 28–29.

Wheeler, S., & King, D. (Eds.) (2001). *Supervising Counsellors: Issues of Responsibility*. London: Sage.

CHAPTER TWO

It is all in the relationship: exploring the differences between supervision training and counselling training

Roger Casemore

Introduction and background

The scoping review of research evidence on the impact of supervision (Wheeler & Richard, 2007, p. 3) showed that, while there is little empirical evidence of the effectiveness of supervision in counselling and psychotherapy, there seems to be an implicit belief in the profession that it is an essential process. A generally held view is that supervision can provide emotional, psychological, practical, and professional support and containment for therapists and enable and possibly ensure maintenance of appropriate standards to protect clients. The history of supervision *training* is that it seems to have developed in a very *ad hoc* manner in the UK since it was first written about in 1988, when it was described as a process of "enabling and ensuring" (Marken & Payne, 1988).

In this chapter, I explore the differences I have experienced between training diploma students to become qualified therapists and enabling experienced therapists to gain a qualification in supervision. This suggests some issues about how supervision courses might need to be structured and run differently from counselling courses.

The relationship is the key

Carl Rogers wrote of the importance of the relationship in therapy (Rogers, 1951, pp. 51–56). He described central characteristics or attitudes of the therapist that need to be experienced by the client within the counselling relationship. He further postulated that these characteristics needed to be developed as an integrated part of the self of the therapist, as a way of being. I have long held the view that, in the person-centred approach, it is through a relationship where the client experiences those characteristics of the therapist that growth and healing takes place. I believe this also to be true of supervision and training relationships. In the same way that the nature of my relationship with a supervisee is very different from that with a client, so the relationships with students on certificate or diploma in counselling and psychotherapy courses are qualitatively different from those with participants on the supervision courses. I note that I have used the term "students" for those on the counselling courses and "participants" for those on the supervision course.

Differentiation

For me, that differentiation between students and participants is one key to differences between counselling training and supervision training. I see the participants in supervision courses as practitioners whose professional knowledge and experience is as valuable as mine, with whom I want to develop a collegial relationship, rather than as students, needing to be taught.

Another reason for differentiating between the training of therapists and supervisors is that supervision is not counselling writ large. Significant differences between counselling and supervision lie in the relationship between therapist and client *vs*. that between supervisor and supervisee. The functions of the supervisor are also very different from the functions of a therapist. I do believe that supervision can be therapeutic in that it enables change to take place, but it should never be therapy as such, or used as a substitute for therapy. I have some very real concerns about those who see supervision training as some kind of extension, or advanced stage, of therapist training, rather than training for a very different role and function. This misconception has led to some individuals wanting to go straight on from completing their counselling diploma to do a supervision course; I think anyone commencing supervision training should have been qualified for at least two years and should have at least four hundred and fifty hours of supervised counselling practice, to enable them to feel confident and competent enough to work effectively as a supervisor and for their supervisees to feel safe in the relationship.

As the purpose and functions of supervision seem to me to be distinctly different from those of counselling, it may be helpful at this point to identify some definitions that will help to differentiate between the two processes.

What is counselling?

The British Association for Counselling and Psychotherapy (BACP) definition of counselling: (BACP, 2007)

> Counselling takes place when a therapist sees a client in a private and confidential setting to explore a difficulty the client is having, distress they may be experiencing or perhaps their dissatisfaction with life, or loss of a sense of direction and purpose. It is always at the request of the client as no one can properly be "sent" for counselling . . .

What is supervision?

The BACP definition of supervision:

> Supervision is a formal arrangement for therapists to discuss their work regularly with someone who is experienced in counselling and supervision. The task is to work together to ensure and develop the efficacy of the therapist–client relationship. The agenda will be the counselling work and feelings about that work, together with the supervisor's reactions, comments and confrontations. Thus supervision is a process to maintain adequate standards of counselling and a method of consultancy to widen the horizons of an

> experienced practitioner. Though not concerned primarily with training, personal therapy or line management, supervisors will encourage and facilitate the ongoing self-development, continued learning and self-monitoring of the therapist. [Mearns, 2007, p. 1]

These definitions indicate that one of the most significant differences between counselling and supervision is the presence or absence of a requirement to attend. For counselling to be effective it must be a relationship of choice by the client; supervision is clearly a professional obligation, or requirement for every BACP practitioner, as defined in the Ethical Framework (BACP, 2007) and it is often a requirement imposed by employers as well.

The requirement for supervision and for supervision training

The Ethical Framework (BACP, 2007b) defines a requirement for supervision as follows:

> Beneficence:
>
> There is an obligation to use regular and on-going supervision to enhance the quality of the services provided and to commit to updating practice by continuing professional development.
>
> Self-respect:
>
> There is an ethical responsibility to use supervision for appropriate personal and professional support and development, and to seek training and other opportunities for continuing professional development.

Thus, BACP is unequivocal about this. I note that this Ethical Framework does not appear to require either therapists or supervisors to be trained and qualified, though it is now considered likely that this will change when regulation of the profession takes effect.

Basic assumptions about learning

I believe that the education of therapists and supervisors should be based on principles of the education of adults, rather than basing it on the principles of educating children, which largely come from Piaget (1972). His assumption is that the teacher has ownership of knowledge and the student will often be treated as an empty vessel into which the knowledge has to be decanted, a process known as pedagogy. Little account is taken of, or respect given to, the student's prior knowledge and experience. Paulo Freire defined this as the 'Banking concept of education' (Freire, 2001).

In *Andragogy in Action* (1984), Knowles defined four assumptions that adult educators should have about adult learning.

1. Adults move from dependency to self-directedness;
2. Adults draw upon their reservoir of experience for learning;
3. Adults are ready to learn when they assume new roles;
4. Adults want to solve problems and apply new knowledge immediately. [p. 12]

Accordingly, they suggested that adult educators should:

- set a cooperative learning climate;
- create mechanisms for mutual planning;
- arrange for a diagnosis of learner needs and interests;
- formulate learning objectives based on diagnosed needs and interests;
- design sequential activities for achieving the objectives;
- execute the design by selecting methods, materials, and resources; and
- evaluate the quality of the learning experience while re-diagnosing needs for further learning. [*ibid.*]

Freire suggested that education should be based on a relationship of dialogue between teacher and student in which the starting point for learning is the sum total of all the knowledge and experience of both tutor and student. Based on this, some years ago, I wrote about what I see as the important principles or assumptions that should form the basis of the approach of any educator working with adults. My points, additional to Knowles, above, included:

Basic Assumptions in the Education of Adults

1 Adults are social beings whose nature results from their interactions or transactions within their social or historical context.

2. Adults have the potential to undergo further qualitative changes in their thinking throughout their entire life span. In so doing, they move towards increasing control over their own thinking and learning.
3. Learning is synonymous with thinking and involves the creation of knowledge, questions, ideas and skills.
4. Knowledge is something that can be used or created.
5. Teaching is a process that involves enabling individuals to think and learn along with others who are thinking and learning.
6. Education is about critical thinking; questioning, problem posing, synthesis and discovery in a continuous cycle of reflection, action and reflection, so that from each end emerges a new beginning.
7. Adults learn best in situations in which they as individuals are valued.
8. The teacher is there to learn as well as to enable others to learn. [Nottingham Andragogy Group, 1985, p. 36]

A developmental objective for all adult educators should be for adults to gain increasing control over their own thinking, feeling, and learning. This process is seriously inhibited if a teacher assumes autonomous control over any phase of learning.

The differences

I have always felt that the structure and format of counselling courses should model the ethos of counselling and of the particular modality being taught, and, similarly, the structure, format, and very nature of supervision courses should model the ethos of and best practice in supervision.

In some counselling qualifying courses, students may have been taught the "skills" of counselling in a quite mechanistic and pedagogical way, and will have been taught how to do and not to do certain things in order to become qualified as therapists. Even in those institutions where more dialogic approaches to education are present, and where there might well have been some negotiation on content and structure, the attitude of tutors and institutions might still be largely pedagogical and didactic. Often, this is most apparent in the ways that tutors retain responsibility for, and the power over and control of, assessment and marking of students' practical and written work. This can lead students to believe that there is one "right way" to do the things that therapists do, and that only the tutors know what that is. I do not believe this to be good educational practice for counselling courses, and it is completely antithetical for supervision courses.

Supervision courses can model good practice in supervision. I am working with experienced professional colleagues to enable them to develop sufficient knowledge, skills, confidence, and expertise to be able to practise effectively as supervisors. They are already trained and qualified as therapists. They are engaged in the same business as I am when I am working as a therapist. I aim to support them to develop themselves as supervisors.

At the start of a counselling course, especially for those students returning to learning in a formal educational setting, unconscious processes and expectations might take over. Some automatically go into "pupil mode", with pens and pads poised, expecting to be "taught" by the tutors. Much to my surprise, I have also experienced this happening at the start of supervision courses, when students begin behaving as though the supervision course is the same as those courses they have been on before. I see it as my responsibility to comment that this is a very different learning situation. This is one in which they are equal partners with me and my fellow tutors in exploring the knowledge and experience we all have in order to enable them to develop their personal construct of supervision and their approach to practising as a supervisor, and one in which we, as tutors, will also be exploring and further developing our knowledge and practice. Through that sharing, each will develop greater understanding of the theory and practice of supervision, personal and professional growth, and even create new knowledge to be shared with the wider world. I also need to watch that I do not re-experience my feelings from previous classroom situations where I have been a more traditional teacher, and begin to behave as though they are pupils in a classroom.

I feel some discomfort in using the term "tutor". There is, of course, the paradox that at the same time as I want participants and tutors to be in a relationship as equals, it is not possible for me completely to abrogate the institutional power that I hold. I need openly to acknowledge that power which the institution places on me, along with the responsibilities that I am expected to carry. At the same time, I need to do my utmost not to let that power get in the way of the relationship between me and the participants, by making sure that I use power sensitively, only when it is essential, and in a way which is commensurate with collegial relationships on a supervision course and never in an authoritarian and indiscriminate way. I am there to learn as well. One of the ways I have of dealing with this is to raise it as an issue explicitly while developing the learning contract that we agree between tutors and participants. This seems to me to be a useful and good parallel with contracting for the supervision relationship.

The learning contract

Since I believe that the relationship between tutors and participants is of paramount importance, I must begin a course by explicitly describing how I see that relationship as a fundamental principle of the course. I need to set out to offer a relationship that will closely model the relationship between supervisor and supervisee, and begin by negotiating a clear and explicit agreement on the structure, content, ground rules, and boundaries of what and how we are going to learn together. I want to make clear that this is a course that is not pedagogic, but is based on the very different principles of a developmental model; the aim of the course is to develop a relationship in which we work together as colleagues who can help each other to reflect on all dimensions of our supervision practice and, through that process, to develop our effectiveness as supervisors. I want to establish a working alliance between us all, in order to enable each of us to gain in ethical competence, confidence, and creativity, and give the best possible service to our supervisees. Importantly, I will want to establish agreement that each of us takes personal responsibility for our learning and for assessing our learning through a joint continuous assessment process. The tutors will not take sole responsibility and total control of marking and assessment of written work and practice assignments, but will share that with all the participants through a process of negotiation.

Starting a supervision course does feel different from a counselling course. Many students on a counselling course might have no real idea of what counselling is, are unlikely to be practising as counsellors, and some might never have experienced therapy as a client. On a supervision course, all the participants will have a pretty good idea of what supervision is, and will have experienced supervision as supervisees. Furthermore, all of them will be practising as therapists and will be in supervision when they start the course. They will have a level of knowledge and understanding about the practice of supervision that will be substantially more than the knowledge and understanding that counselling students will have when they start their courses. It is, therefore, critical that participants' knowledge and experience is fully valued and taken account of. This is bound to have an impact on the nature of the relationship between participants and tutors on a supervision course.

Another difference in the relationship between participants and tutors will arise from an important attitudinal difference that parallels the supervision relationship. As a supervisor, I do not want to be perceived as an "expert". I do want to be seen as having some expertise, even wisdom, to share with my supervisee. I would want this to be the same in the relationship between participant and tutor on a supervision course. In a counselling course, it might be necessary to be seen at times as knowledgeable about theory and about the application of theory to practice, particularly in the early stages, when counselling students have such a steep learning curve to negotiate and there are issues of students' safety and their clients' safety to consider. On a supervision course, without denying the knowledge, experience, and expertise that I have, I really want to communicate a collegial attitude and to encourage all the participants to develop that as well.

Content: differences between supervision and counselling courses

There will, of course, be many differences between the content and structure of counselling and supervision courses, and there will be some similarities, too. This does not seem to be the place to do a detailed comparison and assessment of the differences in their content and structure. However, there are some points I wish to make.

I believe it is important for the content of supervision courses to be based on a balance between theory and the application of theory to practice in both counselling and supervision, and to ensure that participants have enough knowledge about each of the main approaches to counselling. The course content should enable participants to refresh and/or improve this knowledge and understanding, in order that they can be competent to supervise a counsellor who practises in another modality.

In some cases, where a participant might have had training as a counsellor that was clearly inadequate, this could mean that they might need some additional, personalized opportunities to improve their knowledge of theory and their ability to apply it to practice. Careful selection of applicants notwithstanding, I do start all of my supervision courses with a reprise of the various counselling theories to enable participants to have some parity of understanding of theory, which they can share with each other.

In terms of the actual content, I suggest that there should be a focus on the core values of supervision and a substantial element on ethical dilemmas. It can also be very helpful to teach participants a model for the ethical decision-making process. I have written about this elsewhere (Gabriel & Casemore, 2003), and BACP has a range of relevant useful information sheets, too. It is plainly very important to introduce participants to the range of supervision models that exist in order to enable them to develop their own construct of supervision, which they feel confident and competent to practise. I feel it is essential to include a substantial exploration of psychopathology and to have a continuing theme of valuing difference and developing cultural competence throughout the course. Finally, I believe that it is essential to enable participants to have an acceptable level of knowledge of group dynamics theory and practice, particularly if they are going to be doing group supervision.

For me, the most significant difference between counselling courses and supervision courses that needs to be taken into account is in the nature of the relationship between tutors and participants on supervision courses. I would urge those readers who wish to develop a supervision course and those who are currently running supervision courses to take account of the special nature of that relationship. I would also strongly urge those who are running or developing supervision courses to see them as education with adults, based on the basic principles I have outlined above.

References

British Association for Counselling and Psychotherapy (BACP) (2007a). *Information Sheet T1: What is Counselling?* Lutterworth: BACP.

British Association for Counselling and Psychotherapy (BACP) (2007b). *Ethical Framework for Good Practice in Counselling & Psychotherapy.* Lutterworth: BACP.

Freire, P. (2001). The banking concept of education. In: P. Freire, A. M. A. Friere, & D. Macedo (Eds.), *The Paulo Freire Reader* (pp 67–79). New York: Continuum.

Gabriel, L., & Casemore, R. (2003). British Association for Counselling and Psychotherapy, *Information Sheet P4: Guidance for Ethical Decision Making—A Suggested Model for Practitioners.*

Knowles, M. S. (1984). *Andragogy in Action. Applying Modern Principles of Adult Education.* San Francisco, CA: Jossey-Bass.

Marken, M., & Payne, M. (1988). *Enabling and Ensuring.* Leicester: National Youth Bureau.

Mearns, D. (2007). British Association for Counselling and Psychotherapy, *Information Sheet S1: What is Supervision?* Lutterworth: BACP.

Nottingham Andragogy Group (1985). *Andragogy—A Developmental Approach to the Education of Adults* (p. 36). Nottingham: Nottingham University.

Piaget, J. (1972). Intellectual evolution from adolescence to adulthood. *Human Development, 15*(1): 1–12.

Rogers, C. R. (1951). *Client Centred Therapy.* London: Constable.

Wheeler, S., & Richards, K. (2007). *The Impact of Clinical Supervision on Counsellors and Therapists, Their Practice and Their Clients: A Systematic Review of the Literature.* Lutterworth: BACP.

CHAPTER THREE

Training supervisors in multi-disciplinary groups

Julie Hewson

When training people in supervision from a number of disciplines, cultures, and expertise, I am aware of a number of factors that need to be considered.

The first is similar to that of the process of getting to know the client: it involves enquiry and curiosity, like that of an anthropologist getting to understand another professional tribe. The language is different, the culture, norms, and values might be different, the context in which they work different, in addition to the roles and expectations people have of them and they have of themselves.

The second is the modelling they have experienced during their own training. In the past, medical training, for example, was quite often draconian, lacking in emotional literacy, and often exposing and humiliating. With initiatives such as bringing in mentoring and coaching training for GPs and teaching skills of communication and emotional intelligence, those days are long gone.

So, whether supervising or training people in other professions to deliver supervision to their own colleagues, or training people from one profession to supervise those in another, sensitivity is necessary, and an understanding of roles, goals, working contexts, priorities, operational strategies, personal preferences, and differing learning styles.

The necessity for supervision within professions other than counselling and psychotherapy, in different cultures, becomes clear in some of the stories and narratives that follow.

Imagine a wet autumn afternoon, on a busy and efficient ward, with a pervasive air of melancholy, in direct contrast to the bright murals and pictures of happy babies and joyful parents. There had been a death, a tragic death of a neonate in which two members of different professions were implicated, both assuming the other knew a particular procedure, both fearful of admitting they did not. There were the parents, distraught beyond measure, the two young professionals whose working lives were in tatters, and a shocked team whose whole *raison d'être* is to preserve lives of fragile babies. All had been seriously affected by this accident.

A critical incident debrief had taken place, but the nursing and medical staff were dealing with it in differing ways with different outcomes for the staff concerned. The cause of the mistake was, to a great extent, the lack of supervision as part of the professional norm. None of the staff had the regular relationship that those of us in the worlds of psychotherapy, social work, or counselling take for granted. Naturally, during training there had been formal mentoring, but recourse to regular supervision was not part of the tradition then. There was mentoring for some young doctors and tutelage in the nursing profession, but the kind of open forum and reflective space we can hope to expect in the therapeutic services was simply not the norm. The old manner of training doctors was particularly shame-based, and supervision *per se* seemed to be seen as an exposing and shaming process, if it existed at all.

Setting up the first supervision training in Prague, I came across incidents that were very specific to the historical context and culture of the time. The only groups who were able to able to meet without fear of reprisal during the Soviet occupation were the Balint groups for doctors, where patients were ostensibly discussed. Actually, these were the groups that the dissidents were able to use for their political planning to free themselves from the occupier. One example was of a psychiatrist who, for the purposes of being able to work in a particular hospital, had to subscribe to communism, and was faced with either having to commit some of his dissident colleagues to psychiatric institutions or expose them, with the probable outcome of prison or worse. He was not able to get supervision on this moral dilemma at the time, either from the communist authorities or from those of his colleagues who were overt dissidents, who treated him with suspicion. He told me that he had saved the lives of a small number of his colleagues who were under suspicion, but the legacy of his position was cumulative trauma and self-medication.

Another case was that of a psychotherapist, specializing in the field of addictions. She was clearly being ostracized by many of her colleagues on the training programme. Privately, she had told me of her experiences as a loved child, feeling happy and confident, who went to school and faced a wall of incomprehensible hatred. Her father was a communist, and she had no awareness of this or the implications of it until she went to school. She told me that two daughters of another communist sympathizer were killed in the next village. In her training group, I watched a more subtle ostracism taking place, partly created by herself because of the overcompensation for her experiences as a child. Until they had a foreigner who was not party to either side, some of these issues could not be addressed or healed. Who could she go to for supervision on this issue?

These two narratives illustrate a need for supervision that attends to context and culture, outside the normal context of individual case supervision. I have outlined a menu of supervision elsewhere (Hewson, 1999), and others have looked at the tasks and functions of supervision (Carroll, 1996; Holloway, 1995).

Needs differ as experience grows

Initially, like should supervise like. In the early stages of the professional's life, a homoeopath needs to supervise a homoeopath, a social worker a social worker, and so on. This is because part of the nature of the supervisory relationship at this stage is one of mentoring, teaching, and resourcing. Thus, it is essential, as in the first story, that the doctor and the nurse both needed to have been taught a specific procedure relevant to their role, or have a space where they could revisit it or ask for help. At this stage, there is also the position of the role model, demonstrating professional behaviour. This requires emotional intelligence, which is part and parcel of best practice in the talking therapies, but is not necessarily abundant in some of the other professions: the law, medicine, osteopathy, and chiropractic.

However, what becomes very interesting is that some of the most effective supervision at master practitioner level can come from trained supervisors whose original discipline is in another field. They bring a refreshing perspective which is outside the norm and challenges people's comfort zones, while still working from the shared meta-perspective. In a piece of supervision on the training course, a former military policeman placed more emphasis on rational, rather than theoretical, perspectives (using the seven-level model of Clarkson, 1992, pp. 1–27). A psychotherapist had been agonizing about a borderline client's accusations about being late for appointments or running over time. The former military policeman simply asked if she had a diary with her, and, on examination, it was clear on a purely factual and rational basis that the accusation was impossible. This proved to be the universe of discourse that was most needed, not agonizing about transference or countertransference issues, diagnostics, or value-laden discussions about how to manage the client. A simple, factual, rational intervention cleared the air in next to no time and put the supervisee back in the driving seat with her client. I have also observed a teacher supervising an experienced counsellor, in one of the training sessions in which the stated contract was about some help to explore possible interventions with a highly traumatized client. It was clear to all of us that the counsellor herself had become traumatized by the events she had heard, and this had interfered with her being able to resource herself. The supervisor in training could himself have become involved in a parallel process and become deskilled, but, with elegance and agility, he focused on the countertransference and brought the supervisee back to a position where she knew exactly what to do.

Taking account of context and culture

Supervision is a reflective space for a number of professional issues. There is a need to take account of the profession itself, its identity, context, and culture. There also needs to be awareness of safety and what that means to different professional groups. Professions vary widely in how they view supervision. Trainers in supervision have to be aware of the differing emphases and culture about how the supervisor is seen: i.e., as a facilitator, educator, mentor, or coach. These issues are all the more pertinent when considering training a range of professionals in the same group in the art and science of supervision. Significant research based on the work of Fielden (2008) indicates that much early supervision takes an educative function, and the roles are those of the expert and the learner; however, as the practitioner becomes more skilled, there is a shift in relationship, one of more equality and a sharing in dialogue. What this process throws up is the multiplicity of the roles in the supervisor role set. Early on, the supervisor might have an evaluative and assessing role, which leads to a very clear power imbalance that might have unexpected consequences, such as the supervisee hiding ignorance or difficult cases for fear of being judged. The supervisor might be required to be another kind of teacher, enabling the trainee or novice practitioner to become more skilled, knowledgeable, and confident. At this stage, there might be more authoritative interventions (Heron, 1990) as well as facilitative ones. Some examples of working with mixed groups will show how these areas can be addressed.

One of the most useful, if rather obvious, things to say here is: "keep the language clear and simple". I have noticed how Peter Hawkins and Nick Smith (2006) slightly adjust their terminology when describing interventions from Gestalt and elsewhere, to make it understandable to anyone who has not been trained in Gestalt psychotherapy. Demonstrating the process of enquiry has been useful: for example, "I know what . . . [a term or a state] means for me but I do not know what it means for you. Would you help me understand?"

Much of the perceived difficulty is in semantics, and what I internally refer to as tribal languages. Words like "supervision", which seem neutral for one profession, are highly charged in another. I recently happened upon a case of a person who was formerly a schoolteacher, and a very good one. She came into counselling work quite late, and felt drawn to specializing in counselling adolescents. She then began to teach on a Further Education counselling course, and, because she unconsciously identified herself primarily as a teacher, she forgot the importance of supervision for herself in her dual roles. She opted for coaching, and missed a significant difficulty in one of her students that the necessary kind of supervision would have uncovered, with quite serious results. I think she was still unconsciously labouring under the impression that supervision was a judging process rather than a professional support. Teaching a mixed group is a fascinating forum for discussing the function and purpose of these related, but different, perceptions of professional roles.

However, these points aside, what I have also observed when training multi-disciplinary groups in "supervision as a meta-perspective", is that highly qualified psychotherapists can be effectively supervised by a properly trained and expert homoeopath, or a social work manager trained supervisor can be profoundly effective in working with a GP. At this stage, the role of the supervisor is much more that of the facilitator, taking the wider view and attending to broader areas of assessment of the problem, the effect the problem has on the person, interventions, ethical issues and so on. I have played that role to a number of GPs over the years, even though I am not a medic. If he or she needed clinical supervision, a medically trained colleague would clearly be more appropriate, but much of what senior practitioners bring in all fields, which the results of my research showed, was that the areas that most need discussion are those to do with countertransference issues and ethical dilemmas.

We may not know what we want, or what it is called, or even if it exists at all. How can we ask for something we do not know about? This question led me to develop a menu of supervision (Hewson, 1999) with colleagues from a different profession. The very process of listing what could be on offer uncovers the areas or language that seem incomprehensible at first sight, the classic term, for example, being countertransference. This could be explained by asking a series of questions such as: so how did that patient affect you? What was your reaction to them? If you were to consider a metaphor for them what would it be? What was the invitation to you, how did they want you to be with them? You haven't thought about that before? Well, shall we give it a go now?

The central role of contracting

It is important for trainee supervisors to contract explicitly about the specifics of the supervisee's role and clinical knowledge, for to do otherwise would be wholly unsafe and unethical. It is also important to attend to the context of the supervisee's practice, otherwise it is so easy to make assumptions and a crucial piece of information could be lost. If we ask, and ask, and ask again from a position of humility, assuming we will not know, expecting not to understand a particular profession or context, we are more likely to be of use to the professional who has come for a new perspective. Such questioning enables the supervisor to be respectful of the supervisee's dilemmas and clients/responsibilities. An example of this is of an organization specializing in community projects and initiatives which, with good heart, funded one of their team to come on to a supervision training course in order to increase the profile and effectiveness of supervision within the organization. The organization was convinced that the line manager should be the supervisor, which is not unusual outside the counselling and psychotherapy world. During the training, the candidate could see some of the dilemmas of the conflict between these two roles. It became clear, in a piece of taped supervision, that she had been effectively and successful mentoring a colleague, in fact "growing him up", professionally speaking, in a nurturing and generous way. However, a more collegial based supervisory relationship, in which the supervisee is invited to explore his thinking, acknowledge his dilemmas, and make and own mistakes, had been lacking. This had led to a psychological game of "Do me something" (Berne, 1964), in which he was passively waiting for her to provide structure and direction. The organization appeared to lack coherent structures for contracting for the numerous and worthwhile creative projects it was undertaking. Thus, it was "Doing something" for very many community groups, and my colleague's dilemma was a kind of parallel process.

The importance and subtlety of the contracting process might not be immediately evident to professionals in some other spheres. Often, assumptions are made, and the new supervisor goes hell for leather along the route to finding a solution to the problem, without taking account of the process needed for each individual supervisee to get there. Contracts for process as well as content are quite new to many, and are shown to be very important in expanding the richness and safety of the supervisory relationship. If the contract is clear for the manner in which the supervision is conducted, then the danger of hiding difficult and dark areas of professional life is less likely to occur. If the supervisee feels safe in the knowledge that they have a clear contract with their supervisor as to how the process is to be conducted, and how they can resolve the more difficult areas of their professional life, then supervision will truly be able to protect clients and practitioners to the greater good of all. An example of this is to do with shame-based issues. Being unable to express what they know effectively often embarrasses gifted people in the learning process. A contract enabling learning to happen without exposure or judgement would be essential. It could go something like this:

> Let us negotiate how to conduct our sessions in a way that enables you to explore what you already know, what you think and feel and how effective your intuitive hunches have been in the service of the client thus far. It then seems to me that what you are asking for is to feel more confident in expressing yourself using psychotherapy terms, so that you can express what you know through the cognitive categories of the profession. This may help further in accurate diagnosis and treatment planning and enable you to converse effectively with others in your inter-disciplinary team. It will also help you do yourself justice and keep your client safe when discussing your work with the examination board. How does that sound? Shall that be our current overarching contract?

Attending to shame

A slightly tangential example, but one that illustrated for me how much I needed to learn, was when I was training people as supervisors in Dublin. We had been discussing what prevented people from taking supervision or trusting their supervisors with really difficult cases when I mentioned the word shame, and the research I was engaged in on shame and supervision. There was an audible release of breath, almost a sigh, in the lecture room. As I looked at my students, who comprised Christian Brothers, nuns, and non-religieuses, mostly counsellors, teachers, psychotherapists, or coaches, one large and kindly man, showing great emotion, said that just being told that released him from some kind of demon from the past. He said that, for him as a boy, learning had been steeped in humiliation and pain, and although he had become a Brother for some years, he had later left in order to marry. He still worked with the Brothers, and thought very highly of his current colleagues, but he realized how steeped in shame the teaching practices for many of his generation had been in Ireland. What I later learned was that, at that very time, there was a significant investigation going on in Ireland about the abuse of boys by a small number of Christian Brothers a generation or more before, and how terribly this had hurt those good men who were engaged in teaching in the order now.

For some of the nuns, humiliation was the norm when they were girls, and I sensed that many had dedicated their lives to teaching or counselling to redress this at a systemic as well as personal level. To encounter this kind of collective knowing of shame as more of a norm than I had ever come across before was a salutary and important lesson for me to learn.

Necessary strategies and relevant models

What, then, are the necessary strategies for training supervisors in mixed groups within and outside the counselling and psychotherapeutic professions?

1. To return to an earlier paragraph, "ask about the context, culture, ethics, expectations, skills, and assumptions that belong to a supervisee from another professional group".
2. Clarify the significance of language: what do terms familiar to us mean to them, and what do terms familiar to them mean to us?
3. Train supervisors not to make assumptions about almost anything. For example, who is the client? People from each professional group make assumptions about the others' perspective, values, and procedures. We can use the analogy of getting to know the tribe that each professional represents in the team, much in the way an anthropologist might describe

culture, norms, language, rituals, and significance of emphasis. It can be an eye-opener.

4. Give information as to the nature and function of supervision and show how it differs from line management, mentoring, and performance coaching. The notion of a reflective space without fear or favour is new to many groups. It has been noticeable that, early on, people feel the need to fix the problem rather than provide a forum for reflection or a containing relationship. This is why the existence of a range of models of supervision can bring comfort and relief to some professionals who need structure in order to be creative.
5. Clarify the range of relationships that are possible under the umbrella of supervision.
6. Encourage the balance of art and science, creativity and order. This is a gift and a discipline for all of us, whether supervisors, musicians, painters, or photographers. Structure can provide the container in which we can improvise, make associations, and compose.

One of the challenges of supervision training is development of the skills needed to create the reflective space. It requires modelling the process as the trainer, being curious, respectful, facilitative, and supportive. It also requires the knowledge of when to increase the challenge and provide structures and conceptual frameworks that make sense of the creative confusion the client brings into the field.

Some of the models that have been shown to be effective are:

The CLEAR model (Hawkins & Smith, 2006);
The Bands of Supervision (Clarkson & Gilbert, 1991);
Cyclical Model (Page & Wosket, 1994);
The SAS model (Holloway, 1995);
Integrative Transactional Analytic model of supervision (Hewson, paper delivered to Czech Institute for Supervision, 2002).

Supervision training of itself can be an oasis for professionals in a busy, demanding life. It has been my experience that, as the relationships have developed in the context of practice supervision on the course, the theories of contracting, process, menus of supervision, negotiation of responsibilities, and genuine respect and compassion become visible, and this leads to a confidence in the delivery of high quality reflective learning that is both challenging and kind, creative and systematic. We all aspire to be able to learn from each other, and when we have in one training group a range of perspectives that cut across the normal cart tracks of our thinking, it is exciting and liberating.

Offering ideas from a team development model

Finally, as an example of another perspective, I would like to introduce the model from Margerison and McCann, delivered by TMS Development International, which is used to great effect in management consultancy and has its roots, to some extent, in Jung's typology. It notes stages in project management, and identifies the key roles in each of those steps. It identifies the roles individuals enjoy best and what they bring to the feast in a way that differs from the more familiar but equally useful Belbin (2004) material. Although this model comes from organizational culture, it can be valuable to reflect on any project an individual, pair, group, or team undertakes. Certain styles of working will place more emphasis on one part of the project wheel rather than another.

This approach asserts that any project involves eight types of work and an awareness of each of these is useful to run an effective organization (Table 3.1). Noting these roles and positions helps the

Table 3.1. The sequence of types of work.

Advising:	Gathering and reporting information
Innovating:	Creating and experimenting with ideas
Promoting:	Exploring and presenting opportunities
Developing:	Assessing and testing the applicability of new approaches
Organizing:	Establishing and implementing ways of making things work
Producing:	Concluding and delivering outputs
Inspecting:	Controlling and auditing the working of systems
Maintaining:	Upholding and safeguarding standards and processes

supervisor and later (if used in supervision) the supervisee to understand both what they are happiest focusing on, and where that preference fits on a cycle of project management. Such an approach might be useful if working with someone who may be having difficulties discharging their professional duties in a team, where their competence is not in doubt.

The process of co-ordinating and integrating individual work within the team is termed "'ll'inking" (see Figure 3.1). For example, there is a role called the Controller–Inspector. As this kind of supervisor, you might focus on checking recordings, enforcing regulations and being careful and meticulous in your in-depth reflective work with your supervisees. You might expect careful preparation before each supervision session, and regular listening to tapes with typed transcripts. On the other hand, another role, known as the Reporter–Adviser, is more likely to be patient, "beliefs orientated", and flexible, a collector of information, giving space to gather conscious or sub-conscious knowledge. Ultimately, however, they will want to see the work well done, correctly and with the right information.

These are clearly different styles that are reflected in the team roles shown in Table 3.2:

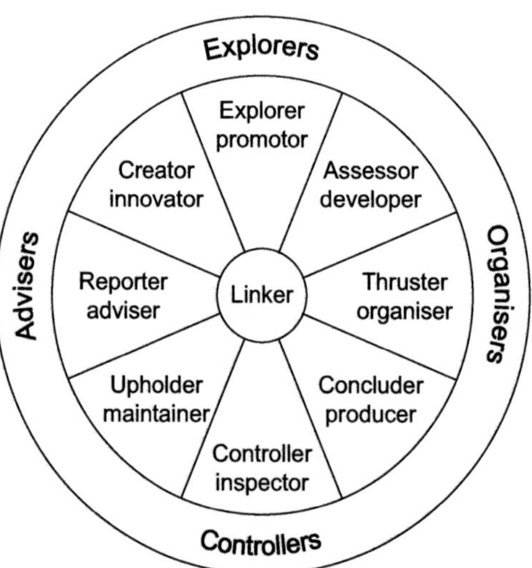

Figure 3.1. The Margerison–McCann team management wheel.©

Table 3.2. Team roles in the Margerison–McCann types of work model.

Team roles	
Reporter–Adviser:	enjoys giving and gathering information
Creator–Innovator:	likes to come up with ideas and different ways of approaching tasks
Explorer–Promoter:	enjoys exploring possibilities and looking for new opportunities
Assessor–Developer:	prefers working where alternatives can be analysed and ideas developed to meet the practical constraints of the organization
Thruster–Organizer:	likes to thrust forward and get results
Concluder–Producer:	prefers working in a systematic way to produce outputs
Controller–Inspector:	enjoys focusing on the detailed and controlling aspects of work
Upholder–Maintainer:	likes to uphold standards and values and maintain team excellence

Each of these roles places a different emphasis on the job in hand and parallels the work areas mentioned. This model is not usually used as a backdrop for supervision, but it illustrates that work with different professional "tribes" enables borrowing of some useful ways of looking, hearing, feeling, and thinking about what is in the field.

Finally, the issues of assessment are central to safe practice. Once again the methods used for assessing safe practice will vary according to the culture and the profession concerned, but the very notion of damage limitation or risk assessment seems central to all professions hitherto represented on our trainings, and when this is emphasized as part of the supervisory contract, interdisciplinary supervision is still as rich and effective at the level of master practitioners who know the meat and the bones of their work.

Concluding comments

The narratives at the beginning of this chapter show not only the need for supervision to enable the exploration of potentially shaming lack of knowledge in a safe environment, but also the necessity to understand the wider historical, political, and organizational context in which supervision and its issues are addressed. Through training a range of professionals, it is clear that effective supervision across disciplines can take place at master practitioner level, because the role of the supervisor, at that stage, is facilitative rather than educative. It also demonstrates the need for effective and structured models of supervision to enable a meta-perspective to have some shape, or container, in which creative interventions can take place.

To summarize, the key aspects of working with professionals from different backgrounds are listed below.

1. Understand the vision of their profession.
2. Understand their operational strategies: how they do things, why they do them, what is their thinking, what are the underlying values.
3. Understand the roles, formal, informal, and team, that affect the way a problem is seen. How people operate in a team, whether that is the supervisor trainer, the trainee supervisor, the counsellor or the client.
4. Consider interpersonal factors: these include preferences in communication, such as thinking, feeling, and then changing behaviour, or feeling their way in, then thinking, then changing behaviour, or, alternatively, enacting, then feeling, and finally thinking about a situation, or quietly linking action with thought and finally feeling.
5. Consider personal preferences in learning styles, and ways of conceptualizing, such as being able to see what a person means, or attend to accurate and elegant language, or take time to embody a notion before fully being able to analyse it intellectually.

To run courses for people as supervisors from different professional backgrounds is like travelling. So many things one takes for granted at home are subtly different, and thus evermore fascinating. Having offered courses to people from the legal professions, the military, drugs and alcohol specialists, teachers, social workers, counsellors, psychotherapists, the health professions, and specialists in complementary medicine, the view of the same landscape is marvellous and different, some noticing the geology, some the flora, some the colours, some the fauna. Some focus on the outer world, some contemplate their internal response to it, some focus on detail, others take in the whole expanse. These are aspects we need to attend to in working with different professionals in a mixed training group.

When different professional tribes get together there is a meeting of minds, hearts, and perspectives and we can all be the richer for this.

References

Belbin, R. M. (2004). *Management Teams: Why They Succeed or Fail* (2nd edn). Oxford: Butterworth-Heineman.

Berne, E. (1964). *The Games People Play: The Psychology of Human Relationships*. New York: Ballantine/Grove Press.

Carroll, M. (1996). *Counselling Supervision, Theory Skills and Practice.* London: Cassell.

Clarkson, P. (1992). *Transactional Analysis—An Integrated Approach.* London: Tavistock Routledge.

Clarkson, P., & Gilbert, M. (1991). The training of counselling trainers and supervisors. In: W. Dryden & B. Thorne (Eds.), *Training and Supervision for Counselling in Action* (pp. 143–169). London: Sage.

Fielden, K. (2008). From novice to expert therapist: the role of clinical supervision in transition. PhD Dissertation, Roehampton University.

Hawkins, P., & Smith, N. (2006). *Coaching, Mentoring and Organisational Consultancy Supervision and Development.* Maidenhead: Open University Press.

Heron, J. (1990). *Helping the Client.* London: Sage.

Hewson, J. (1999). Training supervisors to contract in supervision. In: E. Holloway & M. Carroll (Eds.), *Training Counselling Supervisors* (pp. 67–92). London: Sage.

Hewson, J. (2002). *The Locus of Focus: An Integrative Transactional Model of Supervision.* Exeter: IRON MILL PAPERS [delivered to Czech Institute of Supervision].

Hewson, J. (2007). A wider landscape. In: R. Shohet (Ed.), *Passionate Supervision* (pp. 34–49). London: Jessica Kingsley Publications.

Holloway, E. L. (1995). *Clinical Supervision: A Systems Approach.* Thousand Oaks, CA: Sage.

Margerison, C. J., & McCann, D. (1990). *Team Management; Practical New Approaches.* Aldershot: Gower Publications.

Page, S., & Wosket, V. (1994). *Clinical Supervision: A Cyclical Model.* London: Routledge.

CHAPTER FOUR

Recruitment and access

Caro Bailey

An Internet trawl of counselling supervision courses in February 2008 yielded as extensive a range of entry requirements as there are qualifications. These extend from none at all on both counts, to very specific entry criteria leading to Certificate, Diploma, or post-graduate degrees. Some courses are validated by an external body like ABC or CPCAB, or a university, and others not. At the time of writing, there are no courses validated by BACP. This is a curious state of affairs, since supervision has been and is heavily promoted to be integral to best practice *de facto* since the then BAC Code of Ethics and Practice for Supervisors appeared in 1992, and *de jure* ever since therapy evolved in its own right (Page & Wosket, 2001). Some courses are clear about their course philosophy and modality, others appear not to have either and certainly do not consider it relevant information to provide for applicants. Some courses are as short as ten weeks, others up to two years. The structures are a mix of residential, non-residential, modular, weekly, or weekend. Some clearly state that their level is under- or post-graduate, others float in academic limbo. There appears to be no consistency that the same qualification expects the same, or even similar, entry requirements; for example, I am aware that it is possible to pursue a supervision course *more or less immediately* after having qualified as a counsellor, whereas other courses require a minimum of four years between the two trainings. This infinite variety could be cause for celebration, but it might also be something of a dog's dinner. If the sole purpose is to train in supervision so that a practitioner can claim completion, regardless of qualification, entry requirements, value or worth, it can be achieved. Applicants may choose a training by recommendation, word-of-mouth, reputation, grapevine, knowledge of trainers, or particular modality. In other words, they can choose a professional training on a highly subjective basis. Should this be *the only way*?

Clearer baseline criteria are needed, given the centrality and importance of supervisors as monitors of good counselling and therapy practice. The current state of training on offer suggests that clarity about "essential requirements" would alert those thinking of training to the complexities of the role. This is necessary, on the one hand, to endorse the importance the profession places on supervision, and, on the other, to provide some guidance to those seeking training.

Baseline criteria for recruitment

Readiness

Within the profession, being a supervisor is seen as "career progression". Traditionally, counsellors who had practised for a while and who had notched up experience were often *invited* by colleagues to be supervisors. There is evidence for this in some ongoing research on the career paths of experienced practitioners (Henderson and Bailey, in progress). This still appears to be the pattern among some applicants for training now (CASCADE Supervision Training). This suggests an assumption that being an effective and experienced counsellor equips one to be a supervisor, thus conflating the two activities. This assumption acquires further endorsement from the practice of generally seeking supervision from an individual who has been practising as a therapist with more experience than oneself. This has some validity, I believe. The situation now in the therapy world appears similar to that in the teaching profession before training became an essential requirement. Individuals who had qualifications in a particular subject were deemed qualified to teach those who had either none or fewer. However, in relation to therapy, knowing one's subject and having experience of it does not mean one can necessarily monitor or support the work of others. Therapy and supervision are two distinct, though linked, and separate activities.

In the early years of the profession, there were no training courses in supervision. The two activities were less defined, so individuals who had been practising for a while as counsellors or psychotherapists "slid" from one activity to the other, what Carroll (1996) calls an "inherited role". I did myself. The combination of status and career progression within the profession made this both attractive and flattering. The notion of readiness, that is, "can I do this?" erred perhaps more on the side of the estimation of others than in a thorough examination of one's own abilities. However, as supervision has become more of a discipline in its own right, is seen to be an activity separate from therapy and training, and is now readily available, there is less excuse and more need for those embarking on the supervisory career path to examine what they plan to do and why.

What, though, determines readiness? Certainly the estimation of respected colleagues contributes to the notion. Supervisors themselves often seem to be instrumental in encouraging their supervisees to move into this role. Having practised for a while, some individuals want greater variety in their work and supervision offers this; boredom and waning passion with doing "just" therapy is a related reason. The experience as a supervisee of poor, as well as effective, supervision has spurred others to seek training. Some see supervision training as a way of broadening and deepening their knowledge, skills, and practice of therapy; a means of personal and professional development (CASCADE applicants). It would seem, therefore, that a combination of personal reflectiveness and endorsement by others contributes to the notion of readiness.

A fundamental entry requirement thus includes a capacity for reflectiveness and a thorough examination of why supervision training is being considered at this time, and, specifically, why a particular training is being considered.

Relevant training

At present, the jury has not even been sent out to consider the question of whether an individual not trained as a counsellor, psychotherapist, or in a "related profession" (of which more below) can be an effective counselling supervisor. In theory, this seems possible. Respected drama critics, for example, are not necessarily either failed or practising playwrights; they know their subject intimately and can comment with a breadth and width of knowledge and experience, which can guide others. The roles and skills of a therapy supervisor traditionally build on those, broadly speaking, of a psychological and emotional "helper". The notion of "help", though, is, in part, circumstantial. I can, for instance, feel psychologically and emotionally helped when a plumber does what the job requires and water flows where it should. As a practising therapist, what I need to help me do my job is to be able to consult with someone who shares the same or a similar professional *culture*, with an understanding and knowledge of what my job involves. In this instance, a plumber would not do, however advanced his empathic skills might be.

A similar culture, then, might include complementary therapists (homoeopaths, acupuncturists, reflexologists, and so on), as, in order to administer their therapies, they are likely to have had some training in counselling skills or, if not, have developed good people skills. As Hewson indicates in Chapter Three, members of the medical profession, social workers, spiritual directors, or teachers also can take the role. Yet, they might be in the minority of most training courses, and their individual circumstances would have to be weighed against their being able to share and contribute enough to the prevailing culture to make the experience worth while *for all concerned.* There could be great benefits, as well as possible difficulties in having a more expansive and varied supervision training community from which to pool resources. Clearly, to enlarge the training community in this way would be less possible for supervision courses that arise from specific modalities. However, I am aware of at least one supervisor training course in a specific modality which offers an introductory training course plus reading list for those applicants who apply from other disciplines or different modalities (Temenos).

This does not, however, address the level of previous training required to undertake a supervision course. Currently, the range is wide. Generally speaking, a "professional qualification" or a Diploma in Counselling appears to be sufficient to take a Diploma in Supervision or a post-graduate Diploma to match one in Supervision. This assumes a counselling or therapy training that contains knowledge, skills, and theory within an explicit ethical framework, though the amount of practice it might include can vary immensely. Quite how the picture will change as Foundation Degrees in Counselling become the norm is hard to imagine.

Thus, accountability is relevant for assessing prior training. A supervisor has to be able to account for what she is teaching, advising, assessing, and so on, primarily to her supervisees, and to the wider community as well. Therefore, the level and relevance of previous training has to be sufficient in order to carry this out.

Experience

Generally speaking, this refers to the minimum amount of counselling experience an individual has acquired before embarking on supervision training. Currently, this varies from none at all to anything between two–four years post counsellor qualification. Some training establishments expect a minimum of four hundred supervised hours, which is slightly less than the requirement to seek BACP Counsellor Accreditation of four hundred and fifty hours that have been accrued in not less than three years post counsellor training. The issue here is what constitutes sufficient practice and experience.

In theory, it would be possible to clock up four hundred supervised counselling hours at the rate of nine clients per week over a forty-five week therapy year. While I suspect this is unlikely for many in this overcrowded market of ours, I am also dubious about the wisdom of basing experience on counselling hours alone. I am reminded here of students wishing to undertake counselling training where one of the course requirements is having a Certificate whose training lasts a full year. One rationale underlying this is that students have some experience of being in a large group and confronting aspects of self in relation to others over a period of time that they would not otherwise have. I believe counselling experience also cannot be telescoped. As Brian Thorne stated in relation to person-centred counselling, it is "an invitation to live life to the full" (Mearns & Thorne, 1988). Supervision is no less important an activity. Ideally, it would be wonderful if counsellors could acquire a broad range of experience, in a variety of organizations, in counselling consortia or private practice, with individuals and with groups. With increasing specialization and ever greater calls on placements, this becomes increasingly hard to obtain. I also believe that living life outside of being a practitioner contributes greatly to being a rounded and thriving human being with much to bring as a supervisor.

A third criterion comprises experience as a counselling (or allied professional) practitioner acquired over not less, say, than four years post initial training together with a substantial number of supervised counselling hours. A guide here perhaps lies in the professional body to which the individual belongs and its accreditation guidelines, e.g., BACP, UKCP, probably around four–five hundred hours of supervised practice.

Accreditation

With the imminence of regulation, we are perhaps moving rapidly towards a situation where counsellors will have to be accredited if they want to work in organizations. Until we reach that point, is professional accreditation either necessary or desirable as an entry requirement for supervisor training? That it is not suggests courses might not as yet recruit enough candidates to make them feasible. Increasingly, many advertised jobs for counsellors require accreditation or a "working towards it". To those in the know, accreditation, or membership of a professional register, confers a kind of Good Housekeeping Stamp of Approval or a Kite Mark of Safety. In relation to entry requirements, I would see it as shorthand for the trainers on all the points made above.

To have or not have supervisees on entry to the training

Again there is variation between none required on entry to the course to having at least one or two supervisees or groups at the outset. I have come across at least one student who stated she felt it was unethical to start supervising without having had training, and others who find it difficult to find supervisees. The parallel between therapy and supervision training seems closest at this point; both activities require practice. I have some sympathy with the viewpoint of the student taking an ethical stand, but her position seems to ignore all the experience she herself will have gained as a supervisee. Our initial and ongoing experience as supervisees is similar to the process of "sitting by Nellie", Nellie being the master craftsman from whom we as apprentices learn our craft. The course is likely to have more meaning and make more sense in having practical applicability if the student is able to take her ongoing learning into her work with supervisees.

By the onset of training, a student needs to be encouraged to have at least two supervisees, of whom one may be a group (if the training includes group supervision) or to begin work with these shortly after the course begins.

Selection

One issue here is the extent to which trainers do the selecting. By deciding to undertake training, the applicant has already selected herself and feels ready; she has "self selected", and will have considered why she wants to train at this particular time. The course application form will reflect the course philosophy, both in terms of its criteria and the way in which it is presented. Completing a form invites further reflection by the applicant. If the course criteria are met, the applicant could then theoretically join the next training cohort.

If the course philosophy rests firmly on the belief that students need to base their supervisory practice on use of their own autonomy and exercise of their own authority as well as having satisfied course criteria, the selection process is complete. The consequence of this is that the composition of the training group will be random and left to chance. There will not necessarily be a balance of experience *vs.* inexperience, gender, age, ethnicity, and all the other differences that exist between us. This, I suggest, reflects life itself. Quite apart from posing the question of what a balanced supervision training group might look like and if it is achievable, is it, in any case, desirable?

I am inclined to believe that mix and variety in the training group is itself an essential, providing innate challenge within the training process. In addition, as practising supervisors we will, if we are fortunate, also have a variety and mix of supervisees that will challenge, delight, and appal us. Where better to test our skills and abilities than in our training? It seems to me that, providing the course is absolutely clear about its philosophy and methodology and constantly reviews this, there is no issue of student selection. The issue instead is about how adept and skilled the trainers are in delivering a course that attends to the content of the training on the one hand, while being constantly mindful of the needs of individuals and the group dynamics on the other. This largely mirrors the process of group supervision.

This seems wonderfully straightforward. I believe selection can be, for, if the course represents itself accurately in its promotional literature and trainers are available to answer questions prior to application, the selection process takes place *outside* the course and among potential applicants. There is, I believe, a further parallel here between the *practice* of supervision and the *decision* to undertake supervision training. Both activities demand the use of autonomy and inner authority. A group that is formed to undertake a specific training has an immediate commonality. Groups, whether hand-picked or formed at random, are in any case inherently challenging, which is one of the reasons they are so fundamental to both therapy and supervision training.

I do wonder, therefore, whether issues about selecting students for training reside partly in the course itself not being clear and firm enough about its entry criteria in the first place and, *de facto, not trusting in this process.* And, in the second place, whether there are some trainers who, by virtue of their status and experience, feel they know better than the students about who is *fit to train.*

Working on this basis, the constraints that operate will probably be those of ratio between students and trainers, though this is a moveable feast, and also the size of venue. Courses can be clear about optimum numbers so they might operate on a "first come, first served" basis, with a waiting list if necessary.

Equality and access issues

If we believe that applicants take responsibility for their own learning and, therefore, fitness to train, at the very least it behoves trainers to do the same. It follows that training courses need to be mindful of issues around access in the widest sense of the word and any issue that could be construed as discriminatory. Courses need to comply with The Disability Discrimination Act 1995 and, in particular, to Part 4, Special Education Needs (2001), which relates to how a course is delivered.

Access

Nowadays, this often appears to refer to physical access to the building and only to this: i.e., statements about *disability access to* buildings. Surely, access must mean that which might obstruct potential students from being able to take up and benefit from training. The sub-headings that follow all fall within the umbrella of access, and, if they are addressed, issues of equality will have been at least partially considered, too.

Advertising

The course has to represent itself accurately in its advertising. One way of ensuring this is to have it validated by a reputable authority: that is, ensure it can stand up to external scrutiny. Once established, a course will acquire a reputation and then a network of "graduands" who will attest to its value and worth, as well as recommend it to potential students. Internet access has also made knowledge of courses far more available and, in its fashion, equal than in the days before most of us had access to computers and we had to rely on newspapers, journals, and training directories.

Disability

Here, I believe, we have to take as our base point the reality that human beings are not equal and life is not fair. Attending to this as an ethical practicality, therefore, it would seem essential for all of us who are trainers to do our best not to disbar those who might wish to take up a training by being mindful of issues around equal opportunities, venues, and fees, all of which could be construed as coming under the general heading of equality and access.

Equal opportunities

The "easier" part of this seems to me to be on the course itself, when trainers need to be mindful and aware of discrimination in the training community that might mirror the society in which it takes place. Unpicking this a little, I am thinking here of how groups that suffer discrimination in society at large might feel similarly oppressed on a training course. For example, we need to be mindful of how it might feel to be in a minority of one and check this out sensitively. Trainers should also be prepared to deal with what might well be difficult group dynamics when they become aware of, or their attention is drawn to, discriminatory behaviour, and not shy away from doing so.

The harder part seems to me to lie in the reality that any isolated aspect of society as a whole, such as a supervision training course, cannot redress the balance of its ills as such. I do believe, though, that we must do all within our individual and collective power (in this instance, as trainers of supervisors) to offer as much opportunity as we can to those who are inherently disadvantaged by virtue of culture, class, creed, and so on. Issues around payment can be one fundamental way of addressing this (as follows below), but it is a drop in the ocean compared with other forms of discrimination.

Fees

Most courses, whether in the public or private sector, have to make ends meet: we live in a "bums on seats" culture in which a course has to pay for itself. Once upon a time, we had scholarships or awards that provided direct help for the less financially well off. More indirectly, there was once heavy state subsidy of education. What courses can do today is be willing to offer staggered payments (monthly, termly, and so on) and be as imaginative as they can be in terms of balancing costs while not incurring extra expense when catering for the needs of differently impoverished students. Suggesting taking out insurance against accidents or life events that might prevent the course being completed once started also demonstrates that the course is mindful of its students.

Venue

Problems could occur if courses have been traditionally held in old buildings that might also be listed ones. This is of little worth, however, to someone who cannot access a lavatory in a wheelchair. Accessibility must be made clear on course literature, so that students who have particular difficulties with physical access can decide whether they can cope with the venue before applying to the course. If students have a physical disability, the course venue has to be equipped to cope with this: there has to be wheelchair access to teaching areas, as well as bedrooms if the course is residential. I feel strongly that everyone, "abled" as well as "disabled", should be able to use the same main entrance, the latter not being relegated to the outer reaches of the kitchens and service deliveries entrance, as used to happen once upon a time. Ideally, venues should also be accessible by public transport. Finally, attention needs to be paid to hidden disabilities: provision of induction loops to help those with hearing loss, and meeting particular dietary requirements, encouraging the venue to try to provide much the same food for everyone so that discrimination is neither observed nor felt at every mealtime.

Course delivery

Part 4 of the The Disability Discrimination Act 1995 specifically concerns service delivery, which could be issues with communication, such as dyslexia, for example, that can exist in many forms. Trainers need to ensure that their training methods encompass a variety of ways of learning; they might need to accommodate the needs of some dyslexic students who take a very long time indeed to read and find it easier to be read to. If essays are a course requirement, it might be possible for them to be recorded rather than put on paper. Photocopying can be done on coloured paper rather than white, because that is usually easier for some dyslexic individuals to read. Trainers need to be similarly mindful about any games or exercises they use that might unwittingly exclude a student who has communication difficulties (e.g., conceptualizes in a different way) or, indeed, those of mobility. Students who have particular learning requirements should, in the first place, be able to state this on the application form, and, in the second place, have them attended to by the trainers. It might mean access to more frequent tutorials, and this should be stated as a norm on the course so that no one might justifiably feel discriminated against.

In conclusion

At present, there is a market free-for-all in relation to supervision training. There is, as yet, no requirement (or, it might be said, inducement) for supervisors to be trained. As the quality of training is so variable, those who employ supervisors have few means other than word of mouth and reputation to guide them about the value of a specified training. Statutory regulation by the Health Professions Council is not expected to include supervisors.

More worryingly, the enthusiasm to undertake supervision training might run out. We no longer live in a culture where education is primarily undertaken through courses *for its own sake*. It is more often driven by employment needs linked with career paths. There is little professional incentive for therapy practitioners to undertake a time-consuming and costly training that appears to make little difference to the availability of work. This does seem strange, given the increasing acceptance and integration of counselling in the UK at large, and the general belief that supervision is an integral element of good practice.

References

Carroll, M. (1996). *Counselling Supervision Theory, Skills and Practice*. London: Cassell.

Mearns, D., & Thorne, B. (1988). *Person-Centred Counselling in Action*. London: Sage.

Page, S., & Wosket, V. (2001). *Supervising the Counsellor: A Cyclical Model*. Hove: Routledge.

CHAPTER FIVE

Assessment design and implementation

Caro Bailey

One of the fundamental problems about assessing competency in a supervisor is that we are weighing up a significant contribution to a *relationship*, whether it be as one half of a couple or the facilitator of a group. How can we achieve this? Countless pieces of research and studies on effectiveness in therapy have shown time and again that it is the relationship, *not the therapist alone*, that brings about therapeutic change (Orlinsky, Ronnestad, & Willutski, 2004). There is altogether less research about supervision in the UK, so there is little evidence other than the anecdotal to suppose that supervisory effectiveness might also spring out of the *relationship* (but see Weaks, 2002).

Relationships as such cannot be measured. Sheer subjectivity defies this. Yet, while it is essentially non-quantifiable, as a profession we have to be able to account for what we are doing.

Any training involves acquiring and being able to demonstrate the necessary skills and abilities to do the job, be it for carpentry or supervising. Evaluation is also integral to training. So, while highly subjective processes like therapy and supervision do not lend themselves easily to more standardized methods of evaluation, it has been important to evolve a way of assessing a supervisor who is going to be an ethical, competent, and humane practitioner. To use scales and numerical means of assessment substitutes one form of assessment for another, and still involves subjectivity (Wheeler, 2001). Hence, the notion of ethical subjectivity as a measurement tool to be used. I mean by this that we aim as assessors to use a *felt sense* of what seems to be right in relation to the competencies and abilities of the participant.

What is involved in being a supervisor?

We need to go back to basics for a moment in order to clarify exactly what is being assessed. An effective therapist does not necessarily make a similarly effective supervisor. The latter involves a multiplicity of roles that assume therapeutic effectiveness as a base upon which others have to be acquired. At any one time, I would suggest that these include being a teacher, mentor, supporter, guide, challenger, restorer, assessor, adjudicator (perhaps weighing up the demands of an organization against those of a client, which appear to be contrary), and even judge. Broadly speaking, we expect supervisors to monitor the practice of their supervisees and to help them continue to develop themselves and their practice. In addition, at one end of the spectrum, a supervisor may also be required to assess whether a trainee counsellor is fit enough to qualify. At the other, a supervisor might now more frequently be required to attest whether a counsellor is fit enough to be accredited. And, in between, there is always the possibility that a supervisor might well have to assess whether a supervisee is competent to continue work or whether she should advise time out. All these are weighty and responsible tasks. Woven into the warp and weft of their activities, supervisors are required to assess *themselves and their supervisees* as an integral part of their activities, while at the same time carrying out all the other tasks of supervision to ensure the best possible service to the clients. Bearing all this in mind, it seems necessary and logical to integrate practice at assessing into the training itself.

The problem of supervisory assessment

What we are confronting in any therapy and supervision assessment is the sheer subjectivity of the activity as well as the potential feelings that are evoked in all the parties concerned. We know, for example, that a summative skills session towards the end of a course is as likely to be a test of nerve as ability, and might also encourage performance with an eye on assessment criteria more than much else. Formal examination processes like these tend to focus on one event alone that then appears to bear the weight of assessing all the learning, knowledge, and experience gained through the training. Such events do not embrace the whole person; they are fundamentally partial, and cannot truly reflect the student's growth and development during the course.

The practice of therapy and supervision is not a discrete activity that bears little relation to how we live the rest of our lives. It is an integral part of it. We need, therefore, to address more than the supervision practice itself when we are assessing competence, and find a way of accounting for the whole person. Brear, Dorrian, and Luscri (2008) noted that when therapy courses consider students unsuitable for professional practice, it is primarily for interpersonal or intrapersonal reasons. These continue to be relevant for supervision training, too.

How, then, to devise an assessment process that is both rigorous and fair, which maintains standards and accountability and embraces the rich diversity on offer? We need to be able to tap all the resources in the supervision community and arrive at an ethical and creative assessment process that not only embraces the whole person, but also respects his or her differences. One of the fundamental differences about which we need to be mindful is that each person starts at a different place, has different ways of learning, and variable speeds in doing this. Regardless of how we learn, I do believe we hold the length of a course of training in mind, either consciously or otherwise, as a safe container in which we learn. I have witnessed time and again, on counsellors' and supervisors' trainings, late developers reaching the "winning post" at the eleventh hour. One challenge, then, is accurately to identify the non-developers, who might be counselled off the training or advised well before the finishing line that they will not make the grade. With this in mind, I suggest that assessment of progress and development is as important to a fair outcome as assessment against a desired standard.

The qualities and skills of assessment

I believe there are two main considerations that need to be nurtured in training the supervisor, in addition to the personal moral qualities, and values and principles of counselling and psychotherapy, as detailed in the Ethical Framework of BACP. The first is authority, but not that vested in us by virtue of status or hierarchy. I refer to inner authority, as derived from a mix of competence, experience, congruence, boundary-keeping, respect of difference, ability to learn from experience, humility, ethical practice, skill, ability, and internal locus of evaluation. In sum, we need to develop the ability to distil the essence of all our accumulated knowledge, learning, and experience to enable supervisees to develop themselves to the best of their abilities in order to offer the best possible service to their clients. We need to be able to offer our services with *presence,* that is conviction, without at the same time being authoritarian.

The second is personal autonomy that arises out of the exercise of authority; the ability to be self-determining without being either dogmatic or prescriptive. This involves learning and practising being accountable to self and others through a core sense of self, a knowing and compassionate familiarity with oneself. It can be encouraged by developing a reflexive way of being that carries profound moral dimensions, particularly in relation to our engagement with others. This, in turn, will enhance the possibility of more fully knowing ourselves. The extent to which we have acquired a sense of autonomy through living our lives will already have been honed during therapy training, and might need to be taken a stage further during supervision training.

The supervisory student begins to engage with these issues at the very moment she decides to undertake training, and they form the initial piece of self-assessment.

The portfolio approach

Continuous assessment has long existed as an alternative to final examinations, which can be seen to be an inexact and often inept way of testing ability, particularly when there is a high level of subjectivity involved. It would seem to embrace all the considerations raised above as well as crucially mirroring life's realities. It encourages diversity and difference and is more true to the spirit of the practice of supervision and of the training itself. It is collaborative, ongoing, and cumulative, as well as encouraging reflexivity. It is also immensely time-consuming.

The development of the CASCADE model

To illustrate one way of putting this method of assessment design and implementation into practice, I will use our experience on the CASCADE Diploma in Individual and Group Supervision Training, which is validated by ABC. This is a *process model*, and is fundamentally humanistic while embracing other major counselling and psychotherapeutic approaches. It has always been self, peer, and tutor assessed and takes place over six long weekends bi-monthly over eleven months, or two intensive weeks also separated by months. It can accommodate a maximum of twenty-four students and four tutors. From the very beginning, we require students to assess their readiness to embark on the training and, having joined, to continue to monitor and appraise their progress and that of their peers. Tutors enter into this process alongside students.

Course philosophy

Over time, we have developed our criteria for being an ethical supervisor. This enshrines the course philosophy, to which we work throughout the course and which forms the bedrock from which the assessment process is assessed. Fundamental to the course is the ongoing engagement of each member with the training and assessment process. We believe it is essential to try to parallel the realities of practice, so that we engage in ongoing dialogue with each other and are in constant relationship, with all the responsibilities this entails. In this way, we evolve and maintain a community that celebrates and learns from the differences between us.

It is a hoary old truism that one of the ways of finding out whether we know about a subject is to teach it. Arguably, another way is to assess, which is perhaps a different but comparable way of pursuing understanding. On both counts, we have to know something about the subject and offer our own reasoned argument about why we hold that opinion. Arising out of our course philosophy, it then follows that, while each member is responsible for his or her own learning, she is also responsible *to* others in their learning. This positions assessment as an ongoing, collaborative, integral part of the course that provides crucial practice in an activity that is demanded of us when we practise in the world at large.

Feedback is crucial to the entire course; without good enough skills to deliver this well by each member of the community, both the design and the implementation of the training fails. Therefore, we spend time early on in the course clarifying what we mean by this, we offer guidelines, give practice time, and, every so often, offer refresher sessions throughout the training. This acclimatizes the students to the process. They generally improve both their verbal and their written feedback skills over the life of the course, often to a highly sophisticated degree.

Method of learning

Previously, the importance of developing autonomy and using one's inner authority were mentioned as key factors in the development of skilled and ethical supervisors. We believe the most effective way of nurturing this is through experiential learning. We might visualize this as being at the opposite end of the spectrum from *pedagogy*. Experiential learning demands that we integrate and process our experience for ourselves and with all parts of our being. This seems most closely to accord with the section on Supervising and Managing in the BACP *Ethical Framework for Good Practice in Counselling and Psychotherapy*. Statement 27 states, "Supervisors and Managers have a responsibility ... to acquire the attitudes, skills and knowledge required by their role".

Being a supervisee offers some understanding of this. It seems likely that new attitudes and skills will be more meaningful if they are practised rather than received. The challenge is to balance received wisdom (the learning of others) with finding out for oneself, while at the same time not reinventing the wheel. One way of looking at this in relation to the experiential learning cycle is to see tutor input, for example, as the *experience* that the student then actively engages in through exercises which follow and link the other parts of the process. Experiential learning is tiring, emotionally draining, and without specified end points. Mindful of this, and the demands that being in a large or smaller group can make, we set up peer support partnerships at the beginning of the course. These are chosen at random and comprise three people, none of whom is in the same supervision practice groups. Initially, they help to clarify and refine individual personal learning contracts. They meet at the end of each of the three days, and are intended to provide ongoing support as well as a different forum in which to discuss and share the contents of the day. Students are required here to complete an appraisal sheet to monitor their learning. We are drawing students' attention to *how* they have participated in their learning about theory, the link between theory and practice, their supervisory skills, their participation in facilitated teaching sessions, their personal awareness, and any developmental issues arising.

Without processing, experience *per se* has little or no meaning or value to the recipient of that experience. In this method of learning, reflexivity becomes integral to learning, as it calls on students to assess and evaluate their own experience as it occurs. However, providing supervisory experience in training exists within the very real constraints of time and money. Reflexive experience has to be offered in a variety of ways in order to cater for differences in ways of learning, varied speeds, and aptitudes.

Supervision, like therapy, is practical and requires practice. Crucial to the course, therefore, are supervision practice groups that are formed randomly during the first weekend and thereafter take place at least eight times during the ensuing meetings. These are closed groups of not more than six people, with a visiting tutor at each session. Each group draws up its own timetable to ensure that everyone has practice as both supervisor and supervisee. They meet for an hour, within which two practice sessions are expected to take place, and each session is assessed by the self and the rest of the group. This is a norm on both therapy and supervision trainings. What we expect now, and have put into practice more recently, is *written* feedback, so that the assessment process becomes more overt and evidence based. This, too, lies closer to the realities of increasingly evidence-based practice in the world at large. Given the time factor, we provide the feedback sheets and each student is expected to gather them together to be included within the portfolio. Both supervision practice groups and the peer support partnerships encourage students to hone their assessment skills by giving feedback to one another.

The learning environment

Course design and assessment implementation are inseparable. To make assessment a genuine and active constituent part of the training, there has to be safety as well as challenge, containment without constriction, and rigour that is transparent in its expectations.

What we endeavour to create from the very beginning is a supervisory learning community in which each member is willing to enter into a state of enquiry and collaboration that includes openness and playful qualities. This is immensely challenging, particularly when working with adults, many of whom might well have been working for many years as therapists and have acquired an assurance and standing in that role. It is a lot to ask them to go back to feeling unsure, uncertain, nervous, and lost in a new learning situation, and quite probably feeling that everyone else knows far more. In addition the group will be diverse in terms of supervisory experience, age and stage, culture, gender, biological age, disability, social class, sexual orientation, and so on. At the same time, we do believe that it is a useful reminder for all as supervisors to be thrust back into those feelings of uncertainty and doubt which parallel all those anxieties we can feel when we first experience supervision as trainee counsellors (Turner, Gibson, Bennett, & Hunt, 2008). It also becomes evident for us as trainers early on that by no means everyone on the course has much experience of working in groups, let alone a group that some consider to be a large one. What the large group does provide is the arena on the course in which every single member has a sense and an experience of everyone else as a person, if not necessarily within a supervisory role. It could be seen as the base link in which all other parts of the course come together. Time is spent at the start of the course involving everyone in becoming more familiar with one another, with what the course entails, and the method and means of learning.

As trainers we need to provide containment that has room for challenge within a climate of trust. We need to be prepared to make and acknowledge mistakes, feel foolish as well as joyful, and model what we would like and, in due course, expect of students. It is about *us*, and not *them vs. us*. We are encouraging and working towards every student on the course becoming more able to be genuinely and authentically themselves. Tutors may have more experience, perhaps wisdom and learning, too, but that does not make them automatically better supervisors. It is humbling to discover that students we know are, or are likely to become, more able practitioners than ourselves.

Further development of assessment process

It became apparent to us through our own tutor training supervision and development days that the method of assessment we were using did not fully reflect the spirit of the training, and nor did it seem to be entirely effective. Previously, we used to have a self, peer, and tutor assessed live skills assessment on the fourth weekend. By the end of the course, each student had to produce four items of written work, each two thousand words long. This work was self and peer assessed prior to being handed over to the tutor for final evaluation. Essays had to be marked when the course itself had finished. The course was not contained within its actual lifespan, with the result that we would start the next course while we were completing assessment on the previous one. While all these considerations were important, we felt the most significant were as given below.

- Self and peer written contributions in the usual supervision practice group sessions were often not systematically kept by all except in relation to the live skills session. They tended to look to this significant focal event, which, in turn, discounted the crucial role of the observers on the one hand and the very real value of having an ongoing record of one's development on the other.
- We realized that by focusing on a summative skills assessment and on written work as the method of assessment, this excluded any evidence of the person as a whole. This went deeply against the grain of our course philosophy.
- The supervisory assessment process was too similar to assessments used in therapy training and did not embrace the many

differences between the two activities, particularly that of the authority and autonomy of the supervisor.
- As a whole, the assessment process did not truly reflect the spirit of the course itself, which, above all, concerns continuous process and ongoing development.

The shift we needed to make was less about content and more about making *what* was being learnt in whatever format, part of *continuous, ongoing, and transparent assessment*. Accountability had to be woven into the heart of the process and be more evident.

We have used a portfolio approach for continuous assessment since 2007. Course requirements demand that each student, by the start of the training, has a minimum of two supervisees, either individual or group.

We state some essential requirements for the completion of the portfolio, as detailed below. In addition, we suggest students might also want to include anything else they consider has contributed to their becoming trained supervisors, such as:

- journal entries they might have made over the life of the course;
- workshops attended that might have informed their thinking and practice as supervisors;
- notes on formative books, articles, plays, films, etc.;
- art, or any other work that may have arisen during the training and that can be included within the physical body of the portfolio.

The assessment process

This starts with completion of the application form. Then, on the first weekend, each student draws up a personal learning contract. This forms the baseline from which each student clarifies her focus for learning as both supervisor and supervisee. Many students continue to amend this document throughout the course. The original and subsequent amendments are all included in the portfolio.

Throughout the course, students can request an individual tutorial if they feel they want additional support or guidance.

At each weekend, two students will have practice as supervisor, either of an individual or a group, which is followed by feedback. Self, peers, and a tutor complete evaluation forms, usually after the session. These, too, go into the portfolio.

Either in the third or fourth weekend, according to readiness, each student draws up a self-assessment statement to clarify her process and progress towards becoming an effective supervisor. (By this point, students will have normally have had at least two practice sessions as supervisor.) She will speak to this statement at a learning seminar with peers and a tutor. The self assessment grows out of her personal learning contract, through the feedback evaluation forms and the appraisal sheets drawn up at the end of each day. Each member of the supervision practice group will have a copy of this, so, too, each tutor. We invite students to be creative as well as be mindful that there is limited time for input and there must be room for group discussion. Out of this group discussion will emerge a decision as to whether the student in question is on the way to becoming an ethical, competent, and humane supervisor or not. If there is doubt or dispute, the assessed individual will be responsible, with the help of the group, for setting up a new learning contract that addresses what she needs to attend to. There is then an opportunity to repeat the process over the fifth weekend, if necessary.

While we have deliberately chosen not to continue with a live skills session, there seems no way of avoiding a build-up of tension around what is still envisaged as a summative exercise. We endeavour to emphasize that learning continues after the seminar, but acknowledge that some form of rite of passage has been experienced. We specifically ask for a new learning contract to be drawn up at this stage, and suggest that students who have passed their learning seminar could now draw up their own assessment forms rather than use the ones provided by the course, if they so wish.

Alongside skills assessment, we now ask for a five-thousand-word essay to form part of the learning process. This must include the student's theory of supervision, theory in practice, ethical issues, personal and professional development, and reflective awareness. We do not set topics, but invite students to select an area of interest they would like to pursue, which might be an extended case study or a short piece of original research. We suggest students check their chosen topic with their tutors to ensure relevance and possibility within the word count. The essay must also include reference to other works to show evidence of wider reading. It has to demonstrate that the writer has satisfied the criteria of being an ethical and humane supervisor, and this requires attestation by two peers.

The essay has to be sent to the marking tutor, not the student's personal tutor, about six weeks before the fifth weekend. Included with the essay is a self assessment and assessment by two peers (usually, though not essentially, those in the peer supervision partnerships). By the time the essay reaches the tutor, it will be assumed by the tutor that all aspects of the given criteria will have been reached. If there is dispute or doubt about having met the criteria, it is the responsibility of the relevant student to arrange a meeting of assessors (including the marking tutor) for further discussion. The external verifier talks with the students during the fifth weekend, and reads a sample of their work.

We believe this programme is a rigorous and thorough basis to train ethical, competent, and humane supervisors. Without doubt, it allows for individuality and creativity. We are left with some concerns about whether a less able student might slip through the net, as this approach relies so very heavily on the integrity and professionalism of all concerned. It is hard to fail a peer.

We expect students to be responsible for their own learning, and we spend time clarifying what is meant by that. This is one of the most crucial aspects of the course, and many do not fully appreciate what this means until near the end of the training. We mirror what exists in the "real" world by expecting students to use their authority as assessors of themselves, their peers, their tutors, and of the course itself. They build on the authority they use in living their everyday lives with the help of teaching input and considerable practice.

General concluding comments

I am inclined to believe that the design and implementation of supervisory assessment must include the following to qualify as rigorous:

- a course philosophy that enshrines models and theories of supervision;
- ethical subjectivity;
- ongoing assessment of practice by self, peers, and tutor(s) in order to benefit from three different perspectives in terms of age and stage;
- an awareness of, and attention to, difference in all its variety, as well as specifically as it is manifest in learning
- the courage to tell a colleague that her practice is not good enough and perhaps not competent enough to qualify as a supervisor.

References and bibliography

Brear, P., Dorrian, J., & Luscri, G. (2008). Preparing our future professionals: gatekeeping and implications for research. *Counselling and Psychotherapy Research, 8*(2): 93–101.

Gabriel, L. (2001). Ethical dilemmas: problems in the supervisory relationship. *Counselling and Psychotherapy Journal, 12*(1): 11–12.

Orlinsky, D. E., Ronnestad, M. H., & Willutski, U. (2004). Fifty years of psychotherapy process-outcome research: continuity and change. In: M. J. Lambert (Ed.), *Bergin and Garfield's Handbook of Psychotherapy and Behaviour Change* (5th edn) (pp. 307–390). New York: Wiley.

Turner, S., Gibson, N., Bennetts, C., & Hunt, C. (2008). Learning from experience: examining the impact of client work upon two trainee therapists. *Counselling and Psychotherapy Research, 8*(3): 174–181.

Weaks, D. (2002). Unlocking the secrets of good supervision: a phenomenological exploration of experienced counsellors' perceptions of good supervision. *Counselling and Psychotherapy Research, 2*(1): 33–39.

Wheeler, S. (2001). *Assessing Competence*. London: Cassell.

CHAPTER SIX

Developing trans-culturally sensitive theory and practice

Valerie Batts

Introduction

A white female therapist reflects after her first supervision session with a male Indian psychologist, "How do I know what the impact of my vastly different life experiences are on this prospective relationship? Does it matter?"

A white male supervisor completes a third supervisory session with a black South African supervisee, appearing to have no concerns. The supervisee asks himself, "How do I handle the frustration—and scare—that comes up in me as I realize I am not being seen for who I really am? I wonder if I should ask for another supervisor."

Since the early 1960s in the USA, organizations that support clinicians of colour in a variety of clinical disciplines have been suggesting and demonstrating that "culture" matters (Pinderhughes, 2004). Most clinician supervisors trained in traditional academic settings in the USA and in the UK in the pre-1960s era were taught the accepted western-based psychological frame that neutrality is possible and desirable in supervisory relationships. Although it was generally expected that psychotherapists would engage in their own therapy, typically this action was considered to aid in the development of such neutrality. Further, personal therapy typically did not address cultural issues. Thus, when discomfort across lines of differences occurred, the situation involved risk taking. Examining our responses and behaviour in this situation through the lens of world view enhances our ability to function effectively.

The supervisors mentioned above are facing situations where ignoring difference could needlessly impede their effectiveness. This paper will offer an introduction to options for supervisors to engage trainees and their clients, accounting for cultural differences at four levels: the personal, interpersonal, institutional, and cultural. This model is offered as an important beginning "toolkit" for effective supervisory training and clinical service delivery.

Context

Working with people from different cultural and ethnic groups can be an exciting journey. It can also be a frustrating and puzzling experience for well-meaning supervisors who find that they begin to have repeated "problems" or concerns in such relationships. Early termination or lack of success on other variables is often reported. Supervisors of colour often notice that whites do not typically seek them out for supervision and training or, if white trainees do, they question or express discomfort with, or confusion about, some of the different approaches they might experience. Alternatively, the supervisor of colour becomes a "guru" of sorts, a reflection of an idealization of exoticism that also can have negative consequences on the relationship over time.

Supervisors interested in developing a trans-culturally sensitive practice will need to examine both process and content information. Process is *how* we engage in teaching, training, and other supervisory activities. Many supervisors trained in systems approaches to clinical intervention have been taught to attend to aspects of process: that is, what is going on between clients in the room. Psychoanalytically trained clinicians will attend to issues of "transference": what the supervisee might project on to the supervisor. Less frequently in this model there is also attention paid to how the supervisor might be responding, i.e., countertransference dynamics.

Taking a multi-cultural lens as normative in supervisory relationships, however, means much more. It starts from the assumption that cultural differences inform all aspects of the supervisor–supervisee relationship and that exploration of this dimension can provide vital information for effective clinical change. Exploring these dimensions can deepen and enhance the supervisory relationship, and the supervisee's relationship to the clients she serves.

Attending to cultural differences also means taking time to learn about the world views, perspectives, and "life chances" of different groups in one's community (Knoff, 1986, p. 106). It means recognizing one's own cultural assumptions, values, filters, and judgements. This leads to an increased awareness of the limits of one's own cultural learning and the developing of a cultural humility that allows ongoing learning about self and other to occur (Tervalon & Murray-Garcia, 1998). The supervisory relationship can become a place to unpack this learning, both about self and other. Such a process between supervisor and supervisee involves openness to acknowledging lack of knowledge on both parts, which for many supervisors might reflect a new approach to such work. The power dynamic in the supervisor–supervisee shifts from supervisor as content expert to supervisor and supervisee as learners together in the understanding of how cultural influences are affecting their relationship and/or the supervisee's relationship to a given client of a different cultural background.

It should be noted that this approach to supervision could also have implications for supervisory relationships and client–clinician relationships between people of the same ethnic or cultural group. The approach invites exploring how each person is similar and different from each other person, even within the same social group (Batts, 2002). Social groups are defined, broadly, in terms of those social variables that inhibit and/or enhance the likelihood (i.e., statistical possibility) that a given individual will have equal access to life's chances (Table 6.1).

Thus, a white female clinician from an owning class background may enhance her ability to work with a white female supervisee from a working-class background by exploring both how they are

Table 6.1. Types of oppression.

Types of oppression	Variable	Non target groups	Target groups
Racism	Race / colour / ethnicity	White European Caucasian	Racial ethnic minorities (African, Asian, Caribbean, Arab, Latina / o, Persian / Iranian
Sexism	Gender	Men	Women
Classism	Socio-economic class	Middle-, upper-class	Poor, working-class
Elitism	Education level	Formally educated	Informally educated
	Place in hierarchy	Managers, exempt, faculty	Clerical, non-exempt, students
Religious oppression Anti-Semitism	Religion	Christians, Protestants	Muslims, Catholics, atheists, Jews, others
Militarism	Military status	First and Second World Wars	Falklands War Gurkhas Gulf War
Ageism	Age	Young adults / workers	Elders (40+ by law) / older worker +lower level
Adultism		Adults	Children
Heterosexism	Sexual orientation	Heterosexuals	Gay, lesbian, bisexual, transgender
Ableism	Physical or mental ability	Temporarily able-bodied	Physically or mentally challenged
Xenophobia	Immigrant status / Passport status	UK born UK passport	Immigrant Non-UK passport
Linguistic oppression	Language	English	English as a second language Non-English

similar and how they are different, given their respective class backgrounds.

The goal of learning to apply a multi-cultural lens is to allow the supervisory and the clinical relationship to use the lens to explore and deepen the variety of angles from which to address the given presenting issue of the supervisee and/or the client.

Personal level tools

Emotional literacy

Many supervisors trained in traditional therapeutic models will need to learn to demonstrate "emotional literacy" (Gardner, 1993) in the therapeutic and the supervisory context. Cognitions and behaviours are much more often the focus of intervention (Figure 6.1).

In the psychotherapy context specifically, it might be all right for clients to express feelings as part of "getting cured", yet it can be viewed as a sign of weakness or ineffective countertransference if the clinician is affected emotionally in the client–therapist relationship. Similarly, if a supervisee needs to work through feelings, this is seen as part of their training, but not something that the supervisor should usually be doing as well.

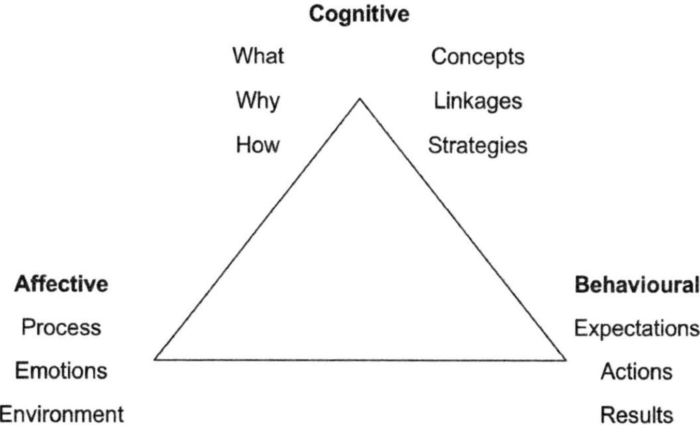

Figure 6.1. Three dimensions of change.

In many relational cultures, the expression of emotions is a normative part of the discourse. Absence of such expression can be viewed as a sign that this person is not real, transparent, or trustworthy. If a supervisor shares nothing about his/her self in the affective domain, for example, in the early stages of a supervisor–supervisee relationship, this can hamper trust building and lead to a less than authentic relationship.

The first task then is to examine how comfortable the supervisor is with expressing affect and to practise affective expression, first with self and then in the relationship.

Increasing knowledge about different world views and cultures and how things are done within them

This knowledge begins with self-awareness. Culturally skilled supervisors have explored their own cultural backgrounds and assumptions and are in a learning journey regarding how these "cultural scripts" (Steiner, 2003) affect their comfort with people who are different. They are also open to noticing how they affect others, irrespective of intent. A white male supervisor who has been trained in private school and university to "speak with authority even if you are not sure" will become aware that his training in taking up space with speculative ideas, and might be ineffective in making contact with a young woman of colour from a family in which she was trained to "speak only when you are sure of what you are saying". Noticing how much he speaks *vs.* how much she speaks in their supervisory sessions can be a clue to such unspoken differences operating.

It is important, further, to acknowledge that learning about cultural differences is a lifelong journey and it is not only all right but desirable to become aware of what we do not know in this area as well.

Becoming aware of barriers to effective cross-cultural interactions

Modern oppression theory (Batts, 1983) suggests that there are five behaviours that can occur among supervisors that inhibit effective supervisor–supervisee relationships, and these are as follows.

- Dysfunctional rescuing: help that does not help and/or that is disempowering, often as a way to handle feelings of guilt or shame from our places of privilege.
- Blaming the victim: putting 100% of the responsibility for lack of success on the part of the "target" person and not seeing systemic barriers.
- Avoidance of contact: no genuine, authentic, equitable contact across lines of difference.
- Denial of difference: the myth of colour blindness.
- Denial of the significance of difference: a belief that all have equal life chances and therefore differences do not matter to the likelihood that a person from a given group will succeed.

It is also important to note that these behaviours can also set up and/or reinforce survival behaviours on the part of the *supervisee* that can also be problematic. These behaviours are given below.

- System beating: figuring out how to get over or around "the system".
- Blaming the system: putting 100% of the responsibility for lack of success on the system and not taking personal responsibility.
- Antagonistic avoidance: avoidance of individuals from social groups because of a blanket mistrust that is hurtful to the person carrying the affect.
- Denial of cultural heritage: denying aspects of self to fit into the larger culture or group.
- Lack of understanding of the significance of difference: minimizing systemic, cultural, historical, and/or social barriers that might inhibit individual success.

The "dance" that can occur in supervisory relationships that do not challenge these barriers keeps both parties stuck in terms of maximal learning and problem solving. The alternatives are noted in Figures 6.2 and 6.3.

Interpersonal level tools

Supervisors who practise the following skills are most likely to develop empowering, transparent, and effective multi-cultural relationships.

Alternative behaviours for modern "ism" and internalized oppression behaviours

• **Functional helping** (instead of *rescuing*)	• **Confrontation/standing up** (instead of *system beating*)
• **Problem solving/responsibility** (instead of *blaming*)	• **Take responsibility** (instead of *blaming*)
• **Make mutual contact** (instead of *avoiding*)	• **Share information/make contact** (instead of *antagonistic avoiding*)
• **Notice differences** (instead of *denying differences*)	• **Notice and share information about one's own differences, culture** (instead of *denying target group*)
• **Learn, ask about, and notice the impact** (instead of *denying the impact*)	• **Notice, ask, and share information about the impact of the "ism on me and on my target group"** (instead of *denying the impact*)

For all behaviours, personal and organizational problem-solving at the personal, interpersonal, institutional, and cultural levels to generate ongoing multicultural structures and processes.

Figure 6.2. Alternative behaviours.

Modern "ism" behaviours	**Internalized oppression behaviours**
• Dysfunctional rescuing	• System beating
• Blaming the victim	• Blaming the system
• Avoidance of contact	• Antagonistic avoidance of contact
• Denial of differences	• Denial of differences
• Denial of the political significance of differences	• Lack of understanding of the political significance of differences

Figure 6.3. Modern "ism" and internalized oppression theory.

- Listening that is active, reflective and empathetic. This typically takes learning to talk less when appropriate and to allow for all perspectives. It takes patience, as well as willingness to make mistakes.
- Developing a non-judgemental attitude *and* learning how to understand and express "judgements" when indicated, in ways that do not communicate that the supervisor's view is more "right".

- Keen observation skills: ability to notice what is happening both within oneself and in others at several levels.
- Knowing how to interpret implicit or covert as well as explicit or overt communication.
- Contracting and negotiation skills: knowing how to clarify who is responsible for what and how accountability will be enhanced. This includes clarifying assumptions about what is needed from the supervisor, which may be different for different cultural groups.
- Being able to see beyond one's own world view.
- Noticing the intent and impact of what we say and how we say it. (See Figure 6.4.)
- Learning how and when to set boundaries, including teaching self and supervisees how to manage how much time is allowed for more talkative, entitled, and/or expressive persons to speak, in the context of group therapy, for instance.

Institutional level tools

A traditionally trained supervisor might tend to think of the supervisory relationship primarily in terms of individual change models. Many supervisees and/or clients coming from cultural groups that have been historically excluded have personal, interpersonal, and systemic barriers to face. They might also have different cultural frames of reference about the sense of self as "I"-based *vs.* "We"-based. Effective supervisors will want to understand when a

- "Try on"
- It is okay to disagree
- It is not okay to blame, shame, or attack, self or others
- Confidentiality
- Practise "self-focus"
- Practise "both/and" thinking
- Notice both process and content
- Be aware of intent and impact

Figure 6.4. Guidelines.

relational world view will enhance effectiveness. Such an understanding supports trainers to teach supervisees how to achieve the following.

- Offer to their organizations the option of team-based decision making that accounts for difference as well as similarity. This might mean faculty examining the institutional "unwritten" rules about what is expected of students in a pass/fail course, for instance. If the course culture assumes that students will be present for all or most classes, even if there is no grade attached, how does the organization communicate these expectations to members of cultural groups for whom this is not normative practice? Assumptions that students are not showing up because of lack of investment or overwhelming circumstances, *vs.* lack of understanding of the institutional expectations, can lead to avoidable cross-cultural misses.
- Examine how decisions regarding client treatment are made through a multi-cultural lens. The supervisee will begin to ask questions such as, "Who is told what and when? Why? What are the assumptions about who can handle what information? How do we anticipate differences when possible and manage the different meanings of such decisions to different individuals within their cultural contexts?"
- Address issues of cultural differences in timing, information sharing, and handling issues such as grief and loss in clinical decisions regarding serious illness or end of life care. Culturally sensitive institutions ask themselves, "How do this client and her/his family handle information regarding this issue? How do we respect their needs in the context of the indicated treatment? How do we support cultural differences in the grieving process as an institution, as a provider?"

Cultural level tools

Supervisory training from a multi-cultural perspective creates and supports the understanding and practising of

- relational cultures where it is all right to talk about differences;
- use of affective as well as cognitive processes for effective problem analysis and resolution;

- a shift in world view so that it is permissible to make mistakes, acknowledge lessons learnt, and continue to enhance supervisee skill and effectiveness.

Summary

Effective supervisory relationships allow supervisor and supervisee to explore the impact of similarities and differences in the client–clinician relationship. They use cultural differences between supervisee and supervisor as one point of reference. Process and content are addressed as they come up, in ways that respect the history and traditions of each group. Understanding and applying the tools described in this chapter allow such encounters/experiences to unfold, and the supervisee's learning from them to be enhanced.

References

Batts, V. B. (1983). Knowing and changing the cultural script component of racism. *Transactional Analysis Journal, 13*(4): 255–257.

Batts, V. B. (2002). Is reconciliation possible? In: I. T. Douglas (Ed.), *Waging Reconciliation: God's Mission in a Time of Globalization and Crisis* (pp. 35–75). New York: Church Publishing, www.church publishing.org

Gardner, H. (1993). *Multiple Intelligences.* New York: Basic Books.

Knoff, H. M. (1986). Characteristics of the culturally skilled counseling psychologist. In: *The Assessment of Child and Adolescent Personality* (p. 106). New York: Guilford.

Pinderhughes, E. (2004). My struggle to understand racism and injustice. *Reflections: Narratives of Professional Helping, 10*(1): 26–38.

Steiner, C. (2003). *Emotional Literacy: Intelligence With a Heart.* Fawnskin, CA: Personhood Books.

Tervalon, M., & Murray-Garcia, J. (1998). Cultural humility versus cultural competence: a critical distinction in defining physician training outcomes in multicultural education. *Journal of Health Care for the Poor and Underserved, 9*(2): 117–125.

CHAPTER SEVEN

Online learning and teaching of supervision of counselling and psychotherapy

Michael Townend and Wendy Wood

Introduction

In this chapter we consider how supervision training can use technology-enhanced learning strategies and be delivered through online learning. We draw both upon literature and our experiences through the development of postgraduate online learning courses in supervision for counsellors and psychotherapists at the University of Derby in the UK.

Online learning (also called e-learning) can be defined as the use of a computer network over an intranet or internet to deliver education and training to individuals or groups. "Technology-enhanced teaching and learning" is a term used when technologies such as the internet, streamed video, podcasts, blogs, or wiki are used to supplement traditional lecture room based teaching and learning.

Important technological advances already influence professional training in health and social care, including the training of psychotherapists and counsellors. Students have access to electronic resources, for example, online databases such as Medline, PsycInfo, ASSIA, access to electronic journals, DVDs, and a multitude of professional organization websites with associated discussion groups.

Thus, the concept of online learning would appear to be a natural progression.

However, developing online learning brings with it some important questions and challenges for professional education. We discuss the challenges that we experienced and how we addressed them below.

The effectiveness of online learning

From reviewing some of the literature in regard to effectiveness, we noted the following points. There is a marked lack of evaluation of claims of the benefits of online learning (Bach, Haynes, & Lewis-Smith, 2007). The literature seems to indicate that in non healthcare contexts, deep learning can take place (Bach, Haynes, & Lewis-Smith, 2007; Gibbs, 1999; Russell, 1999; Welsh, Wanberg, Brown, & Simmering, 2003). Online learning is generally at least as effective as, or slightly better than, classroom-based learning (Allen et al., 2004; Kekkonen-Moneta & Moneta, 2002; Welsh, Wanberg, Brown, & Simmering, 2003). There is also evidence that students who are less confident about computing achieve less (Gist, Schwoerer, & Rosen, 1989). It has also been suggested, contrary to initial predictions, that learning style and gender do not seem to determine the effectiveness or otherwise of online learning (Kass, Ahlers, & Dugger, 1998; Larsen, 1992). There is a trend towards online learning being more effective for short and focused courses that have a less technical content and also emphasize cognitive learning outcomes (Welsh, Wanberg, Brown, & Simmering, 2003). We took these issues into account in the design, development, and teaching of the course.

Some reflections on the design and delivery of supervision e-learning

We have found it essential to create a communication-focused approach to the course. We considered this important due to the nature of psychotherapy and counselling as a relation-based profession (Grant, Townend, Mills, & Cockx, 2008) and also because the literature emphasizes this (Heinze & Proctor, 2004) in order to add value to the student learning experience (Bach, Haynes, & Lewis-Smith, 2007).

Our course at the University of Derby includes problem-based learning in order to facilitate deep learning through individual and group learning activities (Boud & Feletti, 1991; Savin-Baden, 2000). Problem-based learning in an online context is discussed further below.

Educational as well as supervision theories, and counselling and psychotherapy literature indicated a need to demonstrate key supervision competencies and then link the practice of these competencies to the student's own practice by specific learning activities in the work place (Bernard & Goodyear, 2004; Fawbert, 2003; Grant, Townend, Mills, & Cockx, 2008; Hillier, 2005; Watkins, 1997). This was achieved through the production of video-based learning materials with further learning through linked activities of academic and professional debates and discussions in order to facilitate critical and reflective thinking. Video material enhanced students' learning experiences to bring the course to life in a visual and auditory sense (Bach, Haynes, & Lewis-Smith, 2007; Jollifee, Ritter, & Stevens, 2001).

A number of approaches can be useful to stimulate and challenge students within a supportive environment (Uschi, 2002). Writing text-based materials that the learner has to work through in isolation simply will not achieve this, nor will it meet learning outcomes that relate to the development of appropriate professional attitudes or values. Neither will it lead to the development of enhanced skills. Therefore, a successful online learning supervision course needs to be designed to:

- maximize the opportunities for students to engage in interactive activities with their fellow learners and the staff;
- ensure that learning strategies appeal to learners with diverse learning styles and professional background;
- ensure that the four aspects in Figure 7.1 are identified.

Many areas of professional practice emphasize the need for practitioners to become reflective practitioners (Grant, Townend, Mills, & Cockx, 2008; Schon, 1983). Thus, reflective learning was

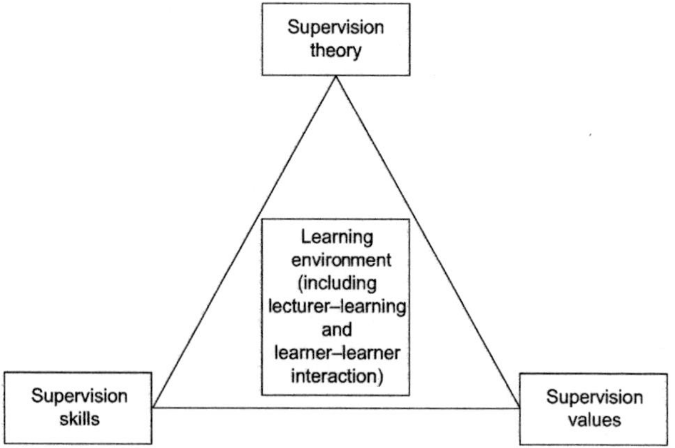

Figure 7.1. The four-aspects model for the teaching and learning of supervision.

also a key feature of the design of the course in order to facilitate the students' abilities to think in an analytical, creative, and "real life" way both on and within their supervisory practice (Kyriakidou, 1999; Schon, 1983; Sutton, Townend, & Wright, 2007).

Having lecturers who were visible to students and interacted with them (Heinze & Proctor, 2004) was important. This included regular contributions to discussion boards, and regular supportive and encouraging e-mails from the teaching team to the group as a whole and to individuals. Telephone or e-mail tutorials were arranged to maintain communication and interactive links (Bach, Haynes, & Lewis-Smith, 2007; Heinze & Proctor, 2004; Hillier, 2005). This aids the early recognition of any problems or anxieties students might have, in order to provide the necessary support.

The design stage of the course also led us to conclude that assessment would need to include students recording their own supervisory practice and submitting this for formal assessment and feedback. This, essentially, would provide direct evidence of the competencies achieved in practice, which we regarded as a necessary behavioural criterion for the demonstration an effective course. This was supported by other assessment activities to measure and evaluate student performance in relation to theoretical knowledge, critical and reflective critical evaluation, and values (Grant, Townend, Mills, & Cockx, 2008; Hillier, 2005; Murphy, Walker, & Webb 2001).

Some reflections on the curriculum model

A curriculum model is, in effect, a strategy that seeks to ensure that the aims of the course and its learning outcomes can be realized by the learner. Curriculum typically consists of learning outcomes, statement of indicative content of the course, how learning will be achieved, teaching methods, and methods and content of assessment.

Academic models of teaching and learning can range from pure lecture room based teaching and workshops to pure online learning. This range is shown in Figure 7.2. Within our course, we have tended to adopt an approach that incorporates a number of methods of teaching and learning, but with no face-to-face contact with the student. There are other education approaches, referred to as blended learning, which is learning that is facilitated by the integration of a combination of different modes of education delivery, models of teaching, and styles of learning (Heinze & Procter, 2004). The Department of Education and Training offers a slightly different definition of blended learning as "learning that combines online and face to face approaches (DET, 2003). Other terms and definitions can also be found in the literature, such as hybrid learning or mixed learning. Thus, there is some dispute in the literature regarding definition and terminology. However, all of these definitions and conceptualizations refer, in the main, to the integration of e-learning tools and teaching strategies and techniques.

In this chapter, we refer to our approach to learning as pure e-learning, which uses a range of teaching and learning approaches.

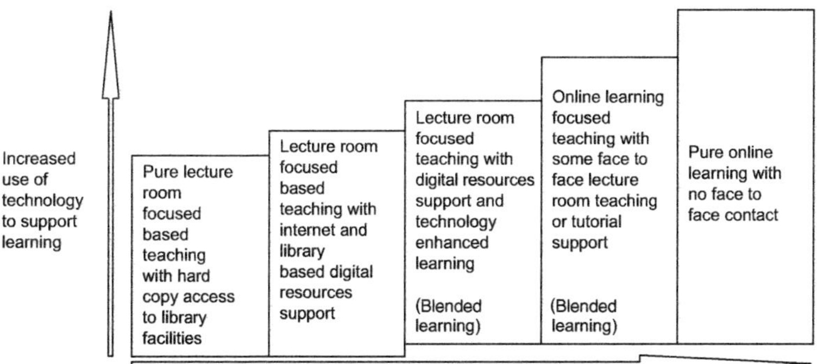

Figure 7.2. Teaching strategies in academic education.

The overall curriculum model is shown in the model illustrated in Figure 7.3.

Assessment strategies

There are two broad categories of assessment methods that are relevant to the assessment of supervision taught through online learning: those that assess knowledge and understanding of supervision theory, and those that assess application in the form of supervisory skills (Hillier, 2005). A list of assessment strategies that can be utilized is shown in Table 7.1.

Reflections on our experiences

Skills development

The development of competency in the skills required for effective supervision is the real challenge for supervision courses that are delivered by e-learning. Such micro skills are traditionally taught through workshops that use a combination of role play, feedback

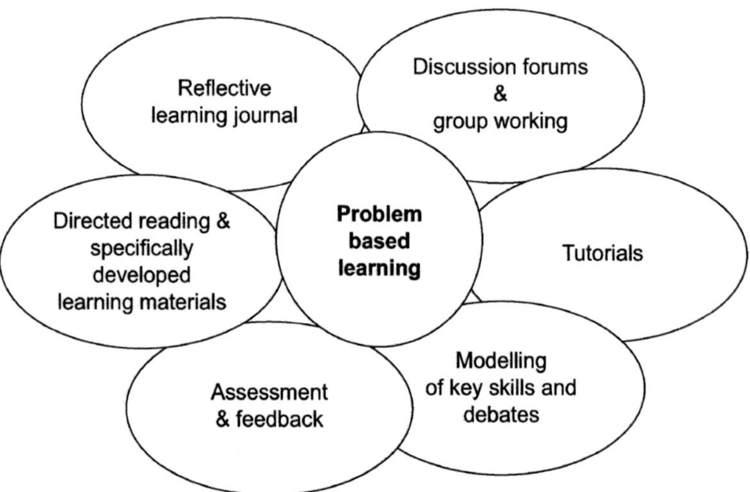

Figure 7.3. University of Derby E-learning Supervision Course Blended Curriculum Model.

Table 7.1. Supervision assessment strategies and online course issues.

Assessment strategies relevant to supervision	Assessment issues in the context of an online learning supervision course
Self analysis of practice	Allows the students to record observe and critique their own performance within a supervision session. The advantage of this method of assessment is that it can clearly help students to demonstrate how theory and skills informs practice as well as giving the team a good example of the student's actual practice.
Portfolios	A popular and important form of assessment within professional programmes of learning and, in this respect, supervision is no different. Portfolios can be used for students to articulate values and provide evidence of both knowledge and skills. They have the disadvantage, within an e-learning context, that electronic submission is not practical and they can be both bulky and time-consuming to mark.
Written assignments	This is the standard approach for assessing theoretical knowledge and the students' cognitive abilities with the critical evaluation of theory. Written assignments can easily be administered through electronic submission systems.
Case studies	Allow the student the opportunity to apply and critically consider theory, values, and application of supervision skills within the context of their own practice. Case studies can easily be administered through electronic submission systems. Confidentiality and anonymity of the subject of the case study needs to be ensured and procedures need to be in place to assure this.
Presentations	These can be carried out live over video links or webcams, or through a presentation being made, recorded, and submitted by the student.

that might use video, and practical demonstrations that model key skills and techniques that are either performed live by lecturers or from video (Bernard & Goodyear, 2004; Fawbert, 2003; Grant, Townend, Mills, & Cockx, 2008; Hillier, 2005; Watkins 1997). The challenge is to reproduce this approach to teaching micro skills through online learning. This is possible to achieve with broadband access that enables the streaming of video materials to demonstrate the skills required of supervisors; these are then linked to specific problem-based or prescribed practice-based activities. Students can video and receive feedback and coaching from the lecturing team on the performance of these activities.

In our experience to date, students have found the video materials produced by the team to be very helpful in that they did provide a way of relating to people rather than just words.

The videos produced by the students certainly clearly demonstrated the development of competency. This included those students who were initially reluctant to produce a video of their practice. As a result of having the facility of a discussion board, we were able to explore the concerns that students had in relation to recording their practice and offer guidance on how to make the best of this learning opportunity, as well as examining the ethical principles surrounding the recording of practice.

Engagement

One of the concerns that we had prior to the development of the course was the possibility that students would find it difficult to engage with the programme as a result of the lack of face-to-face contact. However, our experience has suggested (similar to findings from Tantum, Blackmore, & van Deurzen, 2006) that this is not so, and our students have commented on how much they valued the input of tutors, and that this helped them to engage with the materials. Also, it would appear that the use of problem-based learning also facilitated engagement, which again supports the findings of Tantum and colleagues (*ibid.*).

Concluding comments

In this chapter, we discussed online learning as a process that can enhance the students learning experience. In our work with the training of counselling and psychotherapy supervisors, we have found it to be an effective approach and process for learning the theory, practice, and values to become an effective supervisor, despite our initial reservations and scepticism.

Online learning can enable students who are unable to travel to a university to study for a variety of professional, practical, or personal reasons. Thus, it can support widening access to higher education. Also in terms of widening access, online modules are currently cheaper than traditional university-based diplomas in supervision. It can also add value to the learning process for many students, through supporting the autonomy of the student. This is a particularly important feature for counsellors and psychotherapists who wish to update and develop themselves for continued professional development, many of whom have studied in the HE sector previously. The evidence base for online learning, and our experiences, indicate that it is no more or less effective than traditional forms of learning and teaching. The online learning experience can also lead to the development of high quality learning materials and experiential and other learning activities. These materials are frequently all available to the learner at the beginning of their course. Thus, they are very transparent, and can be accessed in a way that suits the learner as many times as required. Online learning also offers the opportunity for innovative forms of assessment and evaluation, with real-time feedback to the student. Online learning not only enables the counselling or psychotherapy learners to learn about technology as they learn, but also places the learner and the academic at the forefront of the "new world of using information to construct knowledge" (Bach, Haynes, & Lewis-Smith, 2007, p. 188). Finally, as we have argued, the role of online learning is not to replace traditional university approaches in professional training, but offers the academic the opportunity to develop high quality and systemic learning materials and activities that are creative and coherent, and a variety of ways of engaging with learners that can potentially improve the flow of communication and knowledge over traditional ways of learning and teaching.

References

Allen, M., Mabry, E., Mattrey, M., Bourhuis, J., Titsworth, S., & Burrell, N. (2004). Evaluating the effectiveness of distance learning: a comparison using meta-analysis. *Journal of Communication, 54*(3): 402–420.

Bach, S., Haynes, P., & Lewis-Smith, J. (2007). *Online Learning and Teaching in Higher Education*. Maidenhead: Open University Press.

Boud, D., & Feletti, G. (Eds.) (1997). *The Challenge of Problem Based Learning* (2nd edn). London: Kogan Press.

Bernard, J. M., & Goodyear, R. K. (2004). *Fundamentals of Clinical Supervision* (3rd edn). New York: Pearson.

Department for Education and Skills (2003). Towards a unified e-learning strategy, http://www.dfes.gov.uk/consultations (accessed on 6 May 2009).

Fawbert, F. (Ed.) (2003). *Teaching in Post Compulsory Education*. London: Continuum.

Gibbs, G. R. (1999). Learning how to learn using a virtual learning environment for philosophy. *Journal of Computer Assisted Learning, 15*: 221–231.

Gist, M. E., Schwoerer, C., & Rosen, B. (1989). Effects of alternative training methods on self efficacy and performance in computer software training. *Journal of Applied Psychology, 74*: 884–891.

Grant, A., Townend, M., Mills, J., & Cockx, A. (2008). *Assessment and Case Formulation in Cognitive Behaviour Therapy*. London: Sage.

Heinze, A., & Proctor, C. (2004). Reflections on the use of blended learning, www.ece.salford.ac.uk/proceedings/papers/ah_04.rtf (accessed on 8 March 2008).

Hillier, Y. (2005). *Reflective Teaching in Further and Adult Education* (2nd edn). London: Continuum.

Jollifee, A., Ritter, J., & Stevens, D. (2001). *The Online Learning Handbook: Developing and Using Web Based Learning*. London: Kogan Page.

Kass, S. J., Ahlers, R. H., & Dugger, M. (1998). Eliminating gender differences through practice in an applied visual spatial task. *Human Performance, 11*: 337–349.

Kekkonen-Moneta, S., & Moneta, G. (2002). E-learning in Hong Kong: comparing learning outcomes in online multimedia and lecture versions of an introductory computing course. *British Journal of Educational Technology, 33*(4): 423–433.

Kyriakidou, M. (1999). Electronic-conferencing: promoting a collaborative community with learning opportunities for developing teachers. Paper presented at the British Educational Research Association Annual Conference, University of Sussex at Brighton, 2–5 September 1999, www.leeds.ac.uk/educol/documents/0000 1374.htm (accessed 29 March 2008).

Larsen, R. E. (1992). Relationship of learning style to the effectiveness and acceptance of interactive video instruction. *Journal of Computer Based Instruction, 19*: 17–21.

Murphy, D., Walker, R., & Webb, G. (Eds.) (2001). *Online Learning and Teaching With Technology, Case Studies, Experience and Practice.* London: Kogan Press.

Russell, T. (1999). *The No Significant Difference Phenomena.* Montgomery, AL: International Distance Learning Certification Centre.

Savin-Baden, M. (2000). *Problem Based Learning in Higher Education: Untold Stories.* Buckingham: Open University Press.

Schon, D. A. (1983). *The Reflective Practitioner: How Professionals Think in Action.* New York: Basic Books.

Sutton, L., Townend, M., & Wright, J. (2007). The use of reflective learning logs in the training of post graduate cognitive behavioural psychotherapy students. *Reflective Practice, 8*(3): 387–404.

Tantum, D., Blackmore, C., & van Deurzen, E. (2006). Elearning and traditional "face-to-face" teaching: a comparative evaluation of methods in a psychotherapy training programme. *International Journal of Psychotherapy, 10*(2): 7–14.

Uschi, F. (2002). The web as a vehicle for constructivist approaches in language teaching. *ReCall - Journal of Eurocall, 14*(1): 2–15.

Watkins, E. (1997). *Handbook of Psychotherapy Supervision.* New York: Wiley.

Welsh, E. T., Wanberg, C. R., Brown, K. G., & Simmering, M. J. (2003). E-learning emerging uses, empirical results and future directions. *International Journal of Training and Development, 7*(4): 245–258.

CHAPTER EIGHT

The internal supervisor: developing the witness within

Penny Henderson and Caro Bailey

Self-awareness provides an underpinning for the element of reflective practice in supervision. The "internal supervisor" tunes in during a session to how the relationship is going, what might be conveyed unconsciously by the supervisee, and the impact of what they are doing together. In Schon's useful summary (1987), there are two different processes that the internal supervisor uses to support the work. "Reflection-in-action" occurs during a counselling or supervision session. This is the moment when the practitioner takes note of something happening and decides to change tack. Immediacy and, in supervision, self-disclosure, are relevant skills used to support this process. "Reflection-on-action", the other process, takes place after a session, when the practitioner reflects on the work, maybe writes notes, muses, considers the shape of a session, or what, on reflection, was missing; what went well or turned out badly. Preparation for a supervision session also calls on the internal supervisor of the supervisee, to decide what to bring. Learning from reviewing *recorded* supervisions supports "reflection-on-action". Listening to the record, transcribing it, and mulling it over encourages private digestion of a case (Bramley, 1996, p. 42). Being *outside* the session provides some distance; having been *in* it provides connection.

Supervisors need to develop the capacity to see themselves and their work dispassionately, yet with compassion. The ability to stand back and view oneself and oneself-in-relation-to-others occurs developmentally with age and experience. It also needs to be addressed in supervisor training. Some of us might be more inclined towards this more reflective way of being than others. However we have developed our reflectiveness, we need to move towards observant and mindful monitoring and away from self-critical judging. This entails releasing the self from internalized "shoulds" derived from significant others in early life and from inappropriate standards harshly applied by the self to the self. One way of looking at what self-supervision involves is to see this as a "play space"; an internal space in which to reflect, explore, and hypothesize as well as to develop a research way of thinking that evaluates the effectiveness of interventions. Increased awareness of covert processes, thoughts, and feelings distinguish the internal supervisor of a supervisor from that of a less experienced counsellor (Page & Wosket, 2001, p. 266). Habits that support effective practice are built by such practices.

A core aim of supervision must be to help supervisees develop an internal compass for their work. Developing the internal supervisor as an inner companion who is always there is a little like having an Everyman within who "will go with thee, and be thy guide / In thy most need to go by thy side". Reflecting on potential and actual courses of action helps the supervisee expand her vision as well as to feel more resourceful with a client. Ideally, the internal supervisor comes habitually to provide this, so the counsellor-at-work can attend to the process and relationship reflectively while also engaging with the client. Thus behaving as a witness to the working self, this "observing ego" has many components, as this chapter suggests.

By embarking on training, a supervisor might be seeking some knowledge input as well as commentary on her supervisory practice. She will already have been reflecting on self as practitioner, and is likely to have discussed this with her own supervisor.

Most participants will be accustomed to self-supervision. The course itself will hopefully invite further self-supervision through developing new frames of thought, building up skills, and exploring attitudes. Any course that offers multiple perspectives might also enlarge vision and create more flexible habits of, and tools for, reflection. The *skill* of supervision (McLeod, 2007) requires the supervisor both to sustain connection with the supervisee and to hold an evaluative distance in which to reflect on how the work and the relationship are going. At the same time, choices are being made about which focus might be the most useful to offer. Development of critical faculties and frames of mind, and increased awareness of, and a felt connection with, the supervisee are fundamental to the activity of supervision. This is an essential faculty to develop where unspoken issues in the client–counsellor relationship may be mirrored within that of the supervisor–supervisee. (This is known as parallel process.)

The internalized supervisor

In our initial *counselling* training practice, we observed that we often unconsciously imitated a supervisor, parroting them as we learned how to relate in this new, intimately connected but boundaried way. Thus, some of the initial layers of our internal supervisors were actually something different: an *internalized* supervisor. A literal parallel here is watching a small boy imitate the way his father behaves, as if he is taking on wholesale the attributes of someone he wishes to emulate without filtering this through his own ego. This might be especially likely if a trainee idealizes the supervisor. Taking interventions that have been useful in supervision and applying them appropriately to work with clients is part of learning that assists socialization into the role of counsellor. Yet, it is essential for a supervisor to have moved well beyond this stage of rather unreflective regurgitation. There is little thinking for oneself that is involved in this method of practice; above all, it is likely to be incongruent. To have confidence enough to practise as a supervisor demands also that we have the courage to be ever more genuinely ourselves.

Most people who apply for supervision training will have enough experience to have developed a critical questioning element: "Is this what I would do? Should I do it like this?" Thus, the different internalized supervisors the person has experienced become filtered and incorporated into their internal world. Their practice will also rely on personal experience and thoughts, and spontaneous original and creative responses. Remaining open to vulnerability in relationship is also a priority for this developmental process to be sustained.

As Gilbert and Evans say, "The ability to sustain vulnerability is an essential part of relating, and a measure of personal and professional maturity, because it opens the counsellor to resonate with the client" (2000, p. 41).

We see one crucial aspect of being vulnerable as being open to the moment while maintaining an ability to acknowledge not-knowingness when it occurs.

Being 'in' and 'out' at the same time

We are reminded of those little weather-vane houses: when it was dry, a little woman came out of her door, and, when wet, a little man came out of his while she went inside. Here, the picture is of both of them standing in their respective doorways. Metaphorically speaking, and not unlike the weather, we need to develop the ability to be in two places at once: for it to rain with the sun shining, simultaneously.

Like the "participant observer" of sociological research, the internal supervisor has to be "in" the relationship sufficiently to understand the experience of the person she is in relationship with and "out" enough to think, understand, and evaluate the process of the work. Gilbert and Evans (*ibid.*) describe this as combining "inclusion" and "critical subjectivity". For them, "inclusion" is awareness of your own experience *and* that of the client, together with a capacity to stand back and reflect on the dynamic interaction between the two. They quote Wright (1991), adapting his ideas about child development to supervisor development as follows: enlarging our vision depends on being able to move to a broader variety of positions to obtain new and different perspectives on ourselves. This may achieve a multi-perspectival view of the world with an appreciation of "difference" that arises from a systems competence. A third person perspective provides us with a view of ourselves outside of our own immediately lived experience, so that it becomes a "means of scanning both the perceptual field and the inner field of the mind" (*ibid.*).

Gilbert and Evans provide four phases to the process of educating the internal supervisor. They are:

1. Learning to "be inclusive" without losing oneself in the client.
2. Learning to be fully present without losing sight of the other.
3. Holding the polarities, albeit tentatively and sporadically.
4. Being able to move smoothly and consistently between the self and the other while simultaneously reflecting on self in relation to other and the process between.

They encourage supervisors to help their supervisees to deal with any fear of being caught up in transference phenomena by thinking of it as a *treasury of information* and their countertransferential responses as "emotional barometers". Thus, the supervisee can come to value those strong feelings or responses they experience with the client, and seek meaning in them for the therapy relationship.

Self-awareness

The metaphor of a filter is an apposite one for the internal supervisor. As the supervisor hears, observes, and is with a supervisee, she notices what is going on with the supervisee, with herself, and in the space between. As she is observing, she is filtering the information she is receiving in many different ways: personally, professionally, theoretically, imaginatively, to name a few. Thinking of a particular example, as the water of reflection pours through her filters, she notices what trickles through into clearer awareness. With practice and experience, she will also try to note what might be missing that she would normally expect to find. Just as filters need cleaning, so, too, do counsellors and supervisors need personal and professional input in much the same way. We suggest that staying with an issue or problem, rather than giving up, can also help unblock the system.

Group supervision is particularly useful precisely because these personal filters become more obvious in contrast with those of others. It is easier for the supervisor to perceive how her supervisees construe the world in all its differences and diversities as it is presented within the group. She can also become aware of where an individual's empathy is ready and easy and where it is difficult or absent, as well as what is taken for granted as "good enough practice" by them. The supervisor can also note if their practice becomes more flexible and responsive to different styles of learning and views of the world.

Another methodology lies in interpersonal process recall (IPR) (Allen, 2004; Inskipp, 1999). This is best carried out in groups, but it can also be developed as a method of reflecting on recorded practice, either after a session or with one's own supervisor. Reflecting on practice after the event within this framework helps extend awareness of the variety of elements that inform every thought and utterance. While this is a *post hoc* activity, it aims to develop habits of awareness during sessions themselves.

Arguably, too, the more we know ourselves in general, the more we are developing particular and specialized awareness at the same time. We are thinking here about the notion of *ethical subjectivity* that is expanded upon at more length in Chapter Five, on Assessment. This makes heavy demands on us, and rests on the notion that we have an awareness as supervisors of what is apparently going on in a session, what might not be, of undercurrents, of the wider context, and so on, in order for us continuously to assess the ethical probity of our own and our supervisees' practice. And how do we know we can rely on a *felt sense* of what our internal supervisor is adjudging right and proper behaviour? The short answer is that we cannot know. The longer answer is that the sum total of awareness that is organismic is one that, over time, we learn to trust and be guided by, as we also check out our reactions in relation to theory or a supervisor's alternative perspectives, and consider outcomes.

In addition to the above, we would add the importance of retaining a sense of humility coupled with openness. While it is important, and a central requirement of being an autonomous professional practitioner, to be able to acknowledge mistakes and learn from them, it is also humbling when we fall from our own grace. Becoming aware of internalized attitudes to shame, guilt, and humiliation might eventually reduce the need for self-justification and any tendency to denial of responsibility for difficulties in the client–counsellor or counsellor–supervisor relationship. The novice supervisor needs to be able to name uncomfortable issues and to offer assessments of the supervisee's practice, while at the same time encouraging work at a developmental edge. To do this, the supervisor can usefully notice the interventions she most commonly uses and the skills she has, as well as those she has yet to develop (see Hawkins & Shohet, 2006). Thus, increased commitment to work from strengths and also to repair gaps or to extend ways of being can arise from increased self-awareness and habits of reflection that build the muscles of the internal supervisor.

Frames of thought

Frames of thought provide options about focus and choice. They direct the attention of the practitioner to matters to think about. A number of supervisory frames are now commonly taught: the Hawkins and Shohet (2006) seven-"eyed" model provides choices to focus on process within the client–counsellor loop or the supervisor–supervisee one. The Inskipp and Proctor (2000, 2001) model of supervisory tasks draws attention to responsibilities and normative functions, to educative or developmental ones, and to restorative support and the enablement of creativity. Carroll (1996) describes the different roles of a supervisor and proposes training foci for each role. Page and Wosket's (2001) cyclical model draws attention to different phases of a supervisory session. Other frames of thought can be noted in the other chapters of this book, as authors from different perspectives describe key ideas they use.

Bramley (1996, pp. 50–53) describes five elements from her psychodynamic perspective that the process of self-supervision could use for focus, as follows.

- Reflection about the client from the history. Questions to the self of the counsellor might include "what does it feel like to be him?" as well as questions about defences, unconscious strategies, attachments, and so on.
- Reflection about the relationship and working alliance.

- Reflection about the transference. Using trial identification about the client now and at earlier stages of his personal development.
- Reflection about, and examination of, the counsellor's own feelings and reactions to the client.
- Reflecting on an assessment of the client's motivation and readiness to change.

She encourages the internal supervisor to "think the unthinkable, ponder the imponderable, and consider the impossible response". All these very usefully free thinking and encourage the internal supervisor to play with possibilities and connect with intuitive reactions.

A confident grasp of an ethical framework fundamentally supports supervision. It seems to us that supervision training must provide opportunities to work with an ethical framework to underpin good practice. In this way, ethical principles are understood in practice as living, everyday realities, and become a familiar frame for thought, reflection, and choices.

Before leaving the idea of "frames", we note there may well be some "unlearning" that it is equally necessary to do. We are aware that some practitioners can develop what might amount, in other contexts, to be almost a co-dependency on a particular model as holding "the truth". Developing the idea of there being many truths encourages the possibility that supervisees become more open to difference and diversity, and is essential for supervisors who work with people trained in other therapy modalities or allied professions.

Skills

Casement (1985), who created the term "internal supervisor", writes of "islands of intellectual contemplation". He describes these as a "mental space needed even when with a patient for the internal supervisor to begin to operate" (p. 31).

The skills of the internal supervisor are largely those that capitalize on observation and "inclusion", as described above, as well as reflection on the intersubjective experience of supervision. It is particularly important for the identification of parallel process that the supervisor has sufficient analytical capacity to identify and summarize themes and map them on to any expectations within the supervisory relationship. Allied to this, the supervisor needs enough awareness of her own normal responses and those of the supervisee in order to notice and be curious about different or unusual interactions worthy of exploration or comment.

Novice counsellors might need help with the process of distillation that is needed to bring their work to supervision in a focused way. The processes of supervision, and the interventions the supervisor prefers, become tools the supervisee can use for him or her self in future preparation or, alternatively, for self-supervision. Bramley (1996, p. 44) describes supervision as "two people learning how to think together". Within an enabling relationship, the supervisee gradually learns to do it for herself. The supervisee who experiences the supervisor's process over and over, learns to self-supervise as she develops her own internal witness, critic, and commentator. When the supervisor muses aloud about content or process, and offers educated guesses, or, in some contexts, fantasies, generates ideas, and shows how she tests for evidence to back a hunch, the supervisee finds a variety of modes for reflection and can choose those that most suit when doing it for his or her self.

Attitudes and values

It is the attitude to the self that probably makes the most difference to the work of the internal supervisor. When the practitioner develops as much generosity to self as she offers to others, she will have an even-handed sort of attitude to noticing, accepting, and exploring mistakes. A supervisor will aim to encourage this in a supervisee so that this practitioner, too, can hold a reflective attitude, rather than one that avoids responsibility for practice difficulties.

However, the other crucial developmental step is to become aware of personal attitudes to difference, which brings with it the challenges of engaging respectfully with supervisees who differ in class, gender, race, culture, religion, sexual orientation, learning styles, or in other salient ways. A simple example occurred to one of us while reflecting on her mix of current supervisees. One of us (CB) would admit to being very ordered and organized. She has a supervisee who is experienced and a near contemporary (therefore mature), who would come to supervision with a portfolio of papers which would fall and scatter and, in the early days, it seemed as if she had difficulty in keeping a handle on who was whom or why they were working with her. In due course, as CB adjusted to her very different way of operating and developed a fondness for her, she could truly appreciate what a warm and loving individual she was, doing sound work with a variety of challenging individuals. The irritation she felt early on melted away as she acknowledged, and came to value, a different way of working that nevertheless had good results.

Flexibility and style

The more flexible the supervisor and the greater the range of interventions and foci she routinely makes use of, the wider the range of options the supervisee becomes used to. Early on, reflection using one model might be comforting, providing options, or might be rejected if it does not meet the needs or fit with the perspectives or learning style of the supervisee. The less confident and perhaps less experienced practitioner can also find too much choice on offer confusing and muddling, so the supervisor needs to be ever mindful of what she is there for (the supervisee and her clients) and not give in to showing off or performing.

As the internal supervisor develops, so the supervisor-in-training is likely to become more self-reliant and less dependent on the views of others or their approval. Expanding on this, we could surmise that, as we become more assured in ourselves, we are more able to embrace, rather than be scared by, difference. Even very experienced practitioners can seek other views because of the benefit of other perspectives, but they can hold on to their own frames of thought as they add in new angles, valuing the unique insights that arise from the overlay of different perspectives.

Course contributions to internal supervisor development

However we look at the roles and functions of supervision, supervisors are expected to act as the guardians or monitors of good practice in the profession. As we have endeavoured to suggest throughout this chapter, the development of the internal supervisor is vital to maintain this rigour. It would follow, therefore, that supervision training must contain various elements that support and stimulate this growth. The process of observed practice with feedback lies at its heart.

Giving and receiving feedback is at the heart of supervisor training (see chapters on Assessment and Feedback). For the internal supervisor, however, its function is specifically to develop the capacity to evaluate the self and others, and to enhance awareness of the impact of our behaviour. Thus, it commonly expands a view of a shared experience by including others' perspectives on it. Doing this builds awareness of "self-in-relation-to-others". Inevitably, in an assessed course, there will be some comparative and competitive feelings and anxiety about assessment, whether expressed or not.

Empathy exercises, those designed to increase mindfulness of difference, and invitations to reflect individually on responses to self-awareness, prompts participants to increase attunement to self and others. The more subtle and familiar this process of fine-tuning becomes, the more information the internal supervisor has to work with.

Moving outside the supervisory "box" and into creative ways of working stimulates those parts of self not reached by words alone. Sessions during training that use different creative materials, as well as inspiring participants to use what might just be there in a therapy room, encourage flexibility in ways of being. Creative ways of working can take us closer to the edges of examining our lives and, in so doing, keep the internal witness on its toes.

Taking up supervision training often provides the opportunity for participants to become more aware of just how out of kilter their own sense of well being may be. Most are engaged at some level in the triple pressures of work, family, and training, and, as a result, have restricted time for reflection and reverie about their work. Being mindful of energy levels throughout the course, trainers can encourage good practice by abandoning, for instance, what might have been tutor input, for participants to talk among themselves and recoup. This would seem to offer by example the interface between supervision and therapy that can be explored for healthy well being. Planned explorations about resilience, fitness to practise, and the work–life balance expand on this. Becoming more aware about the vital necessity to protect time and develop habits of reflection, the novice supervisors might more readily explore resilience with their supervisees. Almost all will commit to this in principle. It is often the assessment period of the course that reveals the real life pressures that make it challenging in practice. Juggling ongoing and crisis needs of family members, the demands of professional or voluntary work, and the requirements to reflect, think, read, learn, and develop, reveals drivers to perfectionism, effort to please others, hurry up, and be strong.

Comments

The "hawk in your mind" (Bolton, 2001, p. 151) that takes an overview is held aloft by the updrafts of respect for intuitive and sensory awareness as well as critical evaluation. Many participants completing their training on both our training courses comment on the impact it has had on their attitude to their existing supervision and also on their capacity to engage with self-supervision. Most who start their training, complete it. It might be argued that those few who have dropped out over the years are those who are less able to take the wider view that is demanded by the internal supervisor. A few others take longer to finish, often because they are more hesitant to let go of existing certainties in terms of model and practice. These few need more help and more encouragement to expand into the wide-open fields beyond their own self constructed fences (Encke, 2008). Most participants feel free enough to develop their unique styles and yet benefit from observation of the practice of others in an atmosphere of encouragement. If the internal supervisor holds a core value about psychological connection and supports the empowerment of the practitioner and thus the client, a balance between gentle connection and robust review can then be held comfortably.

References

Allen, P. (2004). The use of interpersonal process recall (IPR) in person-centred supervision. In: K. Tudor & M. Worrall (Eds.), *Freedom to Practise*. Ross-on-Wye: PCCs Books.

Bolton, G. (2001). *Reflective Practice*. London: Paul Chapman.

Bramley, W. (1996). *The Supervisory Couple in Broad-Spectrum Psychotherapy*. London: Free Association.

Carroll, M. (1996). *Counselling Supervision: Theory, Skills and Practice*. London: Cassells.

Casement, P. (1985). *On Learning From the Patient*. London: Tavistock.

Encke, J. (2008). Breaking the box: a challenge to free ourselves. In: R. Shohet (Ed.), *Passionate Supervision* (pp. 16–32). London: Jessica Kingsley.

Gilbert, M. C., & Evans, K. (2000). *Psychotherapy Supervision: An Integrative Relational Approach to Psychotherapy Supervision*. Buckingham: Open University Press.

Hawkins, P., & Shohet, R. (2006). *Supervision in the Helping Professions*. Buckingham: Open University Press.

Inskipp, F. (1999). Training supervisees to use supervision In: E. Holloway & M. Carroll (Eds.), *Training Counsellor Supervisors* (pp. 184–210). London: Sage.

Inskipp, F., & Proctor, B. (2000). *The Art, Craft and Tasks of Counselling Supervision, Part 1: Making the Most of Supervision*. Twickenham: Cascade.

Inskipp, F., & Proctor, B. (2001). *Becoming a Supervisor* (2nd edn). Twickenham: Cascade.

McLeod, J. (2007). *Counselling Skill*. McGraw Hill: Open University Press.

Page, S., & Wosket, V. (2001). *Supervising the Counsellor: A Cyclical Model*. Hove: Routledge.

Schon, D. (1987). *Educating the Reflective Practitioner*. San Francisco, CA: Jossey-Bass.

Wright, K. (1991). *Vision and Separation: Between Mother and Baby*. London: Free Association.

CHAPTER NINE

Developing skills: practice, observation, and feedback

Anthea Millar

"Not everything that is faced can be changed, but nothing can be changed until it is faced"

(James Baldwin)

Neela is doing her first observed practice session on a supervision training. As her peers and tutor observe her work she's nervous and uncertain, as if her years of experience as a counsellor are turning to dust. She fears being judged as incompetent and a fraud. She reproaches herself: surely as a counsellor of some professional standing she should already know what to do.

Neela's experience may resonate for you. Certainly I can relate to it. Enrolling on a supervision training could be seen as a statement that we have achieved a certain level of practitioner competence. So, when practice is exposed to observation and feedback, we might feel there is much more to lose than on our core practitioner trainings, and be startled to revisit old feelings of inferiority, shame, and confusion. Yet, there is no running away from it: being observed in practice, and experiencing feedback is a fundamental part of effective supervision education.

Openness to challenge and feedback as essential ingredients to good practice has been well confirmed by Miller, Hubble, and Duncan's (2008) extensive research into aspects of therapeutic change and practitioner excellence. After tracking the outcomes of tens of thousands of clients and therapists, it would seem that success is not determined simply by a practitioner's talent or by gaining years of experience. These alone can actually create a false sense of confidence, with mistakes no longer noticed, and, as a result, learning opportunities are lost or stagnation occurs.

Their findings identify that excellence involves two key aspects that challenge the idea of "natural talent" or "technical prowess". Success involves simply working harder than most at improving performance, and "spending time specifically devoted to reaching for objectives just beyond one's level of proficiency".

In addition, Miller and his colleagues state, "to reach the top level, attentiveness to feedback is essential . . . this extra step lets the person understand how and when she is improving" (*ibid.*, p. 6).

Keeping engaged, even in the face of challenge, is the crucial skill here.

Facing fears and building courage

Miller, Hubble, and Duncan's research underlines what I believe needs to be at the heart of effective supervision education: plenty of opportunity for observed practice that challenges the participants to stretch themselves to engage in new processes, accompanied by very regular and clearly structured feedback to enable mistakes to be made without shame and blame.

Central to these processes (and, ultimately, for all effective supervision) is feedback that provides encouragement. "En-*courage*-ment", with the building of "courage" at its heart, involves having our strengths acknowledged, alongside appropriate rigorous challenge. This provides a potent combination that helps us to face our fears and have "the courage to be imperfect" (Dreikurs, 1970). It is different from the use of praise or rewards, which create extrinsically motivated behaviour and a pattern of winners and losers. Encouragement enables people to develop an inner sense of satisfaction and motivation. For this to happen, a climate of equality and collegiality needs to be created from the outset of the supervision training.

Chris, reflecting on a supervision practice writes,

> The session has been a very useful if painful learning experience. It has helped me to appreciate the consequences of not sharing my thoughts and feelings in the session and given me the impetus and deep motivation to rectify the situation. The key is encouragement—both to myself and in how I appreciate the other. Encouragement becomes the container within which everything else occurs.

Equality: creating a climate of imperfection

"To be human means to have inferiority feelings" (Adler, 1933 [1964], p. 54). Adler suggested that the development of inferiority feelings result in large part from subjective childhood comparisons with other family members. As these feelings are so uncomfortable, we compensate by striving to overcome them through such patterns as superiority and perfectionism. Experiencing inferiority feelings and then compensating for them through some form of "acting out" response happens to most of us when under some stress. The challenge for us all is that if this dynamic is not appropriately identified and addressed, a power imbalance is perpetuated. This, in turn, is likely to create problems in both the training and supervisory relationship.

As an educator, I need to face my own fears and limitations, be ready to share my imperfections and capabilities, and also be open to the skills that participants on the supervision training bring with them. As Caro Bailey has identified in this book, by enabling this mix of competence, humility, ability to learn from experience, and congruence, we are also aiding the development of an inner authority, essential for effective supervision.

The way we observe others, and give and receive feedback, commonly reflects our early experiences. Our interpretation and response to the guidance, discipline, and feedback given at home and school is very likely to be echoed in the here and now, particularly when being observed.

Openly sharing fears and fantasies about receiving and giving feedback at the beginning of a supervision training course can help to dispel the fiction that everyone else feels confident, capable, and in control. It also models a process that can be used in a modified form at the start of a new supervision contract. This can prevent misunderstandings and be particularly helpful in the relationship with participants who might otherwise seem lacking in insight and resistant and defensive around receiving feedback.

The following exercise aims to enable this exploration:

1. *What does observed practice and receiving feedback mean to me?*

Share responses in pairs and then in the whole group.
How do I feel about being observed in practice sessions?
What are my hopes and fears about being observed and receiving feedback from a) peers b) trainers?
What makes it easier for me to receive feedback?
What is particularly difficult for me, when receiving, feedback?
What are my developmental aims for receiving feedback?

2. *What does giving feedback and observing practice mean to me?*

What are my hopes and fears about observing and giving feedback to (a) peers (b) trainers?
What makes it easier for me to give feedback?
What is particularly difficult for me, when giving feedback?
What are my developmental aims about giving feedback?

Observed skills practice

When observed practice is carried out with peers, it provides opportunities for the group to come together with a common goal. Offering a clear statement at the outset of the training that making mistakes is inevitable and valuable frees participants to take risks, fall down, pick themselves up, and discover their own strengths and those of others. This can create a real sense of community rather than competition. Donna illustrates this development in a reflection made early on in the supervision training:

> I did initially feel some angst around returning to "student" mode and working alongside some others who, unlike me, have been

> working in supervisory capacities for some time. However, I felt the playing field quickly level and while our existing experiences may have differed, our desire to learn and personally grow and develop was very similar. This realization enabled me to have confidence to participate more fully than on the first day, where I had felt a little overwhelmed.

On our courses, tutors work to equalize a potential power imbalance by also offering live supervision demonstrations in front of the group. We face our own fears, expose both our skills and imperfections, and aim to provide a base for participants to move on to their own observed practice sessions by critiquing and commenting on the demonstration.

In my experience, when this kind of encouraging environment is created, despite participants' initial fears, the observed skills practice is most consistently identified as being the most beneficial part of the course. Some common forms of this are as follows.

1. Groups of 3–4 participants plus (or minus) a tutor. Each participant takes a turn being: (a) supervisor, (b) supervisee (bringing a real issue), and (c) observer. The tutor (if present) and observer provide more detailed verbal and written feedback to the supervisor. The supervisor and supervisee offer immediate verbal feedback.

   The "supervisor" shares their experience, first identifying what went well, and only then identifying what areas they wish to develop further. This is followed by feedback from the supervisee, then the observer(s), then finally the tutor, if present. All are encouraged to give descriptive feedback using specific examples first of what went well, followed by suggestions for learning edges there could be for the future.

   Whenever possible, recording the sessions will offer additional learning opportunities for the participant in the 'hot' seat of supervisor.
2. Interpersonal process recall (Kagan, 1980). This method is most effective for processing and evaluating very recent video or audio recordings of supervision. The participant and a facilitator (tutor or peer), jointly review the recording, stopping it as it prompts experiences that could otherwise be forgotten. The

facilitator explores further by asking focused lead questions (Bernard & Goodyear, 2004, p. 221).

3. The participant provides a recording (and possibly a written transcript) of a supervision session held outside the course, with an accompanying written reflective analysis. Tutor and/or peers look/listen to it and offer their own feedback.
4. The Goldfish bowl: two participants work together as supervisor and supervisee in front of whole training group. The tutor facilitates feedback from the "supervisor", "supervisee", and group members regarding the supervisor's work.

Each course will have their unique emphases for practice. However, there are core skills and processes generic to most supervision. Wheeler (1999) has created a guide for reflecting on supervision practice that we have found helpful on our courses (Figure 9.1). Although it is unlikely that the whole range of skills described below will be needed in each session, it offers a useful focus for reflection and feedback.

Observation through differing lenses

Having guidelines about what we want to observe is all very well. The real challenge comes in dealing with the many and varied lenses through which each of us sees the world. From my Adlerian base, I draw on the concept of "private logic" (Ansbacher & Ansbacher, 1956). This refers to our uniquely created and biased perception of self, people, and the world that we created during our early relationships. Most of us continue to use aspects of this "private", rather than "common", logic, even if outdated, to guide our movement in our present day life.

Despite the inevitability of our biased perceptions, the more encouraged or secure we feel in the relationship with others, whether as an educator or course participant, the less distorted our vision of the world and others will be. Here, there are parallels with Bowlby's (1988) attachment ideas and "internal working models", where he suggests that those who have experienced more secure attachments are likely to be more flexible and open in their responses.

Creating the relationship

1. Is there a contract between the supervisor and supervisee that creates a working alliance?
2. Does the supervisee feel comfortable to share vulnerability?
3. Is the relationship appropriate to the stage of development of the supervisee?

Extending the supervisee's learning

1. Does the supervisor offer a framework for understanding the client?
2. Are appropriate suggestions/information given in the session?
3. Does the supervisor offer the supervisee an opportunity to reflect on suggestions—and also the safety to reject them explicitly if they appear inappropriate to the supervisee?

Working with personal issues

1. Does the supervisor help the supervisee become aware of personal issues emerging in relation to their counselling work?
2. Does the supervisor respond to the supervisee's personal issues appropriately?
3. Does the supervisor keep the client in focus for the appropriate proportion of the session?

Consultation

1. To what extent does the session focus on each of the 7 eyes (Hawkins & Shohet, 2006)?
2. Does the supervisor take account of issues of difference and diversity?

Monitoring professional and ethical issues

1. Does the supervisor recognize the ethical/professional issues in the supervisee's presentation?
2. Does the supervisor respond to the ethical issues appropriately?

Evaluation

1. Does the supervisor offer the supervisee appropriate feedback? (Use of encouragement and authority.)
2. Does the supervisor provide the opportunity for the supervisee to offer feedback about the usefulness of the supervision to him or her? (i.e., is the relationship equal enough?)

Administration

1. Does the supervisor pick up and work with institutional issues raised, and understand the context in which the counselling takes place?
2. Are appropriate boundaries kept in the session?

Figure 9.1. Guidelines for reflecting on supervisory practice. Adapted from Wheeler (1999).

Another essential aspect to address when preparing for the skills practice and feedback process is building more conscious awareness around issues of individual, developmental, and cultural differences between the observed participant, peer observers, and tutor. Where possible, these need to be addressed openly early on. This involves clear and transparent contracting about the process of feedback and assessment prior to the observed practice that includes clarifying meanings and needs around feedback.

This contracting will be further supported by open adherence to a set of ethical values, principles, personal moral qualities, and guidance of good practice, such as described in the BACP Ethical Framework (British Association for Counselling and Psychotherapy, 2002). This can then create a safe meeting point for direct and clear educative feedback.

Feedback as a meeting point

Feedback is a central activity of supervision. It supports therapeutic competence and safeguards client welfare. As this is such an essential skill, modelling good practice during supervision training is vital. Taught modules related to "giving feedback" are useful; practice, however, is essential. The feedback structures offered as part of the ongoing formative assessment, have, in my experience, made the most impact on participants' learning.

I believe that most of our actions are socially embedded. As such, feedback can be seen as an interaction, or a *meeting point* between individuals, rather than something that one person gives another. Claiborn and Lichtenberg (1989) have identified feedback in supervision as an ongoing process between supervisor and supervisee, the quality of the relationship between the two parties being central to the way feedback is received. One-sided feedback in supervision invariably creates a power imbalance. Page and Wosket (2001) have described how, even when the supervisor shares positive comments, if it is only one-sided, this can still become a misuse of power. Equally, if the supervisee or course participant is the only one sharing their experience, they are left wondering what the other is actually thinking or feeling.

Communication of feedback

Creating structures for regular feedback between all the course participants as well as the tutors from the very start of the course builds a learning culture. The feedback process then becomes a norm that is not attached to the individual's whole personhood, but can become a valuable, rather than dreaded, part of their ongoing development.

For the observed practices on our training, one tutor stays with a group of four participants throughout the sessions in each module. We aim, as tutors, to demonstrate clear, direct, encouraging, and challenging feedback from the outset. We have found the participants themselves soon also offer each other feedback that is specific, balanced, and encouraging, including useful challenge. So, as well as offering valuable input to their peers, they are developing the skills of offering encouraging feedback that will be essential to them as supervisors. Hawkins and Shohet's (2006, p. 134) acronym "CORBS" offers a helpful reminder to the participants of the key principles for giving feedback: it needs to be Clear, Owned, Regular, Balanced, and Specific.

Encouragement is a complex process that is much more than simply expressing positives (Millar, 2007), and for this discussion I will touch on one key aspect. Different from praise, encouragement is largely non-evaluative, focusing on *what* the person is doing, rather than *how* the person *compares* with others. Encouragement can be achieved by avoiding the use of adjectival labels such as "good", "unethical", "clever", "non empathic", and also by keeping in mind the assets and positive *intentions* of the supervisee.

Instead, by using descriptive language and paying particular attention to *verbs*, feedback offered is very specific, identifying what the course participant has actually been doing, without needing to evaluate it. From this base, the tutor can invite the participant's thoughts, add their own view, or provide educative information as appropriate. Here respectful use of "signposting: is helpful: e.g., "I'd like to discuss the ethical issues that may be involved in this situation . . . can we look at this now?" Further space can then be given for two-way discussion with the participant.

As an example, here's a tutor's feedback to Alan, following a skills practice:

> Near the end of the session with B, you opened up some valuable exploration about her client's sexuality that helped identify some issues she hadn't previously addressed. What seemed harder to work with was B's feeling of stuckness in the counselling, which resulted in you also feeling very stuck. I have some thoughts about the dynamics that might be going on here, and possibly how this might be worked with in your future sessions. Would you be interested to explore this further? . . . What do you think about what I've said?

The use of Socratic questions as a form of guided discovery can also help participants focus more deeply on their work, this also keeping a two-way flow of communication.

For example: "What do you appreciate about the way you handled that?"

"How might you do things differently in future?"

"What do you plan to take away from our discussion?"

"What has been useful from this feedback?"

"What has been less helpful from this feedback?"

Written feedback

Some education establishments may require the use of grades, ratings, and tick boxes, and these modes of written feedback can lose touch with an interactive feedback process. However, two-way feedback can still take place in written work, particularly when the course participant has also been invited to evaluate their own work and when the feedback principles described above continue to be addressed.

The following is an extract taken from a much longer piece of written feedback I shared with Suzanne after listening to a tape of her supervision work and reading her own reflections on the session.

> Your written reflection demonstrates mature evaluation of the areas that went well and those you want to develop further.
>
> In the session itself I particularly noted the following:
>
> You provided a free space for your supervisee, X, to share her own reflections and feelings on the client.

You raised an important point when you asked X about the possibility of contacting the psychiatrist.

You helped X make a useful link between her early experiences and her experience now with the client.

You put forward some key insights about the client that proved very helpful to X, e.g., "being anxious is part of her identity".

You drew attention to the need to address the boundary difficulties at the next session.

Learning edge: As you suggest, further focused questioning and clarification of X's experience and inner processes could have enabled greater movement at an earlier stage. There was also a need to explore more openly with X a number of key ethical issues that you had noted, but didn't feel able to address in the session itself. It seems that it was hard in this instance to allow your own considerable experience to be expressed here (maybe a parallel with X's process?). Trusting in your own authority as a supervisor, and voicing it confidently will be an important area of ongoing development.

Wheeler's guide was given to students beforehand, and I used it to structure my own observations and reflections on Suzanne's practice (this extract focuses on the section "extending the supervisee's learning"). I kept in mind the question "*What* is happening?", describing the interventions and intentions I observed. Although I used some evaluative adjectives within the flow, the main focus is on verbs.

This process kept me focused on the specifics of her work and process, rather than falling into the trap of evaluating the person. I then noted and shared my thoughts on areas that I believed would be important for her to develop further. Engaging with Suzanne's written reflections also helped to create a meeting point between us, so that even in written feedback, a two-way process was maintained.

Receiving feedback

Being able to receive feedback in a constructive way is a skill in itself. Whether in the role of educator or a course participant, we are likely to experience some form of defensiveness in the face of feedback, but we can choose what we *do* with this discomfort. Maybe we experience old feelings of shame and defend ourselves by shrinking and losing our sense of capability, or perhaps we compensate for our feelings of inferiority and become aggressive. Either way, this destroys potential learning and growth. The challenge for us all is to be able to listen openly to the feedback, and identify how, if at all, this might support our future practice.

Receiving feedback is far from a passive process. Hawkins and Shohet emphasize that we also have considerable responsibility as "receivers" and offer the following guidelines linked with their acronym "CORBS":

> - If necessary ask for the feedback to be more Clear, Owned, Regular, Balanced, or Specific
> - Listen to the feedback all the way through without judging it or jumping to a defensive response, both of which can mean that the feedback is misunderstood.
> - Try not to explain compulsively why you did something or even explain away positive feedback. Try and hear others' feedback as their experiences of you. Often it is enough to hear the feedback and say "thank you".
> - Ask for feedback you are not given but would like to hear. [2006, p. 134]

Challenges with giving and receiving feedback

A bottom line for supervisors is to ensure the well being of the client. When feedback is given ineffectively or the course participant/supervisee is not able to receive it, there is a real danger of poor practice continuing, and this having an impact on the client.

When course participants seem unable to learn from feedback, and there is real concern about their readiness to become supervisors, it is often much harder to be direct and clear. This is particularly relevant when the relationship is not well established, or we fear the extremes of our own judgements. To compensate for this, we might push down our deeper concerns, resulting in feedback that comes over as vague, general, or inconsistent. Even more serious is when we give only positive feedback, despite having serious concerns. It is always important to identify course participants' strengths, but, as discussed previously, encouragement is also about enabling personal growth through challenge and confronting the areas for further development.

Scaife (2009, p. 325) defines challenge as an invitation to test one's capabilities to the full, which can then generate new perspectives at a cognitive level, and create new options for action. She reminds supervisors that challenging does require them to own their own authority in the role by making requirements clear, using skills of direct communication. Usefully, she invites supervisors to take responsibility for their part of a difficulty in a working alliance: "Since the difficulty is being identified by the supervisor, it is the supervisor who is experiencing the problem and inviting the assistance of the supervisee in its solution".

Similarly, in relation to unsatisfactory performance, Scaife (*ibid.*, p. 328) distinguishes between problematic performance, incompetence, and unethical practice by trainees and qualified counsellors. She recommends preference and purpose statements that make the supervisor's opinions and requirements clear. She is more explicit than most about when and how to fail a supervisee, reminding readers of the importance of record-keeping to ensure fairness.

When offering more challenging feedback in supervision, some of Munson's (2002) suggestions also provide a helpful frame, as follows.

- Challenge only in ways that promote personal growth, and that enables the course participant to use the feedback to their own advantage and benefit.
- Focus only on behaviours that you sense can be changed and be specific in the challenge given.
- Offer the challenge as your opinion not a fact.
- Separate your personal feelings about the course participant from the need to challenge.
- Avoid accusatory comments.

In the following hypothetical example, Daniel has consistently moved into a teaching mode on the supervision practices. His tutor wishes to acknowledge his strengths while also clearly underlining major concerns about his practice that could ultimately result in him not meeting the assessment criteria. Keeping in mind Munson's frame, and using description rather than labelling, she shares the following feedback.

> You have consistently shown well-developed skills in analytic and abstract thinking. These were used to good effect today when you identified possible organizational issues faced by your supervisee, and also in your understanding of psychopathology in terms of the client's mental health. Your sincere wish to offer educative support to your supervisee comes over strongly.
>
> These very skills are also creating difficulties for the supervisory process. During this last practice, you interrupted your supervisee to put forward an explanation of Bowlby's attachment theory when she was expressing her concern about the client's suicidal feelings and her non-attendance that week. Your supervisee responded by stopping talking about her concerns, and the discussion moved to a theoretical exploration of Bowlby's ideas.
>
> For your growth as a supervisor, and to meet the criteria to enable completion of this course, it will be essential for you to show further evidence of working with the supervisee's process. My thoughts are that as a starting point it could be useful for you to review using core listening skills, such as summarizing and reflecting as a means to help you hold back from the teaching role, and so focus on the supervisee's process.
>
> What are your thoughts and feelings about what I have said so far? . . . How do you think you could most usefully build on these skills? . . .

It might be that, despite all apparent efforts, a course participant is still unable to respond well to the feedback process. In this instance, it would be important first to explore whether there is an organizational or systemic issue present. If this does not appear to be the case, then it is unlikely this person is ready to undertake a supervisory role and this needs to be communicated clearly and respectfully. The challenge might be that those who are not able to hear and use feedback to support their progress and development are often bewildered to discover that they have not met the requirements to complete the course.

Conclusion

Returning to Miller and colleagues' research, their findings about practitioner excellence indicate good practice in supervision education. This includes a willingness to engage in repeated and deliberate practice, alongside effective regular feedback, where mistakes can be freely made and accepted as a basis for learning.

If we find ourselves confronting problems with course participants during their skills development, before finalizing our evaluative judgements of the supervisee, it is important first to reassess the feedback processes to ensure that they are not structured in a way that could be contributing to feelings of inequality and inferiority. To minimize power misuse (often occurring unwittingly) and model effective feedback skills, all supervision courses that offer observed practice need to ensure positive structures and processes are in place from the very beginning. Within a climate of equality and encouragement, course participants are able to take risks, make mistakes, and, most crucially, learn without fear. Learning is enabled when initial baselines are identified, effective skills are spelled out, practice is deliberate, and feedback is focused. A key issue is maintaining motivation and engagement in learning despite uncomfortable moments. When assessors can offer challenge in this spirit, all participants can also feel confident that the final qualification represents a fair and rigorous assessment that has not avoided difficult issues.

References

Adler, A. (1933). *Social Interest: A Challenge to Mankind*. New York: Capricorn, 1964.

Ansbacher, H. L., & Ansbacher, R. R. (Eds.) (1956). *The Individual Psychology of Alfred Adler*. New York: Harper & Row.

Baldwin, J. http://quoteworld.org/quotes/907 (accessed 9 May 2009).

Bernard, J. M., & Goodyear, R. K. (2004). *Fundamentals of Clinical Supervision* (3rd edn). Boston, MA: Allyn & Bacon.

Bowlby, J. (1988). *A Secure Base: Clinical Applications of Attachment Theory*. London: Routledge.

British Association for Counselling and Psychotherapy (2002). *Ethical Framework For Good Practice in Counselling and Psychotherapy.* Rugby: BACP.

Claiborn, C. D., & Lichtenberg, J. W. (1989). Interactional counseling. *Counseling Psychologist, 17*: 355–453.

Dreikurs, R. (1970). The courage to be imperfect. In: *Articles of Supplementary Readings*. Chicago: Alfred Adler Institute.

Hawkins, P., & Shohet, R. (2006). *Supervision in the Helping Professions.* Milton Keynes: Open University Press.

Kagan, N. (1980). Influencing human interaction: eighteen years with IPR. In: A. K. Hess (Ed.), *Psychotherapy Supervision: Theory, Research and Practice* (pp. 262–286). New York: Wiley.

Millar, A. (2007). Encouragement and other Es. *Therapy Today, 18*(2): 40–42.

Miller, S., Hubble, M., & Duncan, B. (2008). Supershrinks. *Therapy Today, 19*(1): 4–9.

Munson, C. E. (2002). *Handbook of Clinical Social Work Supervision* (3rd edn). New York: Haworth.

Page, S., & Woskett, V. (2001). *Supervising the Counsellor: A Cyclical Model* (2nd edn). Hove: Brunner Routledge.

Scaife, J. (2009). *Supervision in Clinical Practice: A Practitioner's Guide.* London: Routledge.

Wheeler, S. (1999). Criteria for marking taped supervision (34 competencies). Unpublished paper [reproduced with permission].

CHAPTER TEN

Developing authority from the inside out

Penny Henderson

"The longest journey is the journey inwards"

(Hammarskjöld, 1964, p. 65)

Authority is defined in the online dictionary as "the power to enforce laws, exact obedience, command, determine or judge". The *Shorter Oxford Dictionary* adds that to be "in authority" is to be "in a position of power or control". This might imply a legitimate right to exercise control and power over opinion or behaviour. Associated ideas include responsibility, maturity, consistency, and flexibility, influence and autonomy, obedience and oppression.

Authority within a supervisory role may arise from expectations linked to status or role, personal charisma, expertise, or rules and regulations. It has a quality of entitlement as well as responsibility, that is, it may be something we *have* as well as something we *take* or *use*. It might be experienced through the "presence" of the supervisor, and demonstrated through reflexive and autonomous practice that has the confidence of self-determination. Think of the people you know, or who are in the public domain, that have authority. How do you recognize this? Often confident assertion of a position is part of the impression.

It is important for novice supervisors to develop their clarity about what they are responsible for (or not) and to whom they are responsible. I have seen course participants struggle to become engaged in the issues of authority, responsibility, and boundary setting. Some have to overcome blocks arising from bad experiences as supervisees. Exhibiting strong aversion to being, or being seen as, oppressive, they confuse being authoritative with being oppressive or authoritarian. Others do behave oppressively, and this has to be named. An example of my feedback to one trainee who was not tuning in to her supervisee went like this:

> Your extensive knowledge of theory, and your stated intention to be of use led you to interrupt the supervisee frequently . . . There was little evidence of your "being with" him . . . It could be useful to explore your issues about authority and control with someone, and I'd be happy for us to talk some of this through if you like . . . You acknowledge your tendency to be didactic and this limits sharing of your own responses within the supervision.

Learning to take authority includes many significant developmental steps for new supervisors of almost all theoretical orientations (Henderson, 2006). Under everyday circumstances, it entails taking initiatives and setting boundaries. Participants on courses can experience the positives of authority, and grasp the relevance of reflection about their own attitudes to power, authority, influence, and control if they experience transparent, contractual, respectful, and collegial relationships within supervisor training. For those who have had experiences of oppressive or insensitive supervision, the shift is immense from seeing the gaze of the supervisor as akin to a Gorgon's (that freezes thought and kills self-esteem) to that of a nurturing, boundary-setting care-giver. A supervisor's reflections are most useful if they mirror existing strengths and potential, and offer encouragement to risk professional development (Millar, 2007).

As our course developed, I came to see increased self-awareness and development of an authentic professional style as highly significant to authority. A supervisor has to be willing to consider thinking of herself as a mature practitioner, as if she were an elder of a tribe or a grandparent (Banks, 2002). In other words, be someone who can hold in mind the needs both of the client and the supervisee, as a grandparent may do with two generations. For some novice supervisors this shift in self-perception emerges slowly.

Learning about authority as a supervisor involves lifelong learning from experiences that are often pervaded with tensions. One tension entails staying connected, holding on to empathy and encouragement, without abandoning thinking and standard setting. Thus, the supervisor simultaneously holds in mind both the relationship and thoughts about supervisory issues.

Another tension lies in conflicts between values, skills, and emotions. Attitudes to conflict or risk taking, for instance, reveal willingness to disagree with a supervisee. Skills of direct communication are required to do so on more emotive or serious matters without impairing the relationship irreparably.

Fear of disapproval by the *supervisee* can also influence what the supervisor says, and how the message is conveyed. People can become tentative and very anxious when they have to deliver bad news, and trainee supervisors benefit from encouragement to be compassionate but direct.

Attitudes and core values

Shared exploration of the impact of difference and diversity on supervisory work and relationships underpins this topic during training. Being matter of fact about potentially explosive or uncomfortable issues is essential for exploring differences, whether these are routinely addressed about obvious differences or emerge at a difficult moment in the course of work. Differences in learning styles, culturally and socially biased assumptions, sensitivity to minority concerns, and institutional oppression are relevant, and might pop up during practice or be introduced specifically. Lago and Thompson's (1997) ideas about triangles of difference and presentation of proxy (acceptable) selves provide one vehicle for thinking about relationships where difference is an issue. Some grasp of processes of internalized oppression and institutional oppression is essential, as being authoritative and taking authority can be experienced or misconstrued as raw and biased oppression, whether or not this is intended.

Writers from many different theoretical approaches agree about the nature of a collegial supervisory relationship that will encourage a supervisee to take equal responsibility for the efficacy of the working alliance. Where a supervisor is dogmatic, didactic, confrontational, or authoritarian, the supervisee is most likely to become rebellious or passive (Mander, 2002), or offer "spurious compliance" (Rosenblatt & Mayer, 1975). If the supervisor enables the supervisee to feel safe enough to explore experiences, find meanings, and make decisions about his or her work as an autonomous professional, this facilitation will invite courageous and resourceful reflective practice. The issue of standards and safe practice are central. Wheeler and King's research (2000, 2001) explores experienced supervisors' perceptions of their responsibilities.

The relevance of empathy and congruence as a base for what Hawkins and Shohet (2006) call the "fearless compassion" of the supervisor becomes clear. It is an interesting and sensitive process to support the development of fearless compassion in course participants as relatively less experienced colleagues who are taking up a role demanding maturity and confidence when the very experience of being on a course can re-stimulate feelings of conscious incompetence.

A productive working alliance works best when goals are aligned through careful contracting, and the supervisor aims to see the world from the supervisee's point of view. Thus, skill in co-created meanings, interest in the cognitive style and internal working models of the supervisee, and intersubjectivity are crucial. When a supervisee is afraid, overwhelmed, or unduly uncertain, the supervisor offers containment through attuned regulation of arousal. This occurs through identifying and responding to the actual needs of the supervisee, not the needs the supervisor thinks she ought to have, and it is an essential part of the supervisor's role to monitor the impact of arousal on the work.

Safety in supervision is seen as valuable, because this can create a more secure attachment style, even in adulthood, for people insecurely attached as infants. Secure attachment styles predict flexibility of thought, resilience, and capacity for psychological contact, all of which form a bedrock for professional practice by the supervisee, and a base for the development of their own inner authority within their internal supervisor. Supervisors can also usefully learn that, though their own needs do not take priority in a supervisory relationship, they must be considered if it is to be mutually enjoyable and engaging.

Self-awareness

Reflection about individual responses when anxious or feeling under threat, and ideas about consequences of different attachment or cognitive styles can develop through observed practice. Capacity for "thoughtful delays" (Pryor, 1989) and interest in "blind, deaf, and dumb spots" (Ekstein, 1969) become more obvious through observing peers, and through discussion of some contentious ethical dilemmas.

Inskipp and Proctor (2003, p. 15) remind us of the importance of self-belief in relation to leadership and authority as a supervisor. This springs from self-knowledge and self-acceptance, and confidence in our own judgement. They note the associated need to "exercise systemic power appropriately, elegantly and firmly", with "the humility to recognise that power is limited by the counsellor's consent, and the skill of your support and challenge".

They add:

> Supervisors in training find it quite hard to give themselves permission to:
>
> - Own their own professional judgement of others
> - Contest values, assumptions and even perceptions
> - Invade the established ideas and standards of another, even within the boundaries of an agreed contract.
>
> They assert that it is the right and responsibility of the supervisor to develop these permissions and abilities. [*ibid.*, p. 19]

Discussions can explore the generic personal aims of each participant's behavioural style (e.g., belonging, significance, comfort, control) when feeling under threat or anxious. Similarly, styles of conflict that prioritize the relationship or the task are pertinent to the supervisor and authority. The connections between management of supervisor anxiety and clarity about responsibility can be made. Willingness to stand up and be counted or not can be discussed.

Style differences may emerge and be composed of the cultural, learning, cognitive, or attachment styles of each person. For the new supervisor, it takes time to develop a personal supervisory style, and to discover how this is affected and influenced by the relationship with each different supervisee. Practice on a course with peers can reveal the impact of a good or a difficult match, and the different demands of bonding with another whose style fits easily with one's own, as opposed to bridging between styles that form less straightforward working alliances (Henderson, 2009).

Learning to repair ruptures and rebuild relationships with peers might become necessary when there are any tensions within the course group, or in supervisory experiences. "It's not what we do, it is what we do next that is important" is a stance that conveys the inevitability of being imperfect as a supervisor, and a willingness to engage in repair, taking responsibility for any contributions to the difficulty without self-justification. The novice supervisor can become aware of the impact on others of habitual styles of response (e.g., aggressive, assertive, passive, or compliant) and develop motivation to increase appropriate responses and reduce inappropriate ones. Discussion may identify circumstances when it is necessary to "take a stand" with a supervisee, and, paradoxically, the possibility that a trusting and collegial relationship is already impaired if "taking a stand" is considered the necessary option rather than commenting and "being who you are".

Any supervisor, intentionally or inadvertently, is a model for the supervisee about ways of relating. It is useful to become aware, possibly through recording and reviewing sessions, of the interactions the supervisor most typically initiates or avoids, and how far these are facilitative or controlling. Heron's six-category intervention analysis (1975) provides one framework for observation here.

Self-awareness exercises have a place in supervision courses to add to participants' prior experience of personal development groups or therapy. For example, Peluso's "ethical genogram" (2003) identifies some sources of professional moral values and decision-making styles in experiences of early family life. Luft and Ingham's (1955) Johari window invites a four-option reflection about self-awareness, others' feedback, matters considered too private or shameful to share, and elements of the self not yet known to the self or observers. Any such tools can be used privately in advance, and the results of the reflection can be shared in a discussion. Thus, some origins of attitudes to ethical knots or practice difficulties, dependence, or idealization by a supervisee can be brought to consciousness and explored. Creative writing (Sugg, 2008) and reflective practice writing (Bolton, 2001) also have a marked contribution to make to professional development.

Emotional learning: the place of emotion in supervisory training

The introduction of some emotionally charged material is useful as a means to explore issues of authority, given the emotive nature of the topic. Emotional and experiential sessions provide a vehicle for people to identify and address the luggage of difficult prior experiences, or attitudinal blocks to engagement with the issues. This provides an integrative experience that adds to cognitive development about philosophical and moral thinking that a lecture cannot offer so richly. The process might stir some useful discomfort from increased awareness of difficulties in personal style. It could make the potentially dry process of grasping ethical and legal bases more juicy and memorable.

The process of doing experiential work respectfully always requires transparent instructions, attention to ground rules, explicit permissions to withdraw if engagement is inappropriate, enough time to process emotions or discuss difference in the course group, and clarity about confidentiality about material disclosed at each stage of the process. This should all be familiar to participants from Diploma training as counsellors, but there may be more to lose and potential feelings of exposure for these experienced practitioners.

A number of ethical problem-solving schemas are available and are a useful resource for sessions aiming to provide tools for a working supervisor faced with an ethical dilemma. Carroll's (1996) four-step process, or the British Association for Counselling and Psychotherapy's *Information Sheet P4* (2004) can be used and applied to discussion of scenarios to assist participants feel more confident about routines for reflection about difficult issues. They might also reveal underlying emotions and values generated by, and influencing responses to, the process.

Principles, like lighthouses, give us bearings in stormy seas, and a mature reflective practitioner has to exercise flexibility and caution with awareness of hazards as she negotiates the rocks of conflicting ethical imperatives. Our course has found that even experienced practitioners do not routinely refer to an ethical framework or confidently identify relevant ethical principles (see BACP, 2005).

Responding to projections, expectations, and resistance

Any asymmetric relationship, particularly one where the "elder" partner has the power to influence future work or qualifications, will be affected by each party's attitudes to power and authority. *Being* authoritative, paradoxically, may involve the supervisor not accepting some supervisees' projections about authority and omniscience in order to contribute to the development of the supervisee as an autonomous practitioner. An exercise to explore projections (Inskipp, 1999, pp. 194–196) distinguishes and shares in exaggerated form what each party wants from supervision, and what they think ought to happen. Such negotiation of psychological elements of contracts builds trust about expectations, hopes, and fears for a new supervisory relationship.

Supervisory styles around issues of authority are highly influenced by gender assumptions and styles, as well as cultural gender norms. Each supervisor has to integrate their own inner masculine and feminine strengths, curb the associated weaknesses, and notice their response styles to supervisees of the same and opposite gender. It is useful to talk about previous experiences of supervision and what went well or badly, because it can reveal assumptions about what constitutes a safe and productive relationship.

Issues of inferiority, shame, guilt, and humiliation create a related topic of significance in relation to authority, and a supervisor has to learn to notice when any of these responses is affecting her approach—or the supervisee's—to their supervisory relationship. Good intentions about being responsible and ethical can be articulated in an anxious way that creates shame and fear in the supervisee. Good intentions need to be supplemented by monitoring of outcomes and requests for feedback about process.

Projections from the supervisee about wisdom, experience, and expertise may require a degree of acceptance. Yet, the supervisee can also be made aware that the supervisor has to tolerate ambiguity and "not knowing". Novice supervisors may find both idealization and uncertainty difficult at first, though it is only human to be seduced into narcissistic delight by positive feedback from supervisees. It takes time for each novice supervisor to recognize their unique mix of strengths and weaknesses, and that everyone has a bad day occasionally, and can feel incompetent or inadequate without abandoning the role altogether.

Roles, responsibilities, and frameworks for thought

There may be different expectations of responsibility held by the supervisor, the supervisee, and an employer. Triadic relationships demand many possible foci of supervision, and require the participants to choose between options, each potentially almost equally productive. Exploration of these themes during training normalizes the reality of a supervisor's influence, for good or ill, on the setting up and sustenance of the working alliance with the supervisee and any organization of which they are a part (Hawkins & Shohet, 2006; Inskipp & Proctor, 2001, 2003).

Achieving some coherence in the midst of complexity is essential for supervisors. It takes practice and courage to hold and recall detailed material and multi-layered narratives. Models of supervision, such as the Hawkins and Shohet "seven-eyed model" (2006), or Page and Wosket's cyclical model (2001), offer frameworks for thought that new supervisors can use to remind them of options and choice points when they feel stuck or overwhelmed. Hawkins and Shohet, for instance, indicate arenas for authority issues. When the supervisor listens to details about the client's story she may also consider whether this client is within the experience and competence of the supervisee, especially of a trainee. Interventions and the relationship with the client offer possibilities for encouragement or advice, or for debating appropriateness of behaviour. Shadow issues may arise in relation to the internal response of the counsellor or supervisor to the material being discussed. The supervisory relationship could be tense when assessment of a supervisee who is a trainee is problematic. The supervisor might be a representative of systems or might need to address shadow sides of the organization in which the counselling or supervision takes place. A mistake or ethically inappropriate practice requires discussion.

As Tudor and Worrall (2004) remind us, a developmental element of the role is to support the supervisee to create and sustain an internal locus of evaluation and develop the capacity of the internal supervisor. It is a fundamental element of the role to focus on the development of the supervisee as well as the client.

Because of unconscious processes, exploration of parallel process helps to explore crucial matters that are out of awareness of the supervisee. Parallel process can feel like "magical" intuition to the supervisee, and increase a sense of being manipulated or out of control if not sensitively managed. In the interests of discovery of parallel process, a supervisor may usefully be more overt in self-disclosure. She will often reveal more detail about her thought processes or responses as she "muses aloud" and wrestles with complex issues than when she is working as a counsellor. Learning to share hypotheses or reactions overtly, rather than just thinking them, is part of taking the role.

Skills

The skills of contracting for focus, inviting reflection, speaking about uncomfortable matters in the relationship, and explicitly naming concerns about practice or understanding, rely on generic communication skills familiar to most counsellors. Novice supervisors need to learn to use them more often, or in a timely way, and to feel entitled to offer their own perspective or experience. Skills may include a mix of Socratic questioning and making some direct suggestions; offering affirming feedback about successful interventions, and suggestions for different approaches. Supervisors need to encourage the supervisee in "thought experiments" to consider alternative approaches that might improve outcomes with a client. Management of the session entails more use of summarizing and signposting than might be normal for most counselling.

Novice supervisors might hold back from using these skills for fear of seeming unduly controlling or oppressive. Timing is important. A new supervisor may hope and intend that the supervisee will come to her own understanding about behaviour she should change. She may avoid making comments for fear of being hurtful. She might feel impolite if being too explicit about gaps or misunderstandings in grasping a situation. She could dread the discomforts or potential impact of speaking what it is difficult to speak. Good timing is based on subtle decisions. Generally, it is better for supervisees to discover solutions to developmental or practice dilemmas for themselves. Sometimes, however, it becomes essential, when a supervisee is avoiding an issue, promising to make changes and prevaricating or procrastinating, or engaged in poor practice or malpractice without being willing to change the behaviour or consider the impact on the client, to put this on the agenda, or insist on discussing something uncomfortable. It takes practice to judge how long to bide your time, and when it is desirable or essential to intervene, and requires trust in the process backed by awareness of patterns of avoidance. Particularly when a supervisee tests the relationship or disputes the authority of the supervisor, skills of direct communication are essential. The supervisor has to be able to withstand attacks, and sustain a compassionate acceptance of any of her own unresolved narcissistic needs that are being upset in the process.

Working one-to-one or in groups

Training for group supervision is more fully discussed in Chapter Thirteen. In this context, however, it is important to note how greatly the complexities increase in relation to understanding and managing authority as a supervisor, and creating and sustaining a working alliance with a number of people simultaneously. The twin tasks of building and maintaining the group and managing the prioritizing of the tasks of supervision work create many choices. The supervisor is likely to have a more active interventionist role to engage with disparate individuals than in one-to-one supervision. There is more competition for time and attention. There are complex group dynamics to work with. The supervisor may need more actively to facilitate process and reflection. With greater activity comes all the risks of being misconstrued as the supervisor engages with implicit or explicit rivalries, or different ways of using the space and responding to others' work. There are choices: does the supervisor name an issue or hold back, allow diversions, or remind the group about agreements, teach, or invite others to reflect? These all need confidence, a worked out sense of entitlement to occupy the role for the general good, and understanding of group work and models of group process.

Authority and work with trainees

Supervision must respond to the unique experience, resilience, and level of development of any counsellor, and most particularly of a trainee. More authoritative roles in assessment and feedback pervade this working relationship. Supervisees' dependence has to be acknowledged and accepted without prolonging it as their experience increases. As Crick notes (1991), her learning was greatly increased as a trainee psychotherapist because she noticed the supervisor's style change in response to her increasing skilfulness. A training course that emphasizes collegiality and mutual respect within supervisory relationships can invite participants to consider their archaic habits of response when feelings of competition arise about who is right, or whose ideas should count within supervision. A trusting and egalitarian supervisory relationship has to find the balance of support and challenge that suits both the developmental stage and personality of the supervisee. The supervisor earns the right to challenge by also being supportive, direct, encouraging, and interested. If such invitations are offered in a matter-of-fact descriptive way, within an agreed contract for development, the discomfort or shame of not knowing or getting it wrong can more easily be borne.

Supervisors play a significant role for trainee counsellors. It is in supervision that trainees have a timely opportunity to integrate theory and practice. It is here that the supervisor can help supervisees to take the sting out of difficult initial experiences with clients and feelings of inadequacy, and turn discouragement or shame into learning opportunities. This focus requires the supervisor to be clear about the boundary between restorative or therapeutic work within supervision, and therapy. If the trainee counsellor brings recordings, or is observed while working, feedback can be specific and immediate. Practical ethical issues, such as around touch in therapy, sexual attraction, or responding to a client as "special", can be considered.

The regular frame of supervision offers some security, and helps the trainee counsellor to cope with feeling unsure what to do, knowing that there is a predictable space for supported reflection. To this space the supervisee may bring any preoccupation with fears of doing harm, and, if it is safe enough, any concerns about not doing well enough to pass the course. Regular, clear, encouraging feedback thus serves to inform the trainee about her progress, stagnation, or development, ideally in relation to explicit and transparent standards. Trainees also learn about boundaries here, too: boundaries between therapy and the restorative function of supervision, boundaries about confidentiality, dual roles, self-disclosure, and other challenges of practice.

A supervisor training course that does not address what is unique about work with practitioners at the trainee stage misses crucial opportunities to reflect on related issues of power, authority, feedback, attention to the context, contracting, and creating a facilitative balance between support and challenge. The supervisor-in-training who works with trainee counsellors has to engage with working within organizational contexts, often voluntary ones, and create contracts with all who are involved so that expectations are explicit. Usually, a supervisor relates only to the training course, or only to a placement (but see Herrick, 2007). If there are difficulties, liaison may be necessary with them both, and the supervisor has to learn to hold the needs of client, supervisee, placement, and course in mind. Stewart (2002, pp. 111–114) describes this as like a Rubik's cube, combining many defined roles and fluctuating identifications with each. These processes of liaison entail walking the fine line between not disclosing unnecessary detail from the confidential supervisory relationship while reporting back as required in relation to assessment reports or alerts to the organization about serious concerns about practice or suitability for the work and role. Client welfare is a central component of trainee supervision (Page & Wosket, 2001, p. 10).

"Serving two masters" as a supervisor of a trainee could entail a search for clarity about the curriculum and course expectations, confirmation of expectations for assessment reports, or for liaison from the supervisor, and understanding what is expected of the supervisee to pass the course. Not all courses offer these details, and supervisors need to be clear about the necessity to ask when invited to take on the work.

Supervisors who work with trainees have to learn assessment skills. These include observation, use of pro-formas created by colleagues or course tutors, and how to approach discussion of developmental issues and write reports and references, all calling on skills of direct communication. For some, these skills are easily transferred from other work roles. For others, the responsibility and approach are new. Most particularly, the supervisor has to help the trainee and the course to identify any significant problems in a supervisee's professional development, and assess the likelihood that the trainee will meet required practice standards within the period of training. This calls for regular reviews and communication about assessment criteria, even though it can be difficult and uncomfortable to raise the issue with someone who is sensitive or defensive. These are the very people who most need this feedback, and need it to be done clearly and respectfully. Most supervisors work at some point with someone whom it is apparent should not have passed an initial training. They might need more theoretical underpinning, more practice, or simply be unsuitable for the role. Brear, Dorrian, and Luscri (2008) suggest that course gatekeepers most frequently identify intrapersonal and interpersonal difficulties as reasons for failing students on counsellor training courses. In my view, it is when *surprising* critical feedback is given about such personal matters that recipients can feel most attacked, and the impact on self-esteem, and even a sense of identity, can be profound. Clarity about what is expected and what constitutes a shortfall is humane and necessary for all parties, and most usefully is offered as a basis for identifying developmental steps where that is considered likely to result in future success. Failing a trainee through supervision can be traumatic for both the supervisor and supervisee (Samec, 1995), but supervisors have to develop a capacity to undertake this difficult task.

Here, there is no argument that the supervisor holds some crucial power, and this can be open to misuse by a supervisor who fails to convey difficult messages humanely: supervisors may demonstrate "rating inconsistency", as some are consistently lenient, others have unrealistically high standards (Robiner, Furman, & Ristvedt, 1993). Supervisees who are trainee counsellors might respond defensively when given a message that their practice or personal development means they may not pass the course. It is only human to prefer a defensive strategy under such circumstances, and to limit the amount of honesty about mistakes. Game-playing can then characterize the supervision in very unhealthy ways that impede the development of the trainee. Novice supervisors need to learn how to identify and comment on such games.

Supervisors, thus, have to develop a supervisory style that is encouraging without eschewing necessary comments about development, is authoritative without being oppressive, exercises feedback skills sensitively but clearly, and holds in mind the service to the client. These are core and generic skills, yet are writ large in work with colleagues who are new to a helping role.

It is very common for inexperienced supervisors to supervise trainee counsellors. Stoltenberg and Delworth (see Hawkins and Shohet, 2006, p. 75) suggest that it is hard for a novice supervisor to supervise practitioners *beyond* this level, and they need good supervision of supervision to do it. Because trainee supervisors sometimes offer lower fees while they are in training, this may attract trainees. As they are closer to the experience of training as a counsellor by virtue of being on a course, there could be benefits in empathy and understanding about working within a professionally developing practice. There may be more understanding about the life pressures of working while studying and completing assignments, and coping with family or other responsibilities. However, there is a lot to think about, and competing interests to juggle. It is an opportunity also to consider the personal needs of the supervisor: few courses pay external supervisors to attend course meetings, for example, and some self-employed practitioners find this significantly financially deleterious. Others yearn for any contact, and seek more connection with the course.

Novice supervisors benefit from opportunities to begin considering the issues that arise when supervisees are at an "adolescent" stage, such as some trainees when near graduation. The supervisor has to be able to respond generously and yet hold clear boundaries at this time. Granello (1996) found that the bulk of cognitive development occurs between the mid point and end of training, once a trainee is having supervision. Many opportunities to practise being authoritative can arise in relation to placement or course supervision, together with ethical challenges about confidentiality.

Working with "green L plate" or newly qualified counsellors

Skovholt and Ronnestad (1992) noted that most development of cognitive *complexity* in counsellors occurs *after* formal training. These supervisees may swing between feeling very confident one moment and unsure the next, and still need feedback. The balance of support and challenge shifts too, though sometimes the newly qualified practitioner becomes anxious once more without the support of a course or placement behind them. If the supervisee is in independent practice, the supervisor can usefully encourage explicit clarity about practice pragmatics, such as the supervisee's access to medical or psychiatric consultation if necessary, and arrangements for care of clients via "therapeutic wills" in case of the supervisee's sudden illness or death.

Priorities within supervision change, although development implies neither inadequacy in less qualified supervisees, nor more perceptivity in the person of the supervisor. *Feelings* of superiority and inferiority are common, but not always inevitable, despite real power imbalances arising from role difference.

How stages of development can be addressed within a training course

The course, then, can provide conceptual maps about development, while reminding participants that maps are not the territory, and every supervisee is unique. It can refer participants to ideas and research about cognitive and professional development. Crucially, the course can identify difference in learning styles and sensitivity to equality issues. It can offer empathy exercises that tune participants back into memories of seeing clients for the first time, or going for early supervisions, and, by sharing these, remind the group about the variety there is in development, and the resources practitioners have at every stage. There are choices and choice points to discover, such as when to teach directly and when to wait for the supervisee to discover resources within her own frame of reference. It can aid reflection about participants' development and use of supervision, and what supported this. It can explore roles, skills, and how to co-create a collegial culture with trainees and how that might differ with more experienced colleagues. It can explore feelings about taking authority, and issues of rivalry or oppression.

Concluding comments

Being authoritative and exercising supervisory authority is potentially enabling, sometimes uncomfortable, and an issue for all supervisors.

This chapter indicates that, although ideas and skills are absolutely central to this topic, it is personal awareness and reflection about style and outcomes that underpin these essential developmental steps.

References

Banks, M. (2002). The transition from therapist to supervisor. In: C. Driver & E. Martin (Eds.), *Supervising Psychotherapy* (pp. 23–37). London: Sage.

Bolton, G. (2001). *Reflective Practice: Writing and Professional Development* (2nd edn 2005). London: Sage.

Brear, P., Dorrian, J., & Luscri, G. (2008). Preparing our future counselling professionals: gatekeeping and the implications for research. *Counselling and Psychotherapy Research, 8*(2): 93–101.

British Association for Counselling and Psychotherapy (2004). *Information Sheet P4: Guidance for Ethical Decision making: A Suggested Model for Practitioners.* Lutterworth: BACP.

British Association for Counselling and Psychotherapy (2005). *DG10: The Ethical Framework for Good Practice in Counselling and Psychotherapy within the NHS.* Lutterworth: BACP.

Carroll, M. (1996). *Counselling Supervision: Theory, Skills and Practice.* London: Cassells.

Crick, P. (1991). Good supervision: on the experience of being supervised. *Psychoanalytic Psychotherapy, 5*(3): 235–245.

Ekstein, R. (1969). Concerning the teaching and learning of psychoanalysis. *The Journal of the American Psychoanalytic Association, 17*(2): 312–332.

Granello, D. H. (1996). Gender and power in the supervisory dyad. *Clinical Supervisor, 14*(2): 53–67.

Hammarskjöld, D. (1964). Accessed through www.quotationspage.com/quote/31292.html

Hawkins, P., & Shohet, R. (2006). *Supervision in the Helping Professions.* Buckingham: Open University Press.

Henderson, P. (2006). Learning to take supervisory authority. In: P. Prina, A. Millar, C. Shelley & K. John (Eds.), *UK Adlerian Year Book 2006* (pp. 40–49). London: Adlerian Society and the Institute for Individual Psychology.

Henderson, P. (2009) *A Different Wisdom: Reflections on Supervision Practice.* London: Karnac.

Herrick, J. (2007). Placements: support of confusion? *Therapy Today, 18*(1): 42–44.

Heron, J. (1975). *Six Category Intervention Analysis.* Guildford: University of Surrey.

Inskipp, F. (1999). Training supervisees to use supervision. In: E. Holloway & M. Carroll (Eds.), *Training Counselling Supervisors* (pp. 184–210). London: Sage.

Inskipp, F., & Proctor, B. (2001). *Making the Most of Supervision* (2nd edn). Twickenham: Cascade.

Inskipp, F., & Proctor, B. (2003). *Becoming a Supervisor* (2nd edn). Twickenham: Cascade.

Lago, C., & Thompson, J. (1997). The triangle with curved sides: sensitivity to issues of race and culture in supervision. In: G. Shipton (Ed.), *Supervision of Counselling and Psychotherapy: Making a Space to Think* (pp. 119–130). Buckingham: Open University Press.

Luft, J., & Ingham, H. (1955). The Johari window, a graphic model of interpersonal awareness. *Proceedings of the Western Training Laboratory in Group Development.* Los Angeles, CA: UCLA.

Mander, G. (2002). Supervising short-term psychodynamic work. In: C. Driver & E. Martin (Eds.), *Supervising Psychotherapy: Psychoanalytic and Psychodynamic Perspectives* (pp. 97–105). London: Sage.

Millar, A. (2007). The essential Es. *Therapy Today,* March.

Page, S., & Wosket, V. (2001). *Supervising the Counsellor: A Cyclical Model.* Hove: Routledge.

Peluso, P. R. (2003). The ethical genogram: a tool for helping therapists understand their ethical decision making styles. *The Family Journal, 14*(3): 286–291.

Pryor, R. G. L. (1989). Conflicting responsibilities: a case study of an ethical dilemma for psychologists working in organisations. *Australian Psychologist, 24*: 293–305.

Robiner, W. N., Furman, M., & Ristvedt, S. (1993). Evaluation difficulties in supervising psychology interns. *Clinical Psychologist, 46*: 3–13.

Rosenblatt, A., & Mayer, J. E. (1975). Objectionable supervisory styles: student's views. *Social Work,* May: 184–189.

Samec, J. R. (1995). Shame, guilt and trauma: failing the psychotherapy candidate's clinical work. *The Clinical Supervisor, 13*(2): 1–17.

Skovholt, T. M., & Ronnestad, M. H. (1992). Themes in therapist and counsellor development. *Journal of Counselling and Development, 70*: 505–515.

Stewart, J. (2002). The container and the contained: supervision and organisational context. In: C. Driver and E. Martin (Eds.), *Supervising Psychotherapy: Psychoanalytic and Psychodynamic Perspectives* (pp. 106–120). London: Sage.

Sugg, S. (2008). Creative writing—a tool for developing the reflective/reflexive practitioner? *Therapy Today, 19*(1): 37–39.

Tudor, K., & Worrall, M. (Eds.) (2004). *Freedom to Practise.* Ross-on-Wye: PCCS Books.

Wheeler, S., & King, D. (2000). Do counselling supervisors want or need to have their supervision supervised? An exploratory study. *British Journal of Guidance and Counselling, 28*(2): 279–290.

Wheeler, S., & King, D. (Eds.) (2001). *Supervising Counsellors: Issues of Responsibility.* London: Sage.

CHAPTER ELEVEN

The impact of the organization: the primary care context

Antonia Murphy

Introduction

It is generally agreed that clinical supervision is one of the essential bedrocks of counselling training and ongoing work. In this chapter, I consider particularly supervision of counselling practice in an organizational setting.

The contention of this chapter is threefold:

1. The supervisory relationship is essential to help the counsellor who works in any organisation to manage the complexities of the setting.
2. Such a supervisory process is crucial to developing an ability to understand and integrate the context into further and necessary illumination of the clinical work. In other words, supervisors of counsellors working in an organization need to attend to organizational as well as clinical aspects.
3. Supervisors working with counsellors within organizations themselves need specialist training and/or experience of the organizational setting in order to take an intersubjective approach to the relational dynamics in the setting that then informs the work.

The specific organizational context I want to consider is that of the National Health Service (NHS) and, in particular, primary care.

The primary care setting

The talking therapies—counselling and psychotherapy—have become established in NHS primary care over the past ten years, alongside existing psychotherapeutic provision within specialist secondary psychotherapy and psychology departments and generic community mental health teams. There is, of course, continuing debate about the place of the psychological therapies, particularly primary care counselling, in relation to the treatment of mental health difficulties. Questions are raised as to the validity of such approaches and whether such therapies should be standard fare within general practice. Initiatives within the "Improving Access to Psychological Therapies" (IAPT) project have also raised questions concerning the evidence-based paradigm against which health treatment is measured, and have sponsored the use of cognitive–behavioural methods within this setting. At the same time, the government is concerned to give mental health a much greater priority. Its 1999 National Service Framework states that:

> Most people with mental health problems are cared for by their GP and the primary care team. This is what most patients prefer . . . generally for every one hundred individuals who consult their GP with a mental health problem, nine will be referred to specialist services.

It is against this highly charged and ever changing background that primary care counsellors undertake their work, and this is the "frame" within which supervision of this work is undertaken. The context and environment of primary care is a complex one. The medical and biophysical culture of the NHS has an impact on the psychotherapeutic practitioners who work in this setting and on how the therapy is undertaken. There is so much that is tantalizing and intrusive in the external environment of general practice. There is also a great deal that is helpful.

Psychotherapeutic practice and medical practice sometimes make very strange bedfellows, the former generating self-awareness and ultimately self-responsibility ("working with" the patient) and the latter often offering expert help and generating dependency ("doing to" the patient). Furthermore, it becomes apparent when working in a primary care team that there are very crucial relationships within the team that impinge significantly on the therapeutic work. Counsellors are not working solely within a dyadic therapeutic relationship in which all transference interpretations can be understood in terms of the therapeutic pair, but within a complex web of relationships which, at best, is a threesome (GP, patient, and therapist) and at most a group. Lees reminds us (1997) that the patient may have "ubiquitous transference" to the whole primary care setting, which can help or hinder the unique relationship between counsellor and patient, depending on patient feelings about the other practitioners there.

For these reasons, the supervisory work must bear in mind the impact and relevance of all the dimensions, unconscious and conscious, in play in this setting. Such a complex set of dynamic relationships and clashing paradigms of necessity affects therapeutic work in primary care and it is this multi-layered confection that the primary care counsellor brings to supervision. The supervisor needs to approach the work with an understanding of the organizational dynamics, an eye on the multiple transference relationships, and the many-layered defences that can be played out within the setting and the team. Each surgery also has its own unique culture and administrative systems.

Complex relationships

The counsellor and, hence, supervisor in primary care are working within a set of dynamics which concerns itself not just with the counsellor–patient dyad, but with a whole team of medical and administrative colleagues. Within this system lies a network of transference and countertransference possibilities. Thus, taking an intersubjective approach, primary care supervision is potentially concerned with any number of the following dyads:

- the client–counsellor;
- the patient (client)–practice;

- the counsellor–practice (organization);
- the supervisee (counsellor)–supervisor;
- the supervisor–client;
- the supervisor–practice (organization).

From this, there follows the potential for triads. As Stewart states,

> The patient, counsellor and supervisor all develop transferences towards the organisation and its members, which have to be understood and worked with. The GP/Counsellor/Patient and the Patient/Counsellor/Supervisor matrices both form an oedipal triangle—a three person relationship . . . the psychic realities of all those involved in the work with the patient come together in a complex supervisory picture . . . understanding how these dynamics are played out in the setting and in supervision facilitates analysis and management of both the setting and the work. [2004, p. 358]

Thus, the supervisor of the counsellor working in this setting is required to establish and work within the usual supervisory frame, thinking with their supervisees about all aspects of the work, but also to have the capacity to think about the meta-dynamics, too. In the NHS, the transference of the patient is commonly affected by the patient's prior and ongoing relationship to the GP/surgery. Also, where GP and therapist are both involved with the patient, important mechanisms can be invoked in ways that are often hard to understand, sometimes unexpected and, of course, more often unconscious. The supervisor and counsellor have the task of thinking about, containing, and managing this. They need to be able to maintain a capacity to think about the organizational dynamics of which they themselves are a part, with reference to the therapeutic work. At the same time, the supervisory relationship itself is subject to the fluxes and challenges of the setting, and unprocessed material can be acted out within the supervisory dyad.

Because the patient referred for therapy in primary care is part of a group process, the supervisor needs to be able to view the team and the counsellor's place within it in the service of the patient to find out more about the patient and his/her communications. Jones, Murphy, Neaman, Tollemache, and Vasserman (1994) elaborate on these points emphasizing how

> the divergent ways patients see and act towards the GP and the therapist can provide a greater understanding of the patients difficulties, but only if the therapist and GP can communicate with each other and avoid the temptation of becoming part of these difficulties and acting them out in their own working relationship. [p. 547]

However, not all primary care teams are able to process this material together. The setting of general practice is invariably frenetic. The manic defence is in full flow. It is full of impingements and constantly challenges the possibility of reflective thinking necessary to therapeutic work. Jeffrey (2008) describes these pressures and the difficulty of setting time aside for supervision.

GPs and other health professionals can easily feel overwhelmed when there is an endless supply of patients needing help for "illnesses" which are frequently of an indeterminate nature and from which recovery is slow or incomplete or not possible. They may well feel frustrated with patients who do not get better, and constantly besieged by a never-ending waiting room. As such, they can feel envious of their counselling colleagues, who appear to cherry-pick those with whom they wish to work, and have all the time in the world to see their patients. This can give rise to unconscious attacks on the counselling role or denigration of the process. In contrast, counsellors may well feel lower in the pecking order and envious of the GPs' power and authority. They may feel undervalued, underpaid, and actually ignored and excluded from planning and teamwork.

Hawkins and Shohet (2006) describe how potentially complex can be the enactment of multiple transference within a health setting and how patients can play out their process through the involvement of various health professionals. Describing the experience of a young female client they explain,

> Clearly the client's process is being played out, not within a contained therapeutic situation, but through multiple transference onto four different professionals. The professionals are not only failing to work together to bring about some integration of the various fragments of the client's process, but they are also enacting some of the typical inter professional rivalries endemic within and between each of their roles. [*ibid.*, p. 186]

Supervisors of primary care counsellors will be familiar with the various struggles counsellors often have with respect to rooms, lack of time, waiting lists, noise, lack of communication, boundary infringements, etc. This is the culture of primary care, which is in itself a defensive milieu. Individual time for reflection is rarely offered and perhaps not thought of as valuable in the face of illness and death. Aiding the counsellor to think about these matters that arise in the work in primary care, both in terms of the team dynamics and the patients' own internal world, is an essential part of the supervisor's role. Supervision, when offered with this in mind, helps the counsellor understand and contain the projections they might be holding for the practice. Sometimes, these are powerful, and can result in destructive splits and rifts that are acted out. However, potentially the counsellor is in a good place to aid the collective thinking in the practice. As Stewart again points out, "The counsellor has a unique role within the primary care team, listening in a way that can be very different from the rest of the team" (2004, p. 360).

I would echo that, and extend this to the supervisor, who has a unique place in containing the counsellor and restoring his/her reflective mind, which is sometimes under attack. The supervisory space can be an invaluable place for the whole team, even if they do not acknowledge or know about it. In the best possible environments, the members of the team come together in a collaborative process, but this requires a mature awareness and an appreciation of unconscious mechanisms of splitting and projection as well as acceptance of the real limits of help available. In the absence of whole team awareness, the supervisor is a very necessary container of the counsellor and the team's anxiety. The supervisory process can help to identify where and how and whose damaged parts are being carried.

The supervisory contract

As has been stressed, the counsellor in primary care is working as part of a team alongside doctors, nurses, and other health professionals. Commonly, the counsellor works only part of the time in the practice, and colleagues may see a patient between appointments with the counsellor. In this context, the counsellor needs to be able to talk to colleagues and to establish mutual respect and trust in the interests of all patients. The encouragement of the supervisor is important to facilitate this. This dimension, which sets primary care apart from private practice, has a significant effect on the nature of the supervisory contract as well as on that of the counselling contract. Clear contractual agreements need to be reached, whatever the context of the supervisory arrangement, and supervisors must understand the legal and contractual base of the counselling work.

In today's NHS, arrangements for supervision and the employment context can be very varied. The relationship between the NHS counselling service or individual counsellor and supervisor can take one of several forms, depending on how the service is structured in relation to the NHS commissioning body.

- The supervisor is employed within a counselling scheme and is paid and contracted by the service to provide supervision to all employed counsellors. Clearly, in a large scheme there will be several supervisors, more than likely providing group supervision.
- Individual counsellors choose, contract, and pay for their own supervision, but the supervisors conform to an agreed standard. The supervisor might have a formal link to the counselling service, e.g., through the submission of supervisor reports or regular meetings with the counselling service manager. However, they may well not.
- The service is an out-of-NHS provider. As such, the counselling service provides supervision within its own organizational structure. There may or may not be a link into the NHS trust.
- The counsellor is a lone practitioner working in a GP practice and contracts with the supervisor privately.

We can see from the above list that clarity over lines of communication and matters of accountability with respect to the supervision is variable. In some cases, this is reasonably clear and distinct, in other cases, less so. Where there is a lack of clarity, or uncertainty over the lines of communication, this can lead to a neglect of the processing of the impact of the setting, as discussed above. It could also result in a muddle and confusion which might be less containing for the counsellor. On the other hand, independent supervision can give a refreshing opportunity for independent reflection. Whatever the case, it is important that the supervisor of the primary care counsellor establishes at the outset the parameters of accountability and also of confidentiality.

In their book *Psychological Therapies in Primary Care: Setting Up A Managed Service*, Foster and Murphy (2006) make the case for greater accountability and transparency concerning supervision arrangements within NHS counselling services, particularly in relation to any managerial roles within the service.

> It is important that the manager has a formal relationship with supervisors of counsellors working in the service . . . any issues arising in respect of counsellor competency / counsellor / client safety can hopefully be attended to before work breaks down in some way. The NHS counsellor should have nothing but help from her supervisor and her manager and should not fear the loss of control or creativity in her practice by such arrangements being in place. [pp. 136–138]

In this way, matters of accountability are made clear and distinct. Also, any issues arising in respect of counsellor competency / counsellor / client safety can, one hopes, be attended to before work breaks down in some way. Ideally, the NHS counsellor should have both a supportive and informed manager working together with a clinical supervisor. However, this model presupposes that the counselling service manager exists and is clinically trained in counselling or psychotherapy. The reality of many working counsellors in the NHS is still far from this model. Many might not be formally managed at all, and some might be managed by health service managers from other professional disciplines working with different understandings of patient–professional intervention. This can put greater pressure on the clinical supervisor to act in a managerial role, and also blur the boundaries between supervision and management. The interface between that of supervision and management is particularly sensitive within the primary care setting, and the supervisor will need to be aware of the management context for the counsellor(s) with whom they are working and the particular lines of accountability and responsibility expected of them as supervisors within the service framework.

Training for NHS supervision: specialist features

There are some further dimensions that are particularly relevant to the supervision of the primary care counsellor: supervising across modality, supervising time limited work, and awareness of working trans-culturally.

Supervision across modality

Counsellors working independently have traditionally, but certainly not exclusively, contracted with supervisors working within their core modality. However, with the expansion of integrative trainings, this has become more open. Similarly, to date, most formal supervision trainings have largely been offered within training institutes that follow the modality of a core training. However, with the evolution of the professional primary care counsellor and the accompanying need for specialist knowledge comes the concomitant specialist NHS supervisor. In today's primary care setting, we have growing numbers of counsellors trained in one core model being supervised by a supervisor originally trained in a different core generic model. What has brought them together, ideally, is their additional joint specialist experience of the NHS. So, their core model is often different but their specialism is the same.

It is my experience of supervising the primary care counsellor that shared knowledge of the context may override sensitivities to theory and modality. I have found, over the years, that counsellors from all traditions, ranging from person-centred, psychodynamic, integrative, transactional analysis (TA), etc., seek supervisors for their primary care work who have knowledge and experience of the setting and that this is often a positive determinant in the supervisory dyad. Where issues of modality difference may occur, this can often be fertile ground for exploring ideas and understanding and may well reflect better the "it takes all sorts" flavour of primary care. However, this does call for a high degree of flexibility and creativity in the supervisor, and for a very significant degree of clinical experience. This is in order that the supervisor has the agility of mind and the confidence to hover attentively over the supervision work while retaining their own model, as well as thinking in terms of the other. No mean feat!

Supervising time-limited work

The position with regard to supervising time-limited work also makes different demands on the supervisor and the supervisory relationship. Most counsellors currently work in primary care work in a time-limited capacity, the most common contracts ranging from 6–12 sessions. This puts a very necessary emphasis on assessment skills, and the supervisor will have a role to play in supporting good assessment for brief work. Supervisors may also find that counsellors offer different contractual arrangements: fortnightly sessions, for example, and group work. The supervisory contract needs to take into account the turnover of short-term client work. Will all clients be heard frequently enough, or does the supervisory space offer reflection appropriate to contain clients who may come and go between supervisions?

Trans-cultural sensitivity

Multi-cultural dimensions of counselling work are often encountered in primary care, since this is a place from where clients from all cultures and countries of origin will find their way into counselling. As such, the supervisor in this setting needs to maintain an open attitude to any inquiry and be prepared to relate trans-cultural thinking to all the potential dyads and triads available. This means developing an awareness of one's own cultural assumptions to be free to reflect across perceived difference. Hawkins and Shohet elaborate on this dimension, "supervision plays its part in ensuring that differences are understood and responded to appropriately" (2006, p. 105), and go on to reflect that "supervisory sessions that accept that prejudiced feelings are inevitable, given our cultural heritage, may open up genuine explorations in which these can be challenged and changed" (*ibid.*, p. 124).

The Association of Counsellors and Psychotherapists in Primary Care specialist training course

As a result of an increasing awareness of these special features of primary care supervision work, the Association of Counsellors and Psychotherapists in Primary Care (CPC) developed a full professional supervision training aimed at the NHS supervisor. The course is intended for practising counsellors, psychotherapists, and counselling psychologists working in an NHS setting. It is a specialist, non-modality-specific course that assumes a general relational model of therapy and supervision. The course is based on an elaboration of the concepts and skills necessary to the supervisor working within the dynamics and complexity of the NHS setting. It attends to the particular context of clinical work undertaken in primary care / NHS work and the supervisory requirements of practitioners working with counsellors in such settings. In other words, the training moves from the general to the specific.

The overall aims of the training are summed up as follows.

- Understand and have knowledge of supervisory theory and models. Develop a model or models of supervision in depth and offer an awareness of other approaches including time limited working.
- Understand the nature of the supervisory process, functions and relationship.
- Understand and have knowledge of the functions and processes of NHS supervision over and above generic supervision, in particular in relation to the statutory requirements of NHS practice, e.g., continuing professional development (CPD), audit, evidence-based practice, appraisal, etc.
- Clarify the interface between therapy, supervision, and management in the NHS setting.
- Examine the interfaces between various psychological and medical paradigms and their impact on clinical psychological work.
- Develop an awareness of organizational, ethical, and legal issues relating to supervision in the NHS context.
- Examine and offer critical analysis of clinical practice in the NHS setting.

- Examine supervisory contracting, and identify the specific components of contracting, communication and accountability in the NHS.
- Examine the constraints, limitations, and advantages of an NHS service and setting with respect to counselling practice.
- Articulate the role of an NHS supervisor. An ability to maintain lines of communication and establish collaborative styles of working as required.
- Manage, understand, and explore the impact of the frame in NHS counselling settings on the counselling relationship, therapeutic alliance, and the team dynamics.
- Understand the requirements on both counsellor and supervisor in terms of effective note keeping and records in accordance with NHS and legal requirements.
- Understand the development that takes place throughout supervision

The CPC course was established in 2007, and it was oversubscribed in its first year. This may well indicate a growing awareness among supervisors and counsellors of the "over and above" required specialist elements needed in supervision training for the NHS counselling setting. Further advances in establishing job specifications and employment conditions commensurate with other health professions through Agenda for Change and professional regulation may yet advance the case for specialist supervision training and qualifications together with that of NHS counsellors.

The overall course content is detailed in Figure 11.1.

Conclusion

There are unique features to supervision in the setting of the NHS. The supervision space is, of necessity, a place where the pressures and volume of work can be contained and managed. The supervisors will find themselves containing the counsellor *and* the team at times. Counsellors working in primary care need to be flexible, robust, and able to make therapeutic alliances with a very wide range of patients, and to forge collegial working relationships with fellow health professionals. As Perren (2004) writes of the primary care setting,

- Generic supervision—definitions and models
- NHS supervision—difference and additional aspects
- Theory and practice of supervision
- Personal attributes of the supervisor
- Modality difference/conflict
- Supervisory interfaces: teaching/managing/therapy
- Training supervision/placement supervision
- Assessment
- Supervision in the context of primary care
- NHS organizational context and structures—knowledge of the NHS
- The supervisory process and the dynamics of the supervisory relationship, dyads, triads and groups
- Parallel process and imminent criticism
- Unconscious processes in supervision
- Supervision and power
- Contracting and the supervision frame in the NHS/managed services and contracts
- Working with supervisors from other modalities
- Variations of employment and managed models
- Therapeutic wills: supervisory responsibility
- The interface between the psychological paradigm and the medical paradigm
- Counselling as counter-culture in the medical profession—diagnosis, assessment and formulation
- Collaboration and sharing of information
- Making use of the setting and its impact on the supervisory dynamic
- The dynamics of teamwork; teams within teams.
- The supervisory fit—type, modality, frequency
- Group or individual supervision—requirements of group work
- Supervising short term work—specialism within a specialism
- Working with difference
- Ethics, statutory requirements, the law with particular reference to the statutory sector
- Accountability, evaluation and standards in counsellor supervision in NHS
- Performance and safety of counsellors
- Performance management of supervisees
- Use of CORE forms in supervision
- Notes and record-keeping by supervisors
- The development of the supervisory relationship—levels of supervision
- Requirements of the supervisee at different stages
- Who supervises the supervisor?
- Endings in supervision

Figure 11.1. Content of CPC specialist NHS Supervision Course.

It is a very ordinary space, both satisfactory and unsatisfactory in the way that ordinary things often are. But the very ordinariness of it can mean that patients come for counselling who would not present in other more traditional therapy settings. The real space is often less than ideal but, sufficiently understood, the particular problems posed and opportunities provided by the setting can be used in ways that enable valuable therapeutic work to take place. [p. 351]

The supervisor of the primary care counsellor working in this ordinary space is required to know this real space and to offer, in contrast, a reflective space wherein all that occurs between all the elements can be considered. As such the supervisor aids the counsellor, and the team indirectly, to manage difficult and conflicting feelings that often arise in these tough demanding settings.

It is my belief that this model, emphasizing the specialist context of supervisory work, can be extended to other organizational settings, such as commerce, educational organizations, social care, employment assistance programmes, etc. Knowledge of these particular organizational settings and cultures would be crucial, just as it is in the primary care setting. As such, the particular understanding should be gained ideally through specialist supervisory training and/or clinical experience of the setting, as the CPC course outlined above demonstrates. Supervision can then be a place wherein the relationships between the patient, counsellor, and members of any team can be understood symbolically and all the multiple transference relationships considered.

References

DoH (1999). *National Service Framework for Mental Health*. London: DoH.

Foster, M., & Murphy, A. (2006). *Psychological Therapies in Primary Care: Setting Up a Managed Service*. London: Karnac.

Hawkins, P., & Shohet, R. (2006). *Supervision in the Helping Professions*. Buckingham: Open University Press.

Jeffrey, B. (2008). All at sea. *Therapy Today, 19*(2): 37–38.

Jones, H., Murphy, A., Neaman, G., Tollemache, R., & Vasserman, D. (1994). Psychotherapy and counselling in a GP practice: making use of the setting. *British Journal of Psychotherapy, 10*(4): 543–551.

Lees, J. (1997). An approach to counselling in GP surgeries. *Psychodynamic Counselling, 3*(1): 33–48.

Perren, S. (2004). Psychodynamic practice: working with the patient in primary care. *Psychodynamic Practice, 10*(3): 332–353.

Stewart, N. (2004). Supervising the primary care counsellor within the psychodynamic frame. *Psychodynamic Practice, 10*(3): 354–372.

CHAPTER TWELVE

Training for group supervision

Brigid Proctor and Francesca Inskipp

Introduction: the group supervisor staircase

On reading the expensive offers in the *Observer*, we noticed that one can buy a purpose-built staircase with drawers in each stair. We thought this an engaging metaphor for progression as a group supervisor. Each drawer contains skills, knowledge, qualities, and attitudes needed for a stage of development. We see the steps we describe as leading to a landing surrounded by enticing doors. Individuals might have to retrace steps from time to time before they can finally stand on the landing, assured of some competence and confidence as a group supervisor, or an accredited one!

Elsewhere (Inskipp & Proctor, 2001, 2003; Proctor, 2008), we have offered a generic model of group supervision. It incorporates the *basic* values, attitudes, abilities, and knowledge that we believe necessary to set up and develop effective supervision groups across modalities. We will not repeat the content that we have written or talked about there, except if it is inherently necessary. We will concentrate on the process of training for the role of group supervisor. How practitioners can be helped either:

to climb the staircase systematically, or:
to identify where they already are on the staircase.

In the latter case, can we encourage them to return briefly to the initial steps and rethink their practice in the light of new group experience and reflection?

Collaborative learning

As we reflect, retrospectively, on our experience of offering training in group supervising to a wide variety of practitioners, we become aware that the ability to engage in collaborative learning is the first step for developing effective group supervision. This is true for supervisees and, particularly, for the supervisor. We think that all group supervisor training will benefit from making this explicit, in theory, and from helping participants develop the necessary skill and attitudes to foster collaborative learning in practice.

Practitioners who have consciously engaged in taking responsibility for their own and each other's learning, and have reflected on that process, are familiar with this first step for participating in and leading supervision groups. Participating as a supervisee in an effective supervision group is the next related developmental step. Such participation can counteract the expectation that somehow only "the supervisor" can provide the necessary expertise to lead the group and offer supervision to every participant in it.

As practitioners move up the staircase, they need opportunities for developing further contents for the drawers in order to allow them to become increasingly competent and confident as a group supervisor. Practice in supervising a group and receiving supportive and challenging feedback from trainers and participants is important. This experience and feedback needs to support increasing awareness of the value and problems of diversity in groups, and the ability to capitalize on (or recognize limitations of) heterogeneity. The experience of practice with feedback also needs to support sensitivity to the range of contexts and working cultures in which members may be working.

So, from collaborative learning through the experience of participating in an effective supervision group to role practice as supervisor, with feedback: what a clear and easy passage! The existing professional set-up suggests that, even if this were a generally agreed pathway, few people have had, or would have, the opportunity to follow it so neatly.

From our experience of the complexity of the group supervision field, we were anxious not to suggest that there *could* be a definitive programme for training all group supervisors. Rather, we wanted to think of the essential opportunities that would meet the developmental needs of a variety of practitioners working in a shifting professional arena within a range of changeable contexts. Although we focus on a generic approach, the chapters in this book that cover the strengths and special needs of supervising within a particular theoretical orientation and across orientations will be particularly relevant to group supervision. Trainees in differing theoretical frameworks might need to be supported to interweave their own values, theory, and practice from the outset of a generic group supervision training.

Theory, experience, and reflection

All stages of development need to combine theory, conscious experience, and practice. The tutors may choose:

> to do formal teaching;
> to require directed reading or
> to offer frameworks for thinking about group supervision in a creative or experiential way.

They have choices as to whether theory is approached before opportunities to experience tasks and roles consciously, or to teach through reflection, after, or during, the experience

Dramatis personae

We have invented five hypothetical practitioners in different contexts and developmental stages. This structure has helped us to identify the relevant resources that prospective participants may already have and the additional training that they may need.

Mary, with five years of practice as a counsellor, is already supervising two individual trainees and has been invited to run a group in a voluntary organization. She participated in group supervision on her counselling Diploma course and found it a good experience. She decides to go on a supervision course that offers training in individual and group supervision.

Paul obtained a Certificate in Individual Supervision two years ago. The course was predominately academic, supplemented by in-course one-to-one supervision with other students. There was no special teaching about groups or group supervision; most practical and reflective work was in pairs or triads. He is a member of a peer supervision group. He feels ready to offer group supervision. His chosen course is a follow-up to his Certificate.

Yasmin also has a Diploma in Individual supervision. The course tutors' talked about group supervision, but offered no chance to practise. She had not found being supervised in a group on her counselling training helpful. She is running two groups in different voluntary organizations, which she enjoys, and she wants to learn more. She chooses a course that offers two days of theory and experiential work backed up by specific reading, followed by six half-days fortnightly for group work practice. The course consists of six experienced supervisors, and the format allows each participant to have two opportunities to take the role of group supervisor with feedback from participants and trainer. (We know of no courses targeted and organized like this but think there would be a market!)

Damien is a clinical psychologist who works for an addiction unit. The unit offers only group supervision to all its counsellors. Although he has been doing the job for over a year, and is a member of a supervision group for the supervisors, he has had no training in supervision. He does individual supervision with each counsellor in the group. After talking with a colleague, he would like to expand this into developing collaborative learning in the group and to encourage the supervisees to take a more active part. He has asked for the next annual training day to focus on participative group supervision.

Sheila has a Certificate in Supervision gained on a collaborative learning course. It included doing *individual* supervision practice in a group and receiving feedback from peers and trainer. She works as a counselling trainer on a Diploma course, and is being pressured to lead a supervision group for the trainees. She has been unable to find a dedicated group supervision course and is attending a two-day workshop in Creative Group Supervision to help her to decide whether she should accept this challenge.

Meeting Mary's needs

Step One: becoming a collaborative learner

The course that Mary chose to go on offers training in individual and group supervision. Such a course can model collaborative learning and group working from the outset. The initial Working Agreement sent to prospective participants can contain a clear commitment to collaborative learning. That entails:

- clarity of aims and criteria;
- taking responsibility for your own and each other's learning;
- clarity of roles: tutors, participants, assessors;
- variety of roles to be taken by participants (peer learner, supervisee, supervisor, feedback giver, group member, evaluator, process reflector and commentator, to name a few!).

The Agreement needs to be clear about what "may" happen and what "must" in process and outcome, and to be explicit enough about task and process for the applicant to give informed consent

What the initial contract spells out parallels the decision as to how much should be spelt out in individual and group supervision from the outset. In both cases, the explicit tasks and role implications help participants focus and prepare for the experience of group supervising. We name all the implications at this point to indicate what we understand by the term "collaborative learning".

The coming together of a new training group is an opportunity to model the setting up of a new supervision group. More complicated because of the numbers, members need to be facilitated to get to know each other so that they can estimate how far they can trust each other and the tutors to get down to work. The working agreement that they have "bought into" needs to come alive and have meaning: what has been theoretically agreed needs to be tested in practice. The previous experience of collaborative learning will be very variable in the group. The tutors' management of the group-forming process and of the storming, norming, and performing processes (Tuckman, 1965), which come and go through the life of a course, will provide models for managing the development of a supervision group. The ending experience, too, will give food for thought. Opportunities need to be provided to make these group processes explicit and to allow participants as well as tutors to comment. The manner in which tutors manage power—institutional power, role power, personal and attributed power—and participants' reactions to that will be important in shaping their own individual group management styles.

We think it is desirable for all supervision courses—individual or group—to lay the foundation of a conscious understanding of the processes of collaborative learning. In a course set up to include training in group supervision, the making explicit of group facilitating and development processes through reflection and process comment is fundamental.

Step Two: becoming a skilled small group participant

Mary's course will offer the opportunity for practice as *one-to-one supervisor–supervisee* taking place with one observer or in a group. Dividing the course into permanent small practice groups that take place regularly throughout the course offers a variety of opportunities. Giving responsibility to group members to manage the time and working structure of the practice group collaboratively allows for development of group skills and awareness. It offers practice in co-developing a safe and challenging enough group. It raises awareness of the tensions inherent in this, and different ways that the participants deal with these. Tutors should always be available as, at least, regular visitors and consultants.

As *group supervisee,* one gets the opportunity to become more skilled as *public presenter* of work: being supervised by one person with one observer is still "in public". As *group supervisor in training,* the participant has an opportunity to have access to many different ways of supervising. It also allows time to reflect on the experience of giving and receiving feedback and of becoming more skilled in the art. The ability to give and receive empathic and challenging feedback must be a basic skill for any supervisor. One of the basic tasks is to enable supervisees to receive such feedback openly and reflectively (and, in a supervision group, publicly). Participants need to recognize how this can best happen freely and straightforwardly. Overall, a small practice group offers a conscious experience of taking a variety of roles and of valuing a clear working agreement that will need to be reviewed and adjusted from time to time.

Tutors could take a variety of roles and tasks:

- leader of the practice group;
- group facilitator of the one-to-one practice;
- consultant;
- feeder-back;
- evaluator.

At this stage, there will already be tension between the tutor's institutional and attributed power in (probable) role of final assessor—the normative task—and responsibility for formative and restorative tasks. This is a tension that *needs to be made explicit.* In any group supervision in which the trainees will subsequently be working, such tension will need to be addressed publicly and creatively, even if the supervisor's assessment role is ethical rather than formal. These are the issues of power, authority, and influence that have special implications in a group, as opposed to individual, setting.

Step Three: becoming a skilled and aware supervisee in a supervision group

Mary's course can move on from concentrating on individual supervision to learning to become a group supervisor. One hopes that she approaches with her second drawer—conscious skill and information about being a small group member—well filled. Much of this learning will stand her in good stead for the next step.

A trainee on a group supervision course must have the opportunity to practise supervising in a group with feedback. This necessarily means course members being in the roles of group supervisee.

As supervisee they have at least three roles:

- presenter of supervision work;
- collaborative group participant;
- developing co-supervisor (see Inskipp & Proctor, 2001, Part 1).

They will, therefore, experience being at the receiving end of a variety of group supervisors who are learning to set up a group that works well. They will get practice in presenting economically and accessibly. They will be reminded how easily they can become shamed or resentful at people's responses, and will have opportunities to reflect on what responses help or hinder the work of the group. The issue of time will cease to be theoretical. They will have responses to their own and others' use or abuse of time in the group. They will become increasingly aware of how differing personalities, styles, cultural backgrounds, theoretical orientations, and working contexts can contribute to, or complicate, supervision.

They will discover the importance of being clear about the extent and limits of supervising and commenting on each other's work that their particular working agreement delineates. They may well already be excellent listeners and empathic responders, but here they will recognize the pressures of competition and comparison.

They will also experience the frustration when their peers—or their supervisor—invade their reflective space as supervisee or overload them with advice. They will have a chance to experience being at the receiving end of various verbal and/or experiential methods of group supervising. They will have participated, and developed skill, in group reflection on work and in group reviews.

Underlying all that, they will have opportunities to tie up theories of group process and group dynamics with their own experience. They will have access to comments on group process by the group supervisor. They will have access to the stated experience of others, articulated in the group.

As group supervisee, they will have models of how the supervisor uses authority in managing the group tensions while also concentrating on the task of supervision and the care for individual members. All this learning takes place within a tight time frame.

Participants on the course will have had varying experiences of supervision groups in their professional life. The distinction here is that the conscious recognition of their own and each other's experience, in role of group supervisee, will be part of their explicit learning agenda.

Step Four: becoming a skilled group supervisor

While becoming increasingly aware as a group supervisee, participants will also be having their turn as group supervisor. Well-filled drawers from steps two and three allow this step to be less overwhelming.

Tutors may well decide to demonstrate the process of setting up and working with a supervision group, or to show DVDs of what they consider good practice. They will need to make choices about how to set up groups for group supervision practice (as opposed to one-to-one practice). They will also need to set up a clear contract as to the role they will take with those groups. Their feedback and expertise will be uniquely valuable. They need to be mindful of staying within their contracted role or being explicit if they decide to change or renegotiate it.

If the trainee supervisors are to gain practice of supervising trainees and volunteers, it might be useful for group members to role play a less experienced version of themselves as supervisees (Proctor and Inskipp, 2007). Practice in setting up the contract and working agreement for the group while creating a collaborative and encouraging atmosphere may need them to work in different groups where the participants are less well known to each other. This might be in tension with the desirability of letting a group develop from session to session so that all members can monitor group development over time. (It is surprising, to us, how even short-term groups still seem to display distinct development from forming, through storming and norming, to performing.)

However few turns of practising with feedback that individuals may be able to take, there are two major experiences they need. One is to practise their style and ability for leadership and for being appropriately authoritative in stating "musts". The other is the chance to juggle with competing tasks, together with the awareness of juggling. Good induction of the group members while engaging in the task of supervision is a core skill. It is complex publicly to supervise one member while at the same time teaching all group members to participate helpfully. In addition, the course may have advocated experiential and creative methods of supervision in the group, with the intention of extending supervisees' skill and awareness in using all the senses. Such exercises require additional skill and judgement.

Added to that, monitoring hot issues in the group (e.g., competition, scapegoating, resentments, incompetence), validating diversity and individual working contexts, noticing the stage of development of the group as a whole and of each individual, being aware of the appraisal aspect of the task, and the need to be ethically aware, is formidable, and the conscious preparation and modelling of which we have spoken helps. Feedback from fellow trainees can do a great deal to relieve the overwhelming sense of responsibility that beginning group supervisors can experience.

At this stage, trainees also need to be helped and reminded about becoming practitioner researchers through keeping records, appraisals, and feedback from reviews. They should also be encouraged to consider doing research about group supervision, a sadly under-researched field.

Fifth step: self-appraisal and continuing development as a group supervisor

Throughout the course, Mary will, we hope, have been encouraged to become honest and searching in her own self-appraisal. Becoming a competent group supervisor (and ideally an accredited one) requires ongoing learning from experience of working over time with a group or, preferably, groups. Consultation with an experienced group supervisor is highly desirable, to give an opportunity for continuing self-appraisal and reflection. Peer group supervision of supervision may also meet this need. The course has a responsibility to promote and encourage CPD.

Obviously, Mary will gain from attending supervision conferences and workshops, keeping up with reading and research, and getting continuing feedback on her work from group participants, trainers, and managers. Preparation for accreditation could also intensify her learning.

The staircase (Figure 12.1) illustrates the complexities that underlie the skilled leading and managing of supervision groups. We know that Mary had enjoyed group supervision on her diploma

Step 5. Self-appraisal & CPD
Learning from experience:
reflection; self-appraisal with consultant, supervisor, peer group; conferences, workshops, research, reading; preparing for accreditation.

Step 4. Group supervisor practice
Experience:
finding own authoritative style; supervising in group; contracting a working agreement; juggling time and needs of group; inducting and teaching supervisee and co-supervising skills; managing group process, comments, exercises, reflection, reviews.

Step 3. Supervisee in a supervision group
Awareness, skills, models:
presenting; developing co-supervision; collaborating as a participant; valuing diversity; managing time, power/authority, process comments, hot issues, reflection/reviews.

Step 2. Small practice group
Skills and models:
presenting and supervising publicly; giving and receiving feedback; co-managing agreements and time; commenting on group process; leadership, authority and power in small group.

Step 1. Collaborative learning
Models and practice:
co-creating Working Agreement; getting to know and work; "good group manners"; recognition/management of: healthy group process, 'hot issues', power and authority.

Figure 12.1. The staircase to competence and confidence as a group supervisor.

course, and was looking forward to running a group in a voluntary organization. Some of the learning on her supervision course (for instance, how to be a skilled group supervisee) may not be new learning, but will reinforce and extend the skill and understanding she already possesses and make it more explicit. What Mary lacked when she joined the course was explicit skill and understanding of collaborative learning and any experience of *running* a supervision group.

Using the five-step illustration, we will look briefly at the training needs and possibilities of our other four hypothetical practitioners.

Meeting Paul's needs

Paul has chosen to go on a group supervision course that is a follow-up to his Certificate in Individual Supervision. The course is given over two weekends, to include tutor input, guided reading, practice as group supervisee, and an opportunity to group supervise. It also requires written work. (We consider this to be a minimum time-scale for such training.)

His Certificate course was not organized as an explicit collaborative learning experience, so his group course should fully exploit the opportunity to model the setting up of collaborative learning (Step One).

The length of the course might not allow for much learning in respect of Step Two, collaborative management of a small working group. However, Paul is in a peer group, and will have some experience and models to build on (Step Two).

In his Certificate course, he has had the semi-public one-to-one opportunities of Step Three. In his peer group, he has experience as group supervisee. He can benefit, consciously, from taking the role of supervisee with his colleagues/tutors on this course.

He will even have some experience of supervising in his peer group on which to build (Step Four). Having "tried it" before the course will be immensely helpful in enabling him to develop the skill and ability of Step Four. It will also help to ground his reading and tutor input.

And Yasmin?

Yasmin starts ostensibly at the same "stage" as Paul. However, she has had bad experiences of being in supervision groups as a trainee, but is already quite experienced in supervising in a group. Both give her a solid base of experience against which to test theory and know some of what else she needs in practice.

The first weekend can offer opportunities for developing theory and understanding for underpinning Steps Three and Four. This can be disseminated in a way that models and practises the skills of Steps One and Two, collaborative learning and managing of small working groups.

A course organized to allow six half-days of group supervising and being supervised gives generous opportunities for practising Steps Three and Four, and for the underpinning of Step Five.

But what about Damien?

He has learnt as he has gone along. If he knows that he wants to move to a more collaborative learning style, he needs to do some talking and planning with his fellow supervisors and the unit manager. A day course could be wasted if there were no shared agenda. The training provider needs to talk with the unit manager and ask him to consult with the team and suggest agreed aims for the day and future group supervision support and development (Hawkins & Shohet, 2006).

A tailor-made day on group supervision can teach and model the following.

1. How to set up a safe group: quick ways of getting to know each other.
2. Contracting for how they will work together: the tasks, roles, attitudes, and skills needed
3. How to teach group skills:
   (a) accurate listening and reflection;
   (b) different ways of focusing;
   (c) brief outline of four frameworks of group styles (Inskipp & Proctor 2001; Proctor, 2008).

The trainer needs to take care to set up the training day in the way that demonstrates all these points (Steps 1–3). In demonstrating exercises for teaching trainees the ability to listen carefully and to respond to presentations in an orderly manner, they are also giving participants the experience as group supervisee in a well-managed group that they may not have had.

Finally, Sheila

Sheila has already experienced intentional collaborative learning, She has had a good experience as a group supervisee. As trainer on a course, presumably she has some group theory and experience. Other members of the workshop on creative group supervision might not be so experienced. There is an agreed shared aim that the workshop will be experiential.

In such a workshop, we introduce all frameworks experientially. We ask participants to enact them, holding labels of, for example, different group theories and dialoguing with each other. Through exercises, which they can replicate with group supervisees, we offer a "felt sense" of hierarchy and dynamics in groups. We model designing and leading creative supervision exercises to increase sensory awareness.

It is unrealistic and potentially divisive to offer opportunities for some very few unknown participants to practise group supervision on a two-day course. A demonstration by a supervisor doing group supervision can be helpful, particularly in showing ways to be active in leadership without being bossy or authoritarian.

All such tasters help participants to decide if they are ready to run a group, and to become aware of what they need in terms of CPD. Tasters need to be accompanied by information on the core principles of good practice, or reference to where those can be found (Houston, 1995; Lahad, 2000; Proctor, 2008; Scaife, 2008).

In conclusion

The more we write on group supervision the more we realize the complexities of the roles the supervisor needs to take. One group described it as "being in a sand-pit"—a place to play and create—but watch the sand does not get into your eyes! There is a tension between being grown up and the need for self-protection, to accept and value the child in self and others and to use this to understand participants and clients. Parental responsibilities (according to role) need to be acknowledged while working in adult mode. It helps if the basic attitudes, skills, and understanding of task and processes are already in place before undertaking practice as group supervisor. A clear, ongoing working agreement is probably the greatest help to things going well. Central in that is the reminder that all the training is about helping every *client* to live more resourcefully and to their own greater well being. When it is going well, group supervising and training group supervisors can be hugely enjoyable and rewarding tasks.

Appreciation

Warm thanks to Melanie Lockett, who contributed to our preparatory conversations.

References

Hawkins, P., & Shohet, R. (2006). *Supervision in the Helping Professions* (3rd edn). Buckingham: Open University Press.

Houston, G. (1995). *Supervision and Counselling*. London: Rochester Foundation.

Inskipp, F., & Proctor, B. (2001). *The Art, Craft and Tasks of Counselling Supervision* (2nd edn). *Part 1: Making the Most of Supervision*. Twickenham: Cascade.

Inskipp, F., & Proctor, B. (2003). *The Art, Craft and Tasks of Counselling Supervision* (2nd edn). *Part 2: Becoming a Supervisor*. Twickenham: Cascade.

Lahad, M. (2000). *Creative Supervision: The Use of Expressive Arts Methods in Supervision and Self-Supervision*. London: Jessica Kingsley.

Proctor, B. (2008). *Group Supervision: A Guide to Creative Practice* (2nd edn). London: Sage.

Proctor, B., & Inskipp, F. (2007). *Creative Group Supervision*. DVD: available from the School of Health and Social Sciences, PO Box 180, Newport, South Wales, NP20 5XR, http://newport.ac.uk

Scaife, J. (2008). *Supervision in Clinical Practice: A Practitioner's Guide* (2nd edn). London: Brunner-Routledge.

Tuckman, B. (1965). Developmental sequence in small groups. *Psychological Bulletin, 63*: 384–399.

PART II

APPROACHES

CHAPTER THIRTEEN

Supervision: a psychodynamic and psychoanalytic perspective on supervisor practice and supervisor training

Christine Driver

Supervision within the field of psychoanalytic work could be said to have started with Freud at his Wednesday evening meetings in Berlin (Frawley-O'Dea & Sarnat, 2001). Here, the approach was very much a process of "learning from the master" (Freud himself), with little apparent reflection on the dynamics of transference and process. It was almost fifty years later, through the work of Heimann (1950) and, more especially, Searles (1955) that the significance of transference, countertransference, and unconscious communication in supervision was realized.

The key issue that Searles identified was that the supervisor's emotions are often "highly informative reflections of the relationship between therapist and patient" (1955, p. 158), and that the supervisory relationship is influenced and affected by unconscious processes and dynamics from the patient material and the supervisory relationship. This realization led Searles to coin the term "reflection process" to describe this dynamic and, together with ideas emerging from Ekstein and Wallerstein (1972), supervision began to be seen as a more complex matrix involving at the very least a triangular dynamic (Driver & Martin, 2002, 2005; Hawkins & Shohet, 2002; Mattinson, 1975; Wiener, Mizen, & Duckham, 2003).

What emerged from this is that the role of the supervisor requires the development of an observing ego (Greenson, 1981) and an internal reflective capacity to hold, juggle, focus, and identify the various conscious and unconscious components and communications within the supervisory relationship. This requires the supervisor to sustain an analytic attitude in relation to understanding the impact of the patient's internal world and unconscious communications within supervision, enable the supervisee to develop their awareness of the patient and the patient's internal world, facilitate the supervisee's learning and development, and be aware of the impact of organizational issues on the supervisory relationship. This emphasizes that supervision is a process-orientated focus in which the exploration and interpretation of the clinical material requires dynamic internal activity by both supervisor and supervisee.

Moving from therapist to supervisor

When clinical practitioners train in psychodynamic and psychoanalytic work, the key dimensions which they have to grapple with and understand revolve around the nature of the unconscious, and understanding unconscious processes and unconscious communication via transference, countertransference, and projection within the encounter with the patient. The aim is to facilitate understanding and awareness of the internal world of the patient and their unconscious and emotional complexes so as to enable the patient to make mutative shifts and develop awareness and understanding.

Developing these skills takes time, and they are the prerequisite to moving into supervising psychodynamic and psychoanalytic work. However, becoming a supervisor also requires development of the capacity to manoeuvre between focusing on the patient material, working with the supervisory relationship, considering the overlapping dynamics of patient, supervisee, and supervisor, and analysing the matrix (Perry, 2003) of overlapping processes within the frame of the supervisory relationship.

Training in psychodynamic and psychoanalytic supervision, therefore, requires development of the basic and generic skills such as contracts, boundaries, supervisee development, clinical issues, assessment, organizational issues, and ethical issues, as well as developing a deep understanding of unconscious processes, unconscious logic, and a capacity to process the whole supervisory dynamic so as to develop understanding and awareness in relation to the patient.

The supervisory frame, contracts, boundaries, and unconscious processes

Contracts and boundaries are the fundamental starting points of clinical work, but within the supervisory setting there are additional factors. At a conscious level, it is easy to assume that the supervisory relationship is collegial and that boundaries and contracts do not need to be as specific as those formed with patients. However, the impact of the supervisory frame on the supervisory relationship needs to be carefully monitored and considered, especially in relation to unconscious dynamics such as anxiety, regression, transference, and countertransference.

Langs (1994, 1997) wrote very specifically about the impact of the supervisory frame and, although one might disagree with the extent of his focus on frames, his ideas nevertheless offer an important perspective. For Langs, frequent changes of the supervisory frame, such as changes in session times, rooms, etc., generate unconscious anxiety that results in a disregard for boundaries and frames in the supervisee in their work with their patients. Conversely, Langs identifies that frames and boundaries that remain totally unchanged lead, at an unconscious level, to existential anxiety and a sort of death-like feel, making it hard to stay with the issues and challenges of the clinical work.

Although this creates a view of a "no win" situation, it nevertheless identifies that changes to the boundaries and frame are significant and have an unconscious impact that results in conscious enactments to counteract anxiety. These dynamics are also apparent, on a larger scale, when the organizational demands have an impact on supervision. Changes instigated by the organization, such as increasing fees, changing rooms, changing supervisor, or assessment processes, all affect the supervisory relationship and dynamic.

Such demands may be consciously adhered to, but the unconscious impact on the supervisory relationship and the clinical work with the patient needs to be seriously considered. For example, the demand to increase fees might lead to resistance in the supervisee and a parallel resistance in the patient; a change of supervisor could result in anxiety and uncertainty in the supervisee, leading to unconscious regression or resistance and either a diminished capacity to hold patients or a "do it myself" stance. Assessment of a trainee by a supervisor will also cause a powerful unconscious dynamic. The anxiety generated by this might influence the clinical material brought to supervision and result in an underlying theme of criticism, or being critical, or the supervisee being overprotective or overcritical with their patients.

The supervisory triangle, the patient, and unconscious processes

Understanding unconscious dynamics and the nature of unconscious logic and unconscious communication is, therefore, a key challenge in supervisor training and development. Within supervision, however, the patient that the supervisory work is focused on is absent (Martin, 2002). Martin reflects on this, and identifies that the key challenge for the supervisor is to enable the supervisee to stand back from the pairing with the patient and develop a more asymmetric relationship in which both supervisor and supervisee reflect on the transference, countertransference, and unconscious dynamics that are occurring between the patient and the supervisee (*ibid.*, p. 15).

What the supervisor has to juggle is a simultaneous monitoring of the conscious dialogue about the patient as well as reflecting on the unconscious dynamics and communication from the patient material within the supervisory relationship. This is an intrinsic part of psychoanalytic and psychodynamic supervisor training. Learning to develop these reflective and analytic skills requires the supervisor to reflect on his or her own countertransference reactions to both the patient material and the supervisee's presentations and use this awareness in their discussions and interpretations to the supervisee.

Developing awareness of unconscious communication, however, is a challenge, because, by its very nature, the unconscious is unconscious. Training in supervision enables supervisors to develop the skills and techniques to identify such phenomena and to develop awareness and understanding of unconscious processes and unconscious logic. A useful tool to develop this capacity is observed supervision. This enables feedback from the observers about the unconscious communications and transference and countertransference issues, and provides insight into the ways in which awareness of these dynamics can be achieved.

This is the challenge of psychodynamic and psychoanalytic supervision. It is relatively easy to comment on the concrete content of the session, symbolic material, and technique in terms of theory and conceptual understanding, but it is a much bigger challenge to catch hold of the way issues from the patient are unconsciously communicated or projected into the supervisory relationship. This requires awareness of the difference between assimilative learning, the gathering of new information and "increasing already existing knowledge" (Szecsödy, 1997, p. 109), and accommodative learning. This latter is a much more dynamic process of those "ah ha" moments, in which awareness at a conscious and unconscious level occurs and insight and understanding, at both a cognitive and emotional level, deepens. Accommodative learning requires an internal shift (Driver, 2005, p. 19; Martin, 2002) and enables previously held knowledge to be restructured and a new understanding and awareness achieved by the supervisee and, ultimately, the patient.

Supervisee development: the conscious and unconscious frame

Studies by Stoltenberg and Delworth (1987), Hawkins and Shohet (2002), and Stewart (2002a) about supervisee development have identified that beginners start clinical work with high anxiety, dependence on the supervisor, and with a degree of self-focus. This makes it difficult, initially, for the supervisee to consider transference, countertransference, and unconscious processes from a more objective perspective, or to reflect on the internal world of the patient. The supervisor, therefore, needs to model a process of discourse and internal reflection on the transference and counter-transference issues emanating from the patient, and possibly reflected in the supervision, to enable understanding and mutative shifts (Martin, 2002) within the supervisee about the patient.

Maintaining and facilitating supervisee development also brings to the fore issues relating to assessment. Assessment requires a careful handling of both conscious and unconscious processes. It also requires an ability to identify and evaluate the "skills, competences and abilities, or lack of, in the supervisee" (Driver, 2008, p. 331), as well as the supervisee's capacity to work and think psychodynamically and psychoanalytically. In addition, when assessing the supervisee's work, the supervisor needs to distinguish between what is emerging from the patient and what is intrinsic to the supervisee. Unconscious dynamics and communication from the patient via the reflection process (Searles, 1955) can create confusion within the supervisory relationship of what is being perceived. For example, a "fragmented and disorganised patient can often make a supervisee's presentations fragmented and disorganised" (Driver, 2008, p. 337) and make thinking difficult. In such a situation, the supervisor needs to separate the dynamics of the patient material from the supervisee's learning needs in order to develop understanding and awareness.

Supervisee development, therefore, requires the supervisor to be cognizant of both conscious and unconscious dynamics and to differentiate between the clinical material and the supervisee's capacities as a clinician. It is a delicate process that requires sensitivity in order to maintain a creative dialogue and a process of learning, but it is an important part of the supervisor's skills in enabling supervisee development and maintaining and developing good practice.

Supervising across modalities

Psychodynamic and psychoanalytic supervisors often work in counselling and psychotherapy agencies or NHS settings, supervising clinicians trained in various modalities. The key to any supervisory process is dialogue, and the challenge for the supervisor is to find a common language with their supervisees to generate understanding about the patient. The psychodynamic and psychoanalytic field contains a range of theories and theorists which inform the work and thinking about the internal world of the patient. However, reflection on the patient material can be examined more generically in relation to key figures such as mother, father, siblings, family dynamics, etc., to generate a dialogue about the patient's internal world.

A supervisory process that enables understanding will always benefit both practitioner and patient and the development of the work. Psychodynamic and psychoanalytic supervisors work from the basis that unconscious processes are key to understanding the internal world of the patient, and that the patient's material and the interactive dynamics will throw light on this. Psychodynamic and psychoanalytic work, therefore, aims at developing understanding within the patient of the "internal struggles and relationship patterns" (Driver, 2005, p. xvii) that they are caught up in, in order to enable internal and external mutative shifts and changes.

In many respects, this presents a challenge for cross-modality supervision. Many modalities have a primarily conscious and cognitive focus, whereas psychodynamic and psychoanalytic supervision focuses on affects, emotional complexes, defences, and unconscious dynamics. Cross-modality supervision is creative and enlivening because it challenges the assumptions made by a specific modality, but it also has to deal with the differences and maintain a balance between creativity and limitations.

Conclusion: the challenge of training supervisors of psychodynamic and psychoanalytic work and the future

The key challenge in training psychodynamic and psychoanalytic supervisors is finding ways to consider and reflect on the unconscious dynamics that enter into the supervisory relationship. These may be from the patient, the supervisee, the organizational setting (Crowther, 2003; Stewart, 2002b), or even from the supervisor (Stimmel, 1995).

Training in supervision needs to incorporate not just the generic components, but also opportunities to think about and reflect on issues relating to unconscious processes and unconscious dynamics. Understanding cognitively and consciously what the patient material is about is not enough. Unconscious processes, by their very nature, are not immediately known or perceived, but, in order to enable the supervisee and ultimately the patient to develop understanding and awareness, it is vital that the supervisor enables a process that brings to conscious awareness the unconscious communication and unconscious processes that influence and disturb the supervisory relationship, so as to enable understanding about the internal world of the patient and the learning needs of the supervisee.

The need for supervision training is vital to enable the practitioner to understand and develop both a theoretical and dynamic understanding of the skills and competencies that a supervisor needs. There are now many more trainings in supervision and a growing awareness of the need for them, but training in supervision needs to extend beyond the counselling and psychotherapy profession and include practitioners working in such roles as nurse practitioners, support workers, and other professionals who undertake a supervisory role in the caring professions, so that they, too, can gain and develop understanding and awareness of the generic and specific components of being a supervisor.

Looking ahead, in five, or perhaps ten, years' time, all clinical supervisors will probably be required to be trained and registered. Within the psychodynamic and psychoanalytic arena, supervision will be much more of a process-orientated dialogue, with more attention given to unconscious communication by practitioners in all orientations. Training in supervision will also incorporate research into the practice and efficacy of supervision and the development of a critical and analytic attitude to the dynamics and process of supervision.

This chapter reflects a resumé of where supervision and supervisor training within the psychodynamic and psychoanalytic field has reached. The past twenty-five years have seen a massive increase in the training and understanding of supervision and the impact of unconscious communication within this. As awareness and understanding develops, the next ten to twenty years will see further developments and insights in this field.

References

Crowther, C. (2003). Supervising in institutions. In: J. Wiener, R. Mizen & J. Duckham (Eds.), *Supervision and Being Supervised: A Practice in Search of a Theory* (pp. 100–117). Basingstoke: Palgrave Macmillan.

Driver, C. (2005). Language and interpretation in supervision. In: C. Driver & E. Martin (Eds.), *Supervision and the Analytic Attitude* (pp. 17–33). London: Whurr.

Driver, C. (2008). Assessment in supervision: an analytic perspective. *British Journal of Psychotherapy, 24*(3): 328–342.

Driver, C., & Martin, E. (Eds.) (2002). *Supervising Psychotherapy*. London: Sage.

Driver, C., & Martin, E. (Eds.) (2005). *Supervision and the Analytic Attitude*. London: Whurr.

Ekstein, R., & Wallerstein, R. (1972). *The Teaching and Learning of Psychotherapy*. Madison, CT: International Universities Press.

Frawley-O'Dea, M., & Sarnat, J. E. (2001). *The Supervisory Relationship: A Contemporary Psychodynamic Approach*. New York: Guilford.

Greenson, R. R. (1981). *The Technique and Practice of Psychoanalysis*. London: Hogarth.

Hawkins, P., & Shohet, R. (2002). *Supervision in the Helping Professions* (2nd edn). Buckingham: Open University Press.

Heimann, P. (1950). On countertransference. In: M. Tonnesmann (Ed.), *About Children and Children No-Longer* (pp. 55–59). London: Routledge, 1989, 2005.

Langs, R. (1994). *Doing Supervision and Being Supervised*. London: Karnac.

Langs, R. (1997). The framework of supervision in psychoanalytic psychotherapy. In: B. Martindale, M. Mörner, M. E. C. Rodríguez, & J.-P. Vidit (Eds.), *Supervision and its Vicissitudes* (pp. 117–134). London: Karnac.

Martin, E. (2002). Listening to the absent patient. In: C. Driver & E. Martin (Eds.), *Supervising Psychotherapy: Psychoanalytic and Psychodynamic Perspectives* (pp. 11–22). London: Sage.

Mattinson, J. (1975). *The Reflection Process in Casework Supervision*. London: IMS Tavistock Institute.

Perry, C. (2003). Into the labyrinth: a developing approach to supervision. In: J. Wiener, R. Mizen, & J. Duckham (Eds.), *Supervision and Being Supervised: A Practice in Search of a Theory* (pp. 187–206). Basingstoke: Palgrave Macmillan.

Searles, H. F. (1955). The informational value of the supervisor's emotional experiences. In: *Collected Papers on Schizophrenia and Related Subjects*. London: Maresfield Library, 1986.

Stewart, J. (2002a). The interface between teaching and supervision. In: C. Driver & E. Martin (Eds.), *Supervising Psychotherapy: Psychoanalytic and Psychodynamic Perspectives* (pp. 64–83). London: Sage.

Stewart, J. (2002b). The container and the contained: supervision and its organisational context. In: C. Driver & E. Martin (Eds.), *Supervising Psychotherapy: Psychoanalytic and Psychodynamic Perspectives* (pp. 106–120). London: Sage.

Stimmel, B. (1995). Resistance to awareness of the supervisor's transference with special reference to the parallel process. *International Journal of Psychoanalysis, 76*(6): 609–618.

Stoltenberg, C. D., & Delworth, U. (1987). *Supervising Counsellors and Therapists*. San Francisco, CA: Jossey-Bass.

Szecsödy, I. (1997). (How) Is learning possible in supervision? In: B. Martindale, M. Mörner, M. E. C. Rodríguez, & J.-P. Vidit (Eds.), *Supervision and its Vicissitudes* (pp. 101–116). London: Karnac.

Wiener, J., Mizen, R., & Duckham, J. (Eds.) (2003). *Supervision and Being Supervised: A Practice in Search of a Theory*. Basingstoke: Palgrave Macmillan.

CHAPTER FOURTEEN

Training for supervisors of transactional analysis practitioners and others

Charlotte Sills

In this chapter, I aim to do two things. The first is to highlight the ways in which transactional analysis (TA) supervision might be different (or at least have different emphases) from generic supervision and, in doing so, identify what particular strengths the TA supervisor might have to offer practitioners of any approach. The second is to identify one or two challenges that face TA supervisors in supervising practitioners from different disciplines and also in responding to developments in the field, both within and outside of transactional analysis. Although, inevitably, they tend to be different sides of the same coin, I will try to separate them into strengths and challenges.

As far as I know, TA is the *only* approach to counselling and therapy that has developed a complete structured training for supervisors of its practitioners. This training takes the form of several years of supervision practice under contract with a mentor, alongside other formal and informal learning experiences, regular supervision of supervision, and a commitment to take part in the organizational life of TA. Each developing supervisor's learning journey is individually designed with his or her primary supervisor, so that, although there may be periods of "workshop style" learning in groups, each person has their own pathway and time frame. The journey culminates in an examination comprising two viva exams, in which the candidate responds to questions from an international board of peers, as well as doing live demonstrations of supervision at practitioner level and advanced level. The candidate is required to demonstrate a depth knowledge of TA theory and practice as well as other psychological approaches, along with a coherent supervision philosophy and method that are congruent with the ethics and principles of TA. The decision about readiness for examination is partly administrative: in other words, the completion of clearly prescribed numbers of hours of formal learning, supervision and practice; it is also a more subjective assessment of readiness by the candidate herself and at least two supervising supervisors. The final examinations lead to the qualification of Supervising Transactional Analyst (STA); they are usually, though not always, as some supervisors do not want to teach, combined with a further viva exam on teaching skills and methods, the whole day leading to the grand title of Teaching and Supervising Transactional Analyst (TSTA).

Perhaps understandably, the people who have devised this challenging supervision training—let alone those who have undergone it—are rather protective about their achievement! Consequently, only TSTAs and endorsed "Provisional" trainers (PTSTAs) who supervise under the guidance of a TSTA can offer official training and supervision in TA; in other words, to acquire the relevant hours of training and supervision necessary to qualify as a practitioner of TA, one must be working with these endorsed trainers/supervisors. The implication is that being a supervisor of TA trainees and practitioners is a very different activity from generic supervision and, therefore, the training of TA practitioners can only be entrusted to those further up the TA hierarchy.

As the reader might imagine, this situation has led to a deal of discussion and debate: is this exclusivity justifiable? Trainees sometimes feel constrained by the closed market of the (dare I say it?) pyramid; and then there is the inevitable possibility of becoming overly self-referential if "foreign" ideas are not integrated.

However, the thought and care that goes into the training and accrediting of supervisors has led to the TA communities being centres of real knowledge and excellence in the field. Even as I write

(2008), I am involved in some extensive international research, both quantitative and qualitative, into the training of effective supervisors. This is commissioned and funded by the European TA Association (EATA). What is more, the requirement of TSTAs to demonstrate that they can locate TA in the wider field of psychological thought and integrate theories and methods from other approaches goes a long way to offsetting the concern about an ideological closed shop, as does the international multi-cultural nature of the organization, including the examination boards. Concerns about dual relationships and conflict of interest are also largely unnecessary (though might not have been thirty years ago). In the UK alone, there are around sixty TSTAs, and there are TA organizations in upwards of thirty European (Western and Eastern) countries, as well as in Australasia, the Americas, South Africa, and so forth. It is almost always possible to ensure neutrality and fairness in the system.

What may be the particular strengths of transactional analysis supervision?

For a depth exploration of TA supervision, consult Tudor (2002), who offers an excellent overview of the nature of transactional analysis supervision and its history in the literature; also the April 2007 edition of the *Transactional Analysis Journal* (Cornell & Shadbolt, 2007a), which has the topic of supervision as its theme. This chapter, however, focuses more on what the TA supervisor brings to the craft of supervision generally.

Despite the fact that the concepts and theories of TA draw greatly on both the psychoanalytic and the cognitive behavioural movements, the philosophy and principles of TA locate the approach firmly in the humanistic tradition of therapies. First, there is "OKness", immortalized in that deceptively trivializing phrase, "I'm OK—You're OK". This aphorism captures the existential statement: I am and you are *separately existing yet connected*, with the additional value of OKness, which is understood to mean equally worthy of respect, valuable, important. The whole speaks of the aspiration to mutual respect in the relational dance of power and intimacy.

The second tenet states that all human beings have the capacity to think, and make decisions about themselves and their lives (albeit sometimes unawarely), and that these decisions can be changed. The principle of self-responsibility and empowerment is very strong in TA, which in the 1960s and 1970s grew as a "radical psychiatry".

These positive and optimistic statements lead to two cornerstones of TA practice: the contract and open communication. These may be two of the particular strengths of TA supervision.

The contract

It is well documented (e.g., Bordin, 1994; Lambert, 1992; Wampold, 2001) that one of the elements necessary to successful therapy outcome is a clear agreement between therapist and client as to the goals of the therapy, including a general understanding of how this will be achieved: the tasks of the work. These agreements are key parts of the working alliance that is so essential to effectiveness. It is, undoubtedly, also true for supervision. Of course, the supervision contract is well respected and discussed by many writers in the field (see, for example, Proctor, 2006); but the contractual method has a particular place at the heart of TA practice and supervision (Berne, 1966), where it is used not simply as a tool for clarifying and structuring, but as a subtle and dynamic part of the work. As such, it can become surprisingly powerful as a container, guide, boundary, diagnostic tool, and transference identifier. A TA supervisor will expect to make a clear contract, not only for the overall development of the supervisee and the manner of the supervision (including, where relevant, the theories to be used, the methodology, and so on), but also for each session, revisiting and updating it if necessary and checking its completion. Frequently, the contract will articulate the part each person will play in the session's encounter. The TA supervisor will also be highly aware of the implications of context and setting and the necessity of the multi-handed contract (English, 1975; Micholt, 1992; Tudor, 2006), and this makes her an ideal supervisor for a multi-approach agency or counselling scheme.

The contract (be it for therapy or for supervision) should appeal to all ego states; it should emerge from careful and committed inquiry and understanding of the situation and should involve an exchange of benefit between supervisor and supervisee and be within the law (Steiner, 1974).

Open communication

The definition of TA supervision (e.g., Barnes, 1977; Cox, 1998) stresses that its intention is to improve the service to the client by developing the effectiveness of practitioners *through the use of TA.* This requires supervisors to have a more than working knowledge of the theory and the language of TA in order to practise. There is a reason for this. Of course, there is a sense in which TA, like any theoretical approach to understanding human beings, looks at the structure of personality, how it develops, the causes of problems, and, crucially, how change occurs. That being the case, the particular concepts and language of one approach can normally be "translated" into another. What makes TA unusual is that it has a wealth of theory and methods that use direct, precise, and straightforward language to describe both the complexities of conscious and unconscious intrapsychic life and its development and also how that is manifested and maintained in the co-created interpersonal relationship. This is contained in the notion of "script", the patterned course of the person's life: self-determining *yet changeable.* The concepts are clear, simple without being simplistic, and understandable to practically everyone. TA's theory embodies the values inherent in its philosophy and principles, and it is important that the supervisor models these. The triad of philosophy, practice, and theory is thus shaped and contained by the accessibility and immediacy of the concepts.

Respectful open communication was always a feature of TA; Berne encouraged his clients to read his books. Supervision has always been considered an important part of effective practice. Supervision and supervisor development is frequently carried out in "cascade" format with practitioners, supervisors, and supervising supervisors working together and each making a contract for their development. Sometimes, patients are involved in practitioner development, a tradition started by Berne (1968), who held staff–patient staff conferences at the psychiatric hospitals where he worked. He considered that if a thing is worth saying, it must be sayable in front of the patient. So, he structured the ward rounds and case conferences in such a way that all the staff—doctors, nurses, support workers, therapists—talked about the patients' progress and treatment in a circle group while the patients sat around the outside of the room listening. Then the patients were brought into the circle to discuss their own progress—and their thoughts about the effectiveness of the staff—while the medics sat around the edge and listened. These staff–patient conferences were aimed at challenging the patient–therapist divide and were designed so that they gave all staff and all patients an equal opportunity to have a voice and discuss the treatment being carried out. (For a modern account of this challenging form of open communication, see Cornell, Shadbolt, and Norton, 2007b.) It is reported that the patients found this system much more comfortable than the staff.

Standards of assessment

Thus, an integral part of TA supervision is the notion of a robust attitude to asking for consultation and help, while staying responsible for one's own work. The stage and experience of the practitioner is always considered, and the supervisor is expected to vary her style: being ready to provide information and education about theory and skills if necessary, monitor ethics, or offer support where relevant, and also be able to provide a space for reflection, or enter into a more subtle conversation about relational dynamics, parallel process, and the like.

Based on its philosophy and principles, the international TA communities have identified and articulated a number of essential competencies for a TA supervisor (first developed by trainers and trainees at Metanoia Institute, London: see Clarkson, 1992, p. 275). These form the basis of the final examination to become an STA. They are: contract made and fulfilled; key issues identified; probability of harm reduced; developmental direction increased; appropriate process modelled (i.e., transference–countertransference and parallel process attended to); and equal relationship maintained. Mazzetti (2007, p. 94) developed these into a seven-point operational model of TA supervision.

- Establish a clear and appropriate contract.
- Identify key issues.
- Establish effective emotional contact with supervisee.
- Attend to the safety and protection of both client and supervisee.
- Increase developmental direction.
- Increase awareness of and effective use of parallel process.
- Develop an equal relationship.

As will be obvious, nothing in this list presents a problem in supervising counsellors and therapists from other disciplines, as long as their philosophies are compatible with TA's humanistic principle of self-responsibility and autonomy. If the TA supervisor is willing to put her language on one side and make the effort to translate concepts into other terms, there is no reason why she should not be an excellent supervisor of practitioners of any discipline whose philosophy is compatible. However, as I discuss below, in order to engage with the more emergent process of a relational or psychoanalytic supervision, she will need to widen her repertoire.

Supervising TA trainees: challenges for the future

Each of these strengths gives rise to a potential challenge or shadow. I hailed the contract as a powerful tool for facilitating effective work, particularly in supervision, where there is unlikely to be an advantage in allowing the transference and countertransference dynamic to develop. However, the shadow of this clarity of the contract is that it risks being too concrete. Traditionally, the TA contract would be outcome-focused, observable, measurable, and verifiable, a fact which led TA to be considered purely as a cognitive–behavioural therapy for many years. Of course, the existence of a clear and measurable outcome contract lends this sort of cognitive TA to carrying out the type of research that is prized by health services and fund holders. However, the contract implies certainty—even foreknowledge—on the part of the supervisee, who is expected to articulate (often near the start of the supervision session) exactly what he wishes to learn. This inevitably means that, by definition, the goal of the session is one that is envisaged within the current frame of reference; no second order learning is anticipated or invited. What is more, there is a danger that specifying a contract might upset the delicate balance between respecting that which is known and honouring that which cannot be known. Therapists must allow themselves to stay with the messiness of emergent feelings and images, and not believe that everything should be neatly boxed. Recently, there has been a move to develop the contract's more flexible role as part of the relational dialogue. For example, the contracting matrix (Sills, 2006) identifies four types of contact, the latter two of which honour the emergence of "implicit" experience in the therapeutic space (Figure 14.1). There remains some inevitable and perhaps necessary limiting quality to any contract other than the purely administrative, and yet it allows space for the therapeutic or supervisory encounter to discover new ground.

Here lies a paradox for the TA practitioner and supervisor. On the one hand, TA, with its contractual method and its articulated competences for practitioners, lends itself very well to creating research trials, even randomized control trials (RCTs). Practitioners of TA could clearly articulate the concepts and treatment plans associated with specific problems (for example, eating disorders, self harm, depression) and create "manuals" for practitioners that could be applied and tested using one of the outcome measures. However, a move in this direction would not only jar with the humanistic "philosophy" of the approach, it would directly oppose the recent developments in the practice of TA that have been

Clarifying —	**Behavioural change —**
Exploratory —	**Emergence —**

Figure 14.1. Contracting matrix.

welcomed by therapists who felt that there was something missing: the relational perspective.

The relational trend in TA

While the principles and values of TA are humanistic, its theory is, in part, cognitive–behavioural (for example, stroke theory, racket theory, script decisions, and so on) and very largely psychoanalytic (ego states, impasses, games, etc.). Berne himself undertook training as a psychoanalyst before seriously falling out with his institution. It is likely, therefore, that he assumed that any TA practitioner would automatically bring a psychodynamic awareness and thinking to his or her client work. However, he was determined to challenge what he saw as exclusivity, obfuscation, and time-wasting in his psychoanalytic colleagues. Therefore, he developed TA methodology in the more cognitive–behavioural tradition (although writing as he did in the 1950s and 1960s, his ideas actually pre-dated many of the original CBT thinkers) in order to create a way of working that was speedy, accessible, and understandable. As a result, the significance of some of his most important theories was partly overlooked.

In recent years, there has been a movement in TA to recapture the richness of its psychoanalytic roots (in particular, the existence of "the unconscious", or unconscious processes) while attempting to retain some of its pragmatism. This was especially developed in the Italian TA institutes in the 1980s (e.g., Moiso, 1985; Novellino, 2003) but has spread all over the world (for example, see the April 2005 edition of the *Transactional Analysis Journal* [Hargaden, 2005]). The relational movement has (for all sorts of theoretical, sociological, and geopolitical reasons that are beyond the scope of this chapter) begun to gain sway in the worlds of philosophy, modern science, organizational theory, and psychological therapies. This trend is mirrored in transactional analysis with what is now called Relational TA (Cornell & Hargaden, 2005; Hargaden & Sills, 2002). Berne was ahead of his time. Perhaps it was his passion for equality that drove him to develop theories that acknowledged the co-created nature of meaning and of behaviour. His theories of ego states contain a meaningful object relations theory, explaining how personality is formed in relationship. His theories of transactions and games track the transferential dance of mutual enactment. Relational TA builds on these theories and connects them both to their roots in unconscious processes and also to recent understanding of neurobiology and of connection in social processes. Relational TA involves letting go of a search for "the answer" and allows for a multiplicity of truths in the co-created here and now, acknowledging the communication of the relational unconscious through feelings, emotions, body signals, symbols, and images.

This inevitably brief outline suffices to point to the second obvious challenge to future TA supervisors, both of TA practitioners and others. Working with uncertainty, with careful inquiry into meanings and responses, does not lend itself to the efficient container of the contract and a twenty-minute supervision. Neither does it sit comfortably with TA's facility to name what is happening quickly, confidently, directly, and often with a touch of humour. Embracing the idea that we all shape, and are shaped by, our context and our relationships challenges the confident location of a script, a game invitation, or a racket within the individual patient. On the contrary, it means that practitioners and their supervisors need to become as skilled as possible in listening to their own feelings and transferential and countertransferential stirrings, in order to engage with a client in collaborative encounter. This means possibly blurring the boundary between personal work and education, and including in the contract a willingness to explore all sorts of ways of understanding relational unconscious processes. An acceptance that supervisor and supervisee are also shaping their relationship calls for new discussion about difference, power, and authority in supervision. These ideas about relational supervision are elaborated by Hahn, Hargaden, and Tudor (2009), and Fowlie in an unpublished paper.

The challenge is, therefore, how can the TA supervisor allow space for this sort of uncertainty and exploration while retaining all that is reassuringly accessible in TA and that gives useful tools for taking charge of one's life and the supervisory process?

And this brings me to my last current, ongoing, and future challenge: the language of transactional analysis. It is dated, unmistakeably Californian, arguably a little "glib", and often sexist (whoever would think of talking about the envious attack of the paranoid schizoid position as "Now I've Got You, You Son of a Bitch"?). Is there a way of finding other language—catchy, straightforward, and even humorous—that will continue the ethos of being accessible to all, while fitting better with the twenty-first century and respecting the complexity and "unknowability" of human beings?

References

Barnes, G. (1977). Doing contractual supervision. In: M. James (Ed.), *Techniques in Transactional Analysis for Psychotherapists and Counselors* (pp. 166–175). MA: Addison Wesley.

Berne, E. (1966). *Principles of Group Treatment*. New York: Grove Press.

Berne, E. (1968). Staff–patient staff conferences. In: M. James (Ed.), *Techniques in Transactional Analysis for Psychotherapists and Counselors* (pp. 153–165). Reading MA: Addison-Wesley, 1977.

Bordin, E. S. (1994). Theory and research on the therapeutic working alliance. In: O. Horvath & S. Greenberg (Eds.), *The Working Alliance: Theory Research and Practice* (pp. 113–137). New York: Wiley.

Clarkson, P. (1992). *Transactional Analysis: An Integrated Approach*. London: Routledge.

Cornell, W. F., & Hargaden, H. (2005). *From Transactions to Relations*. Chadlington: Haddon Press.

Cornell, W., & Shadbolt, C. (Eds.) (2007a). Theme issue: supervision. *Transactional Analysis Journal, 37*(2).

Cornell, W. F., Shadbolt, C., & Norton, R. (2007b). Live and in-limbo: a case study of an in-person transactional analysis consultation. *Transactional Analysis Journal, 37*: 159–172.

Cox, M. (2003). A method of doing supervision: using a mix of transactional analysis and developmental theory. Presentation at the Insitute of Transactional Analysis Conference, Swansea, UK.

English, F. (1975). The three cornered contract. *Transactional Analysis Journal, 5*: 383–384.

Fowlie, H. (2008). Relational supervision. Unpublished paper.

Hahn, H., Hargaden, H., & Tudor, K. (2009). The supervision of relational psychotherapy (in press).

Hargaden, H. (Ed.) (2005). Transactional analysis and psychoanalysis. Theme Issue. *Transactional Analysis Journal, 35*: 106–211.

Hargaden, H., & Sills, C. (2002). *Transactional Analysis: A Relational Perspective*. London: Routledge.

Lambert, M. J. (1992). Psychotherapy outcome research: implications for integrative and eclective therapists. In: J. I. Norcross & M. R. Goldfried (Eds.), *The Handbook of Psychotherapy Integration* (pp. 94–129). New York: Oxford University Press.

Mazzetti, M. (2007). Supervision in transactional analysis: an operational model. *Transactional Analysis Journal, 37*: 93–103.

Micholt, N. (1992). Psychological distance and group interventions. *Transactional Analysis Journal, 22*: 228–233.

Moiso, C. (1985). Ego states and transference. *Transactional Analysis Journal, 15*: 194–201.

Novellino, M. (2003). Transactional psychoanalysis. *Transactional Analysis Journal, 33*: 223–230.

Proctor, B. (2006). Contracting in supervision. In: C. Sills (Ed.), *Contracts in Counselling and Psychotherapy* (pp. 161–174). London: Sage.

Sills, C. (2006). *Contracts in Counselling and Psychotherapy* (2nd edn). London: Sage.

Steiner, C. (1974). *Scripts People Live*. New York: Grove Press.

Tudor, K. (2002). Transactional analysis supervision or supervision analysed transactionally? *Transactional Analysis Journal, 32*: 39–55.

Tudor, K. (2006). Contracts, complexity and challenge. In: C. Sills (Ed.), *Contracts in Counselling and Psychotherapy* (pp. 119–136). London: Sage.

Wampold, B. E. (2001). *The Great Psychotherapy Debate*. Englewood Cliffs, NJ: Lawrence Erlbaum.

CHAPTER FIFTEEN

Person-centred supervision training across theoretical orientations

Rose Battye and Anna Gilchrist

"Imagine you are on your way to your supervision session, and think of all the things you don't want to talk about," said Dave Mearns.

We were in a seminar about supervision, in the second year of our counselling training in 1986. We both had placements, and plenty of ideas came into our minds, such as when we overran our sessions, the times we found we were talking about ourselves, clients who bored us or made us feel uncomfortable, and the times we felt out of our depth. There were sessions where everything seemed to be going swimmingly and there just was not anything to say.

Dave waited for us to scribble down our thoughts, and then he said very seriously, "And these are the things you *need* to take to supervision."

It was a moment we never forgot, and when, twelve years later, we were planning our course in the person-centred approach to counselling supervision, we agreed that our experiences as supervisors and supervisees had confirmed the wisdom of Dave's words. For the benefit of client and supervisee, we feel strongly that supervision needs to be a place where the supervisee is able to bring *everything* about themselves with regard to their work for discussion and reflection. Because we believe this is important for supervision generally, we offer our training to people from all theoretical backgrounds. This conviction greatly affected the way we designed the course, which is perhaps more structured than is typical for a person-centred training and also contains theoretical input from other perspectives.

The course

We initially faced the challenge of offering training in supervision that provides a learning experience based on person-centred principles while respecting and working with perceptions and beliefs from different theoretical modalities.

The challenge was met chiefly in the way we delivered the training. We discovered that the person-centred approach to training shares much with the person-centred approach to supervision. Both are underpinned by the clear acknowledgement of "the profound personal development demands for working at relational depth" (Mearns, 1997, p. 94). In our first course, we hoped to create a person-centred learning environment by embodying the approach's principles ourselves as fully as we were able. Reflecting afterwards, we realized that something unexpected had happened; the way we had been during the course had incorporated all the key elements of the supervision relationship. While learning about supervision, the trainees had experienced it for themselves within the process of their training. With subsequent courses, we have been more mindful of this process, and now understand it as one of the training roles described by Tudor and Worrall (2007, p. 214):

> To manifest the attitudes of the person-centred approach, not so as to model them—since the notion of modelling derives from a learning theory that is antithetical to the person-centred approach (see Wood, 1995)—but in a spirit of congruence, and so as to offer students an experience of receiving what they might be aspiring to offer.

Roger Casemore describes similar experiences in Chapter Two.

Focus on the perspective of the supervisee and the trainee

A key feature of person-centred supervision is the focus on the supervisee, "so that they can explore non-defensively what the counselling process means to them, and how they experience themselves in relationship with their clients" (Merry, 2002, p. 173). Of course, there would be no supervision activity without the existence of clients. Supervision is for the benefit of the client, but the underlying principle is that the client is best served by supervision that enables the supervisee to become the best counsellor they can be. Mearns and Cooper (2005) describe a potentiality model of supervision, "where the aim is to help the supervisee to develop further the skills and sensitivities they have" (p. 156). We hope to enable each trainee to become the best supervisor *they* are capable of being, which entails developing their individual skills and sensitivities during the actual time spent on the course.

In both supervision and training, this release of potential happens through a relationship characterized by the necessary and sufficient conditions for therapeutic personality development postulated by the person-centred approach. Mearns and Cooper describe these as "A Single Core Condition" (*ibid.*, p. 35).

> The full power of the therapeutic relationship—as manifested in relational depth—is best regarded as a gestalt comprising the core conditions in high degree and in mutually enhancing interaction. [*ibid.*, p. 36]

The learning environment of the course enables trainees to experience this gestalt for themselves, and so learn its value in the supervisory relationship.

The integrative power of the core conditions in supervision and supervision training

One of our first exercises is to ask trainees to identify, from their experiences as supervisees, the characteristics that distinguish helpful and unhelpful supervision. Being understood, being accepted, trusting the supervisor, and feeling judged, criticized, misunderstood, and generally not feeling safe, always come out as key characteristics. It is immediately clear from this exercise that Rogers' core conditions of unconditional positive regard, empathy, and congruence (1957, p. 96) provide what is needed to create the helpful supervisory relationship which is our starting point. This exercise brings the group together in a spirit of shared understanding and purpose, whatever differences may be present from past experience and various theoretical orientations.

As well as the expected differences, given the mix of theoretical backgrounds, there are commonalities where people have developed their own understanding of the core conditions as a result of professional and personal experience. At the same time it is not uncommon to discover widely differing attitudes and beliefs from people apparently coming from the same tradition, including the person-centred approach itself. The interactions and dynamics between trainees give plenty of opportunities to practise and deepen their understanding of the "integrative power" (Mearns & Cooper, 2005, p. 37) of the core conditions.

Empathy has a powerful role in deepening this understanding in both supervision and training. If the supervisor is able thoroughly to enter the frame of reference (Rogers, 1957, p. 96) of the supervisee, to get a clear sense of where they are coming from and what it is really like for *them* to be listening to their client, there is a much better chance of the supervisor understanding the attitudes, beliefs, and experiences which are driving and influencing the supervisee's reactions and interventions, and, therefore, a greater chance of being able to feel accepting towards the supervisee. We extend this empathy to our trainees, hearing and valuing each individual's experiences and background as their unique frame of reference, whatever their theoretical position. As a result, we see them become less defended and more able to explore and discuss their beliefs. The core conditions work together; better understanding leads to greater acceptance, and the training experience becomes more effective.

While feeling accepted and understood clearly helps the supervisee or trainee bring parts of themselves or their work that may otherwise be avoided or neglected, "cosiness" (Houston, 1995, p. 16) and collusion are obviously not desirable. Supervisees and trainees alike need to be willing to reflect on and, if necessary, question their perceptions, behaviour, and motivation. The supervisor's ability to be congruent and authentic helps to keep the relationship as a place of keen reflective practice. Again we see the interweaving of the conditions, as Elke Lambers explains, the supervisor

> who offers the supervisee her congruent acceptance, creates in the supervision relationship an excellent basis for support, challenge and for open respectful exploration about both therapeutic and ethical issues. [2000, p. 211]

If supervision trainers can embody this kind of authenticity, trainees will learn its value by experiencing it. In both supervision and training, it is the interplay of the core conditions that facilitates "collaborative enquiry" (Merry, 2004, p. 192) as well as support and encouragement. As trainees become willing at least to try to extend integrated core conditions to each other, we see increasing respect towards different approaches as well as different positions within the same approach, and we know that, as supervisors, it is more likely they will be willing and able to hear the unique perspective of their supervisees.

Balancing experiential learning with theoretical understanding

We believe in the effectiveness of experiential learning. Our course takes place over five weekends at two-monthly intervals. Each day (apart from the final weekend) includes supervision sessions in triads to enable trainees to examine their practice in depth. Every trainee is observed by one of the trainers each weekend, to monitor their development. Each day also includes a supervision group, which the trainees take turns at facilitating. These groups end with process time, so the facilitator can receive and give feedback and group process can be examined. We encourage mindful, reflective practice wherever possible, so that trainees can develop the habit of enhancing awareness of what they do and why. Assessment develops awareness through the submission of two essays, the analysis of a recorded supervision session, and the analysis of the supervision relationship, which are marked at a postgraduate level. Along with Professor Brian Thorne, our participating consultant, we believe that it is extremely important that supervisors are able to conceptualize their work as well as that of their supervisees. The writing of these pieces is more challenging for some than for others, but, through the process, all trainees develop increased insight and improve their ability to link theory and practice.

> Experiential learning which is unsupported by sound theoretical understanding is likely after a while to leave the trainee confused or incapable of describing and analysing the processes he or she is experiencing. [Thorne & Dryden, 1991, p. 8]

Similarities and differences between being a trainer and a supervisor

The way we are as trainers exemplifies key qualities of being as a supervisor, through embodying the core conditions as best we can. More overt and practical similarities between being a person-centred trainer and supervisor include:

- keeping focused on the agreed task;
- checking understanding;
- being open to ideas that might be helpful;
- being aware of an individual's personal process, our own process, and group process;
- responding in a way that encourages people to open up, to be curious;
- creating an atmosphere where spontaneity, humour, and fun can emerge;
- monitoring for over-working and the importance of work–life balance;
- sensing when to move things on and when more space is needed;
- providing containment by respecting time constraints.

However, for us there are differences, too. As supervisors, we do not have a specific agenda for the supervision session, but as trainers we do: we believe certain subjects should be addressed within supervision training. This is a considerable challenge for us: how to maintain the person-centred learning environment, give time for these essential subjects, and make sure the trainees have enough time to honour their own process. Evaluation forms are filled in anonymously halfway through the course in order for us to have an additional way of checking whether trainees have any problems. Forms are also given out at the end. Ever since the first course, the consistent honesty of the feedback has suggested that trainees have experienced a powerful person-centred learning environment, and we have thus met our challenge.

In the person-centred tradition, there are community meetings at the beginning and end of each day in order that trainees can encounter trainers and colleagues freely and reflect on their experiences during the course. Other activities include presentations chosen, designed, and led by trainees, private and learning journals, small study groups between training weekends, and peer and self assessment. We hope to create a place where trainees can feel "held not confined", the refrain in Seni Seneviratne's beautiful poem at the beginning of Tudor and Worrall's *Freedom to Practise* (2004). Within this place, we introduce the subjects that we think are necessary for supervision training.

colour changing
pastel to bold

held not confined

fluid in honesty
growing asking changing

held not confined

being energy, questions, difference
moving out of safe to scary

held not confined

meeting self changing self
a place of feeling

held not confined

[Seneviratne, 2002]

The "essential" subjects of our core curriculum and our openness to ideas from other approaches

Our core curriculum includes looking at four models of supervision, all of which consider key issues such as the supervisory process, the alliance, contract, and functions and roles from different perspectives, so that trainees can find a way of working that best suits them. Some people create their own model.

Other core subjects are practising the giving and receiving of feedback, awareness of ethical dilemmas, and fears associated with essay writing. These can be difficult subjects to examine deeply, because they often involve hidden feelings and beliefs that challenge the self-concept: "the person's conceptual construction of himself" (Mearns & Thorne, 1999, p. 7); "The individual preserves his self-concept by completely evading any conscious contact with experiences or feelings which threaten him" (*ibid.*, p. 14).

Self-concepts can become unusually fragile when confronted by new tasks or the potential criticism of tutors or colleagues. Trainees may be restricted from being the most effective supervisors they can be by not recognizing their prejudices and fears as well as their denied strengths, and we believe these can be identified by developing awareness of fluctuations in their self-concept. We invite trainees to notice when they become defensive, or feel held back in any way from being fully congruent, empathic, or accepting, and also to respectfully challenge their fellow trainees if they sense they are overreacting or inhibited in some way. Other orientations often describe this in terms of the shadow and its unsuspected influence. "The shadow is the unacknowledged side of the self, that part of ourselves which we dismiss to 'the shadows' or recesses of our conscious awareness" (Page & Wosket, 2001, p. 123).

The gestalt of the single core condition, co-created by the trainers and trainees, makes deep personal reflection and the commitment to awareness possible. In the safety of such a community, even the most difficult aspects of "the shadow" can be faced.

> Not surprisingly the shadow side of those of us in the helping professions often includes those parts of ourselves which are antipathetic to our chosen field. Thus a counsellor may, for instance, have in their shadow desires to bully, inflict or witness pain, judge, or exert power over others. Uncovering and facing

> these aspects of ourselves can be quite shattering at the time; indeed, doing so inevitably breaks a psychological defence we have previously had in place. [Page, 1999, p. 124]

It is extremely important to remember that the shadow is also understood to contain positive qualities. Unacknowledged strengths, described in the language of psychosynthesis as "the refusal of the sublime" (Assagioli, 1993, p. 48), may be discovered there.

Just as understandings about "the shadow" can inform exploration of distortions of "self concept", we believe there are many ideas from other theoretical orientations which can enrich person-centred conceptualizations and one of us has written more extensively about this (Battye, 2003). We feel that our courses have greatly benefited from the exchange of ideas as a result of including trainees from different modalities. We agree with Hitchings:

> Whilst I do believe that concepts from other models need to be translated into a person-centred language and frame of reference, to ignore what other compatible therapeutic systems might have to offer, is in my view, irresponsible. [2004, p. 216]

Conclusion

We hope that the trainees who complete our course will feel able, if they so wish, to supervise practitioners from other orientations; we hope they do not feel threatened by new and different ideas, and know that what ultimately matters is giving attention to the process of the supervisee.

> If we see ourselves as responsible for helping the therapist to articulate the relationships he sees between his practice and whatever theory he believes himself to be working to, and for helping him to explore his experience of his work in the light of that articulation, we do not need to be familiar with the detail of whatever theory he works to. [Worrall, 2007, p. 206]

We believe our training, with its emphasis on self-exploration through experiential learning, backed by theoretical understanding, can lead to the inner confidence that this requires. Worrall says it

> demands supervisors who are comfortable in their own ignorance; who don't need to impress, control or teach; and who are genuinely willing for their supervisees to be accountable and responsible for their own work, even and perhaps especially when they think and practise differently. [*ibid.*, pp. 206–207]

Not every person-centred practitioner will agree with this. Hitchings summarizes a diversity of person-centred approaches and refers to Rennie's (1998) distinction between the literalists and the experientialists.

> The experientialists, whilst generally arguing that they remain true to core theory and especially Rogers' therapeutic conditions, pay more explicit attention to the client's overall process and their own interrelated process. Where they depart from the literalists is in the apparent directivity of their responses. [Hitchings, 2004, p. 204]

It will be clear from what we have been saying that, in the training of supervisors, we place ourselves in the experientialist camp. We are dedicated to the core theory and to the therapeutic conditions but our training is arguably directive in that we follow a structured programme. None the less, we consider our work to be a valid and proven training in the person-centred approach to supervision and one which has much to offer at time when the boundaries between different orientations are becoming more permeable, to the potential benefit of both therapist and client.

References

Assagioli, R. (1993). *Transpersonal Development: The Dimension Beyond Psychosynthesis.* Rome: Aquarian Press.

Battye, R. (2003). Beads on a string. In: S. Keys (Ed.), *Idiosyncratic Person-Centred Counselling* (pp. 151–171). Ross-on-Wye: PCCS Books.

Hitchings, P. (2004). On supervision across theoretical orientations. In: K. Tudor & M. Worrall (Eds.), *Freedom to Practise: Person-centred Approaches to Supervision* (pp. 203–224). Ross-on-Wye: PCCS Books.

Houston, G. (1995). *Supervision and Counselling.* London: Rochester Foundation.

Lambers, E. (2000). Supervision in person-centred therapy: facilitating congruence. In: D. Mearns & B. Thorne (Eds.), *Person-Centred Therapy Today* (pp. 196–211). London: Sage.

Mearns, D. (1997). *Person-Centred Counselling Training*. London: Sage.

Mearns, D., & Cooper, M. (2005). *Working at Relational Depth in Counselling and Psychotherapy*. London: Sage.

Mearns, D., & Thorne, B. (1999). *Person-Centred Counselling in Action* (2nd edn). London: Sage.

Merry, T. (2002). *Learning and Being in Person-Centred Counselling* (2nd edn). London: Sage.

Merry, T. (2004). Supervision as heuristic inquiry. In: K. Tudor & M. Worrall (Eds.), *Freedom to Practise: Person-Centred Therapy Today* (pp. 189–200). Ross-on-Wye: PCCS Books.

Page, S. (1999). *The Shadow and the Counsellor*. London: Routledge.

Page, S., & Wosket, V. (2001). *Supervising the Counsellor: A Cyclical Model* (2nd edn). Hove: Brunner-Routledge.

Rennie, D. (1998). *Person-Centred Counselling: An Experiential Approach*. London: Sage.

Rogers, C. (1957). The necessary and sufficient conditions of therapeutic personality change. *Journal of Consulting Psychology, 21*(2): 95–103.

Seneviratne, S. (2004). Poem. In: K. Tudor & M. Worrall (Eds.), *Freedom to Practise: Person-centred Approaches to Supervision*. Ross-on-Wye: PCCS Books.

Thorne, B., & Dryden, W. (1991). Key issues in the training of counsellors. In: W. Dryden & B. Thorne (Eds.), *Training and Supervision for Counselling in Action*. London: Sage.

Tudor, K., & Worrall, M. (2007). Training supervisors. In: K. Tudor & M. Worrall (Eds.), *Freedom to Practise Volume II: Developing Person-Centred Approaches to Supervision* (pp. 211–220). Ross-on-Wye: PCCS Books.

Wood, J. K. (1995). The person-centered approach to small groups: more than psychotherapy. Unpublished manuscript.

Worrall, M. (2007). Person-centred supervision across theoretical orientations. In: K. Tudor & M. Worrall (Eds.), *Freedom to Practise Volume II: Developing Person-Centred Approaches to Supervision* (pp. 205–209). Ross-on-Wye: PCCS Books.

CHAPTER SIXTEEN

Training for supervising cognitive–behavioural practitioners and others

Alec Grant

Introduction: cognitive–behavioural supervision overlaps with therapy and teaching

In a seminal text on clinical supervision in Beckian-derived cognitive psychotherapy, subsequently supported by Liese and Beck (1997), Padesky (1996) argued for supervision to parallel the process of therapy. Specifically, that supervisor and supervisee should establish a supervision problem list, set goals, collaboratively conceptualize roadblocks to attaining these goals, set agendas for supervision, and utilize Socratic dialogue and behavioural experiments.

Arguing also that supervision overlaps with teaching, Padesky was mindful of competency development in her view that supervision methods should be tailored to meet supervisees' level of expertise and needs. To this end, the revised cognitive therapy scale (CTS-R) (Blackburn et al., 2001) could be utilized to measure supervisee knowledge and competency level, and growth as a function of supervision. This would be appropriate, for example, if a supervisee has good knowledge of cognitive therapy methods but poor conceptualization and related skills:

> the supervisor might ask the supervisee to role play a problem clinical situation ... This role play could be followed by questions about how these interventions generally proceed ... and how difficulties occur with this particular client. [Padesky, 1996, p. 283]

Padesky stressed that video, audio, or live supervision is fundamental to the supervision relationship. In her view, supported by others working in cognitive–behavioural and related modalities (Sloan, 2003; Townend, Iannetta, & Freeston, 2002), retrospective reporting, or verbal summaries of supervision, at best only capture elements of current awareness or understanding.

The picture of supervision among accredited CBT therapists in 2002

In 2002, Townend and colleagues surveyed a random sample (50%) of therapists accredited with the British Association of Behavioural and Cognitive Psychotherapy (BABCP). The results of this survey, which have not been replicated since, contrast with Padesky's advice on supervision. The aim of the survey, which had a 61% (number 170) response rate, was to describe the current supervision practices of UK accredited cognitive–behavioural therapists, in order to highlight areas of good practice and, conversely, identify areas requiring attention. A further aim was to identify issues to address in clinical supervision training programmes for both cognitive–behavioural therapists and others who utilize cognitive–behavioural approaches.

The survey found that, whereas 65% said they engaged with regular planned supervision, 17% reported having irregular planned supervision, while 11% reported that they had supervision on an "as needed" basis. The form of supervision described was mostly informal, operationalized as "case discussion on an unplanned basis when a problem occurred". This was stated as happening "sometimes" (47.8%) or "often" (38.5%).

In terms of models of supervision, either a cognitive–behavioural or rational emotive therapy model was described as influencing the supervision of most respondents. Padesky (1996) and Liese and Beck (1997) were most frequently cited as influences on their supervision practice. However, direct examination of practice through the use of audio- or videotapes of therapy sessions were used often by only 5% of respondents, although a further 13% reported that they sometimes used this method. Direct observation of practice was reportedly used even less frequently, with only 6% stating that they used this method "often" or "sometimes". Only half of those who supervised were receiving supervision for their supervisory practice, which poses questions about the training, or lack of it, to prepare supervisors for their supervisory role.

Dual role relationships

A dual role relationship is one where the supervisor has another relationship with the supervisee along with the supervisory one. Townend and his colleagues sought to ascertain the prevalence and impact of such relationships. With regard to managerial and professional relationships, 38% of respondents reported engaging in dual relationships. A line management relationship was the most common, with 19% indicating that their supervisor was also their manager. Another type of dual relationship, indicated by 13% of respondents, included having supervision with a colleague at the same level as themselves in the service. It also emerged that a personal relationship alongside the supervision relationship was described as relatively common (27%). Such relationships included friends, friends' partners, and, on one occasion, the supervisor was the therapist's partner. Interestingly, only ten respondents reported that a personal relationship interfered with supervision, and that only rarely or sometimes.

Weaknesses in clinical supervision among accredited therapists included the fact that, whereas therapists espoused the need to follow a formal model, such as Padesky (1996) or Liese and Beck (1997), this did not appear to be adhered to in their day-to-day clinical practice. Another major weakness of supervision practice was the limited use made by experienced therapists of audio- and videotapes, or real life observation, and the competency development-based use of instruments such as the Cognitive Therapy Scale (CTS). This indicates a clinical practice to supervision slippage, and vice versa.

The fact that a high number of respondents voiced satisfaction with their supervision is equivocal. That it may have reflected high standards of supervision is unlikely, given the above data. What is more likely, according to Townend and his colleagues, is that it demonstrated a generally low level of expectation from both supervisor and supervisee. Similarly, the impact and danger of dual role relationships has to be viewed as a weakness, indicating a lack of awareness of ethical and other dimensions of supervision.

Cognitive–behavioural supervision in relation to supervision in mental health

Although widely regarded as important (Department of Health, 1998), supervision has been a strikingly poorly researched topic within mental health (Scaife, 2001), referred to as an "alarming state of affairs" (Russell & Petrie, 1994). The traditional assumption that supervisors are meant to develop competence by drawing on their skills as therapists and on their past experiences as supervisees has been argued as unlikely to form the basis of competent supervision (Hess, 1987). What is arguably needed is a CBT-specific form of clinical supervision (Townend, Iannetta, & Freeston, 2002) which has an educational basis and which derives from both theoretical understanding and empirical investigation.

Educational approaches to cognitive–behavioural-specific supervision

To this end, a number of helpful guides to good cognitive–behavioural supervision practice now exist (Lewis, 2005; Liese & Beck, 1997; Padesky, 1996; Townend, 2004). Further, in a definitive and important article, James, Milne, Blackburn, and Armstrong (2006) argued that there are a number of educational approaches to supervision that make it more successful. Although the evidence base does not as yet justify being too prescriptive, James and his colleagues asserted that some theories enhance and should underpin cognitive–behavioural supervision. These authors proposed the following series of steps:

Step 1: *Assessing learning needs*: The supervisor should spend time assessing the supervisee's experiences and background early on in the supervision relationship. Such learning should be matched to the supervisees' educational needs, which will include their existing competencies and learning context (context includes the learning opportunities available, the expectation of duties to be performed and competencies to be demonstrated).

Step 2: *Establishing baselines and developing competencies*: At this stage the supervisor looks for the supervisee's baseline competencies. This may usefully employ the Cognitive Therapy Scale-Revised (CTS-R) (Blackburn et al., 2001). This in turn utilises the Dreyfus competence taxonomy (Dreyfus, 1989). This will help quantify the presence and absence of specific skills.

The Cognitive Therapy Scale-Revised (CTS-R) scale (Figure 16.1), is the most widely used competency scale in cognitive–behavioural therapy (Figure 16.2):

Step 3: *Working in the zone of proximal development (ZPD)* (Vygotsky, 1978): The ZPD defines the distance between what a supervisee can do independently with respect to a skill versus what s/he can potentially achieve with maximum supervisory assistance. For example, at the beginning of a cognitive behavioural course, a supervisee might score 28/72 on the CTS-R, and, realistically, by the end of the course the best s/he is likely to achieve is 38/72. This ten-point range would therefore be her/his zone with respect to these competencies. The relevance of the zone in relation to a specific skill is that it can help identify those aspects of the skill "yet to be developed" that will enable the learner/supervisee to perform the skill independently.

Step 4: *Applying effective techniques in supervision*: Based on a review of leadership techniques in teaching, training, therapy, coaching, managing and supervision, Milne et al. (2002) provided a synthesis of supervisory activities in an observation tool called Teachers' PETS (Process Evaluation of Training and Supervision). PETS identifies 13 activities typically engaged in by a CBT supervisor. These are listening/observing, managing, supporting, questioning, formulating, informing, feeding back, challenging, disagreeing, evaluating, guiding experiential learning (e.g. modelling, role play) and "other" (e.g. social chat, paper work and setting up equipment). These techniques are supported in guidelines to professionals (e.g. British Psychological Society, 2003), advocated in textbooks

CTS-R Items	Score	Comments and how you could improve on your score
1. Agenda setting and adherence Did the therapist set a good agenda and adhere to it? **2. Feedback** Were there statements and/or actions concerned with providing and eliciting feedback? **3. Collaboration** Were there statements and/or actions encouraging the client to participate appropriately, and preventing an unequal power relationship developing? **4. Pacing and efficient use of time** Were there statements and/or actions concerning the pacing of the session, helping to ensure the time was used effectively? **5. Interpersonal effectiveness** Was a good therapeutic relationship evident (trust, warmth, etc)? **6. Eliciting appropriate emotional expression** Were there questions and/or actions designed to elicit relevant emotions and promote a good emotional ambience? **7. Eliciting key cognitions** Were there questions and/or actions designed to elicit relevant cognitions (thoughts, beliefs, etc)? **8. Eliciting and planning behaviours** Were there questions and/or actions designed to elicit dysfunctional behaviours and engage the client in planning for change? **9. Guided discovery** Were there questions and/or actions designed to elicit dysfunctional behaviours and engage the client in planning for change? **10. Conceptional integration** Were there statements and/or actions designed to promote the client's understanding of the models underpinning CT? **11. Application of change methods** Did the therapist facilitate in-session learning and change through a change method (cognitive and behavioural)? **12. Homework setting** Did the therapist set an appropriate homework effectively?		

Figure 16.1. The Cognitive Therapy Scale-Revised (CTS-R) scale.

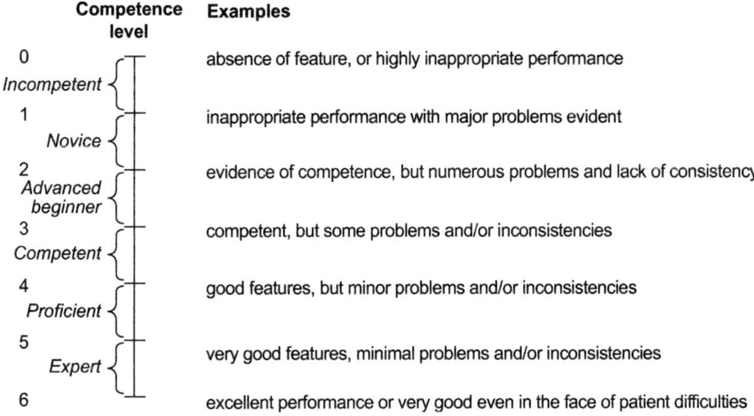

Figure 16.2. The Dreyfus scale is incorporated and informs item ratings within the CTS-R.

on supervision (e.g. Falender & Shafranske, 2004) and found within successful studies of supervision (Milne & James, 2000).

The learning process proposed by PETS has recently been operationalised in the "Tandem" model (Milne & James, 2005). The Tandem analogy provides a practical and accessible way of construing and examining key conceptual, relational and structural issues in supervision. This model contains at least seven key axioms. For example, there is a need for the supervisor to take charge in the early stages of the relationship in order to "steer" a developmental course. Furthermore, the front wheel of the tandem, under the control of the supervisor, is essentially the educational cycle. This describes the inter-related steps of engaging in "needs assessment", "agreeing learning objectives", "using appropriate change techniques" and "evaluating performance".

In contrast, the back wheel represents the experiential learning process that is closest to the experience of the supervisee, in the tandem's "stoker" (back seat) position. The tandem's back wheel is used to depict Kolb's (1984) experiential learning cycle. According to Milne and James (2005), it is the essential role of the supervisor to ensure that the supervisee moves around the learning cycle appropriately (the functional definition of successful supervision). Other aspects of the tandem, such as the frame, gears and pedals, are also used analogously (for example frame as "framework" and gears as mechanisms of change). They relate to the various interpersonal process and teamwork issues required in the delivery of effective supervision.

Step 5: *Evaluating progress*: The PETS instrument also examines the impact of the supervisor's actions on the supervisee. The resultant supervisee behaviour categories are: reflecting, experimenting, conceptualizing, planning, experiencing emotion (for example expressing discomfort; providing details of emotional state in therapy). In relation to step five, there are straightforward tools that can be used by the supervisee to foster self-monitoring and for the supervisor to enable formative and summative evaluation. These include the CTS-R (Blackburn et al., 2001) and the Therapist Evaluation Checklist (Hall-Marley, 2000 reproduced in Falender & Shafranske, 2004).

The present and future

In summary, it has been argued that there are sound empirical, theoretical, and conceptual models of clinical supervision available for cognitive–behavioural practitioners engaged in appropriate formal supervisory relationships. However, these may have had a relatively insignificant impact in actual supervision practice among BABCP accredited therapists in recent years.

So far, the discussion has focused on the supervision of trained cognitive–behavioural therapists. However, an immediate and future challenge is cognitive–behavioural supervisors providing supervision for those who are either barely trained in, or who are learning, the cognitive–behavioural approach, having come from a different modality. This phenomenon should be viewed in the context of the interrelated cognitive behavioural dissemination agenda and evidence-based psychotherapy.

The importance of empirically-supported psychological therapies has been accorded a high profile in policy literature in the last decade (Department of Health, 1996, 2001, 2004, 2005). Cognitive–behavioural approaches remain consistently the "front runner" in this context, reflected in clinical practice guidelines (NICE, 2008). Since the publication of the Depression Report (LSE, 2006), and the Labour Government's manifesto commitment in 2005 to increase the psychological treatments available to those suffering from anxiety and depression, backed up by an investment pledge of £173 million, the 2008 profile of cognitive–behavioural therapy has arguably never been higher.

All of this has resulted in a trend of therapists from different modalities training in cognitive–behavioural therapy. However, not all those who "jump ship" to cognitive–behavioural training will do so willingly, because of issues such as the wholesale neglect of modalities such as person-centred therapy from the government and evidence-based psychotherapy agendas. How well prepared is the cognitive–behavioural supervisory community to meet this challenge, and what is the nature of the challenge? Supervisees with other prior training and a different set of conceptual thinking will need to learn a completely new psychotherapeutic vocabulary and conceptualization skills. This will require cognitive–behavioural supervisors to be mindful not just of the formative, competency developmental demands of supervision, but of its normative and restorative dimensions. Anxiety management and confidence building must, of necessity, be centre stage. A further demand will be that of sensitivity. Explicit respect must be accorded to supervisees' prior modality training and the need to build on this.

Formative, and, to some extent, normative and restorative supervision development should sensitively utilize the forms of competency development previously discussed in this chapter (Blackburn et al., 2001; Dreyfus, 1989). In addition, it will be important for novice cognitive therapists' development to relate to the three systems of learning inscribed within the "DPR" (declarative, procedural, and reflective) model (Bennet-Levy, 2006; Grant, Townend, & Sloan, 2008). According to Bennett-Levy, student cognitive–behavioural therapists develop in relation to *declarative* and *procedural* systems which amount to knowledge of factual information, or "knowing that". This is associated with novice learning, and refers to mastering cognitive–behavioural techniques. The *reflective* system is more advanced, relating to "when-then" rules (the awareness of the moment-by-moment opportunities in therapy when techniques and procedures can and should be applied sensitively).

This clearly has implications for cognitive–behavioural clinical supervision training to proceed alongside cognitive–behavioural training programmes. This should enable effective and graduated competency skills to be developed and maintained through systems of feedback on performance and the transfer of knowledge from the classroom into practice (Grant & Townend, 2007; Grant, Townend, & Sloan, 2008; Townend, 2005; Townend, 2008). However, this task is compounded by a range of assumptions which clearly illuminate the conceptual ambiguities that still exist around cognitive–behavioural supervision (Armstrong & Freeston, 2006; Townend, 2008).

A related problem is the fact that, according to the supervision competency development work of Roth and Pilling (CORE, 2008), the BABCP had only forty-six accredited cognitive–behavioural supervisors compared to around 1300 accredited practitioners. This may well reflect a relatively low priority still being accorded to supervision as a serious clinical activity.

And what of the ethical dimension to supervision? A useful illustration of one aspect of this is the infrequent use of live or real-time equivalent supervision reported earlier in this chapter that may, for example, be usefully compared with the development of counselling psychology. Ladany, Hill, Corbett, and Nutt (1996), in a survey of 108 supervisees in the USA, found that nearly all admitted to non-disclosure of varying kinds. A substantial amount of such avoidance related to material that could be central to learning and competency development, including personal issues raised by clinical work, perceived clinical mistakes, and negative reactions to clients.

The trend of retrospective reporting forms of clinical supervision, as opposed to live or real-time equivalent forms, makes it highly likely that selective non-disclosure currently remains a feature of supervision in cognitive–behavioural psychotherapy. This places the onus on cognitive–behavioural supervisors to model good supervision practice by have recordings of their clinical work as the basis for their own supervision.

It is to be hoped that the above developments, inscribed within the increasing profile of competency development in cognitive–behavioural psychotherapy and supervision discussed in this chapter, may gradually close the gap between good cognitive–behavioural supervision and related educational practice represented by writers such as Padesky, James, and Bennett-Levy, and the debased variants exposed by Townend and colleagues. Time will tell!

References

Armstrong, P. V., & Freeston, M. H. (2006). Conceptualisation and formulating cognitive therapy supervision. In: N. Tarrier (Ed.), *Case Formulation in Cognitive Behaviour Therapy: The Treatment of Challenging and Complex Cases* (pp. 349–372). London: Routledge.

Bennett-Levy, J. (2006). Therapist skills: a cognitive model of their acquisition and refinement. *Behavioural and Cognitive Psychotherapy, 34*(1): 57–78.

Blackburn, I. M., James, I., Milne, D. L., Baker, C., Standart, S., Garland, A., & Reichfeldt, F. (2001). The revised cognitive therapy scale (CTS-R): psychometric properties. *Behavioural and Cognitive Psychotherapy, 29*: 431–446.

British Psychological Society (2003). *Policy Guidelines in Supervision in the Practice of Clinical Psychology*. Leicester: Division of Clinical Psychology.

CORE (Centre for Outcomes, Research and Effectiveness) (2008). Website: www.ucl.ac.uk/clinical-psychology/CORE/supervision_framework.htm (accessed 15 June 2008).

Department of Health (1996). *NHS Psychotherapy Services in England: A Review of Strategic Policy*. London: Department of Health.

Department of Health (1998). *A First Class Service*. Leeds: Department of Health.

Department of Health (2001). *Mental Health Policy Implementation Guide*. London: Department of Health.

Department of Health (2004). *The NHS Knowledge and Skills Framework (KSF) and the Development Review Process*. www.dh.gov.uk (accessed 30 December 2007).

Department of Health (2005). *Chief Nursing Officer's Review of Mental Health Nursing*. London: Department of Health.

Dreyfus, H. L. (1989). The Dreyfus model of skill acquisition. In: J. Burke (Ed.), *Competency Based Education and Training*. London: Falmer Press.

Falender, C., & Shafranske, E. (2004). *Clinical Supervision: A Competency-based Approach*. Washington, DC: American Psychiatric Association.

Grant, A., & Townend, M. (2007). Some emerging implications for clinical supervision in British mental health nursing. *Journal of Psychiatric and Mental Health Nursing, 14*(6): 609–614.

Grant, A., Townend, M., & Sloan, G. (2008). The transfer of CBT education from classroom to work setting: getting it right or wasting the opportunities. *The Cognitive Behavioural Therapist*, 5 August: 27–44.

Hall-Marley, S. (2000). Unpublished instrument, available as an appendix to C. Falender & E. Shafranske (2004), *Clinical Supervision: A Competency-based Approach*. Washington, DC: American Psychiatric Association.

Hess, A. K. (1987). Advances in psychotherapy supervision: introduction. *Professional Psychology: Research and Practice, 18*: 187–188.

James, I. A., Milne, D., Blackburn, I.-M., & Armstrong, P. (2006). Conducting successful supervision: novel elements towards an integrative approach. *Behavioural and Cognitive Psychotherapy, 35*: 191–200.

Kolb, D. (1984). *Experiential Learning*. Englewood Cliffs, NJ: Prentice-Hall.

Ladany, N., Hill, C. E., Corbett, M., & Nutt, L. (1996). Nature, extent and importance of what therapy trainees do not disclose to their supervisors. *Journal of Counseling Psychology, 43*: 10–24.

Lewis, K. (2005). The supervision of cognitive and behavioural psychotherapists. *BABCP Magazine: Supervision Supplement, 33*(2): 1–4.

Liese, B. S., & Beck, J. S. (1997). Cognitive therapy supervision. In: C. E. Watkins (Ed.), *Handbook of Psychotherapy Supervision* (pp. 114–133). New York: Wiley.

LSE Centre for Economic Performance (2006). *The Depression Report. A New Deal for Depression and Anxiety Disorders*. London: London School of Economic and Political Science.

Milne, D. L., & James, I. (2000). A systemic review of effective cognitive–behavioural supervision. *British Journal of Clinical Psychology, 39*: 111–129.

Milne, D. L., & James, I. (2005). Clinical supervision: ten tests of the tandem model. *Clinical Psychology Forum, 151*: 6–10.

Milne, D. L., James, I., Keegan, D., & Dudley, M. (2002). Teacher's PETS: A new observational measure of experiential training interactions. *Clinical Psychology and Psychotherapy, 9*: 187–199.

NHS National Institute for Health and Clinical Excellence (NICE) (2008). www.nice.org.uk.

Padesky, C. (1996). Developing cognitive therapist competency: teaching and supervision models. In: P. M. Salkovskis (Ed.), *Frontiers of Cognitive Therapy* (pp. 266–292). New York: Guilford.

Russell, R. K., & Petrie, T. (1994). Issues in training effective supervisors. *Applied and Preventive Psychology, 3*: 27–42.

Scaife, J. (2001). *Supervision in the Mental Health Professions. A Practitioner's Guide*. Hove: Brunner-Routledge.

Sloan, G. (2003). Audio recordings of nurse-patient interactions. *Nursing Standard, 17*(29): 33–37.

Townend, M. (2004). Supervision contracts in cognitive behavioural psychotherapy. *BABCP Magazine: Supervision Supplement, 34*(3): 1–4.

Townend, M. (2005). Interprofessional supervision from the perspectives of both mental health nurses and other professionals in the field of cognitive behavioural psychotherapy. *Journal of Psychiatric and Mental Health Nursing, 12*: 582–588.

Townend, M. (2008). Clinical supervision in cognitive behavioural psychotherapy: development of a model for mental health nursing through grounded theory. *Journal of Psychiatric and Mental Health Nursing* (in press).

Townend, T., Iannetta, L., & Freeston, M. (2002). Clinical supervision in practice: a survey of UK cognitive behavioural psychotherapists accredited by the BABCP. *Behavioural and Cognitive Psychotherapy, 30*: 485–500.

Vygotsky, L. S. (1978). *Mind in Society: The Development of Higher Psychological Processes.* Cambridge, MA: MIT Press.

CHAPTER SEVENTEEN

Learning to supervise using a solution-focused approach

Carole Waskett

How do we teach people how to supervise others? The multiplication of courses, and requirements for supervision qualifications are fairly new. We used to trust counsellors and psychotherapists to "just know" how to supervise. When looking for a supervisor we searched out someone with experience and a good reputation, perhaps someone who used the model we were comfortable with, who was willing to take on the role. That was how I found my first supervisor, and how I started to do it myself.

Then, after training, having supervision, and practising in a solution-focused (SF) way for some years, I learned more about SF supervision at BRIEF (www.brieftherapy.org.uk) in a two-day course. I went on doing that with my supervisees. Eventually, the world wagged a finger and said, "Two days is not long enough to be properly trained in supervision". So I completed a longer university module, based on the person-centred and Hawkins and Shohet (2006) models. I appreciated the tutors' input, enjoyed the company of the rest of the group, did my best with the work, and passed comfortably. But the course seemed to make supervision unnecessarily complicated, and I have always been a fan of KISS—Keep it

Short and Simple. So I continued to supervise my various supervisees in a simple SF way. But now I had a certificate that "proved" I could do it. It was all rather confusing.

Supervision applied to a variety of helping professionals

Now, as an NHS trainer who also runs a private training and supervision practice, I teach both mental health professionals and a variety of other helping professionals (mostly the latter) how to supervise and support others. In my working world, the meanings of "supervision" for therapists, counsellors, and other mental health workers, and "clinical supervision, or practice supervision, or professional support" for nurses, allied health professionals, prison officers, social workers, and others, share permeable boundaries.

SF supervisors have to have some common qualities and skills, whoever they are supervising. Because these qualities and skills are, in the main, dedicated to being curious and supportive about what the *other* person is saying or doing, there is no need to do anything special or different for different disciplines. It is the supervision partner—the supervisee—who will be doing or saying or thinking the different or distinctive things according to their discipline. The SF supervisor does not have to know more than the supervisee, or be wiser about the supervisee's practice. They have only quietly to use their supervision skills of taking their part in a helpful conversation (checking quite frequently that it is, in fact, helpful) and maintaining ethical practice.

These are the three qualities or skills that seem to me to be essential to the SF supervisor:

- a willingness to tune in to the ordinary working language and world view of the supervisee;
- an interest in any strengths, resources, helpful behaviours, and forward movement towards the preferred future, which belong to, or are possible for, both the supervisee and their clients;
- enough learning and practice to know how to have a SF conversation with its different tools.

Two further elements are common to all good supervision:

- an ability to keep one's own ego out of the way, and an understanding of how to adapt one's side of the conversation to the supervisee's natural timing and pacing;
- a clear understanding of the appropriate ethics, boundaries, and professional responsibilities of a supervisor.

It seems to me that, if an SF supervisor is confident and comfortable with each of the above elements, they can do supervision safely, ethically, and properly with anyone who requests it, whatever the supervisee's professional background and practice.

More about a solution-focused approach to supervision

In this approach, we assume that the supervisor, like the SF therapist, is "non-expert". However practised one's empathy, it is impossible accurately to be inside the mind of someone else, either supervisee or client, or to know very much about the relationship between supervisee and client. So the SF supervisor will be open-minded and curious about these areas.

We make no formulations or hypotheses. We do, however, make an assumption: that the person we are working with has all the resources necessary to run their own professional life and make good decisions for themselves; likewise for any client being discussed. The supervisor's job is to be interested in and nurture the supervisee's desired forward movement in their practice while not getting in their way. In this approach, supervisors tend to be more interested in the supervisee than in the supervisee's clients. Helping to enable the supervisee's best work will feed through to the benefit of their clients, and the supervisee is the only person we have a mandate to work with.

Provided the supervisee is willing to work with the supervisor, it is irrelevant whether the supervisor is aligned with the supervisee's discipline, model, or approach, neither does it matter if the supervisor is senior to the supervisee. This is an egalitarian and non-expert model, in which the only expertise the supervisor offers is the ability to use SF language skills in co-creating a helpful conversation with the supervisee: that is, a conversation which helps the supervisee to work at their best. This dialogue will often consist of thoughtful questions and answers to highlight the skills and know-how of the supervisee and help them to consider their work and think ahead.

These conversations are not always specifically about cases. The supervisee might wish to talk more generally about their practice, and we may, for instance, have a conversation around how good a practitioner they feel they are, perhaps using scaling thus:

> "So if 10 means you feel you are already an excellent practitioner, and 0 means you're definitely in the wrong job, where on the scale would you say you were at present?"
>
> "And what makes you think you're at X rather than further down the scale?"
>
> "And what do you think you (or the client) will be doing differently at one step up?"

This respectful curiosity really embodies the supervision. The supervisor holds the boundaries of time, place, and their own ethical practice firmly, while being open and interested in how the supervisee works and how they see forward movement happening in the work they are doing, with respect for *however* the supervisee chooses to do it.

In their own clinical work, an SF practitioner will often be more interested in the client's *behaviour* than in their expressed *feeling*, and in general will not use ideas about unconscious processes, transference and countertransference, or the parallel process. She is more inclined to stay on the surface than probe the depths. However, as a supervisor, her interest is in what the *supervisee* believes and does in their work. If she is working with a person-centred practitioner, she may echo the supervisee's person-centred language: "feelings", "congruence". With a practice nurse, she is likely to respond in familiar nursing language, such as "patient" and "treatment".

If the SF supervisor is invited to work with someone wanting to look at unconscious processes and parallel process, again they will adapt their language to fit, following the supervisee's lead. Working with someone from another counselling model is similar to working with someone from another discipline altogether. The SF supervisor will be interested in the supervisee's views of how unconscious communications affect and assist the therapy under discussion. This work across models can be stimulatingly fruitful as supervisor and supervisee create pathways and bridges towards each other's beliefs and professional experiences, and learn how to collaborate with each other for the benefit of the supervisee's clients and work.

Each supervisee is unique, and the supervisor will also be aware of learning about what *this* supervisee means when they use *these* particular words. We try to make the conversation smooth and easy for the supervisee, not snagging or distracting them with jarring language.

Teaching SF supervision to SF trainees

It is quite simple to teach SF practitioners to use SF as supervisors, although it takes learners practice and attention to become skilled. These trainees already understand the philosophy and elements of the approach (MacDonald, 2007; O'Connell, 1998). Solution-focused therapy and solution-focused supervision work in parallel. All the elements of SF are revisited and used:

- tuning in to the language/world view of the supervisee, and being guided by the supervisee's agenda;
- recognizing the supervisee's existing strengths, skills, and resources;
- respectfully acknowledging problems and difficulties while not encouraging further problem talk;
- inviting the supervisee to describe and develop ideas about the preferred future (for their own work generally, or their work with a particular case);
- using circular questioning, that is, questions from the viewpoints of others, e.g., "What would the client's mother think of this?";
- looking for exceptions to the problem;
- finding out what the supervisee and their client are doing that works for them (both in the supervisee's practice and in the

client's way of running their life), and being interested in what will happen when they do more of that;

- collaborating to chart progress by various means, including using scales.

Briggs and Miller (2005), Trenhaile (2005), and Pichot (2005) each describe in much more detail some aspects of SF supervision.

In general, the central needs of these students are to grasp the double vision of holding both supervisee and their supervisee's clients in view, to master the additional more formal responsibilities of the supervisor, and to gain confidence.

Teaching trainees from other helping professions

It is also surprisingly easy to teach professionals from other disciplines, such as nurses, allied health professionals, drugs workers, or social workers how to do SF supervision. These workers tend to be interested in the precise yet simple language skills used, and are often attracted to the positive and pragmatic attitudes of SF thinking. While many (for example, nurses) use the medical model in their normal work, they are usually very willing to try something new when it comes to supervising colleagues.

Teaching trainees who are non-SF psychological therapists

Psychological therapists trained in other models might find it more difficult to learn to supervise in a solution-focused way, and often, understandably, prefer to supervise from their own approach. However, those who attend SF supervisor training willingly and with interest, seem very able to absorb this way of working. For some, this means that they will take on the SF approach fully in their supervision practice and perhaps even begin to use it in their therapeutic work; others may just pick up a few concepts or tools to incorporate into their usual style.

At first, learning the approach can feel awkward. As an illustration, in a recent SF training session with trained and experienced but non-SF therapists, pairs worked together to practise the use of scaling. Embedded in this exercise was the concept of non-expertness: the supervisor (or therapist) did not need to know the details of the problem. The interviewee was asked to silently imagine a change they wished to make, without describing the change and why they wanted to make it. The interviewer then asked their partner, "If 10 means you've made this change successfully, and 0 = the opposite, where are you now?", and explored details of "How did you get to X?", and "What will be different one step up, or as you move up the scale?"

In feedback at the end of the exercise, several interviewers expressed frustration that they were not told about their partner's problem and why the change was desired, and said they found it very difficult to restrain themselves from asking about these matters. They were naturally curious, and they honestly felt they were not being as helpful as they wanted to be. The speakers, though, to everyone's surprise, expressed pleasure and a sense of space and accomplishment in the short conversation. The interviewer's interest and encouragement was fully present, without the contamination of their views on the actual situation. This exercise demonstrates how beneficial—and how difficult—it can be for us as supervisors to leave our own ego or advice out of the conversation and simply focus on the supervisee's thinking.

Final thoughts

Mental health practitioners such as counsellors, psychotherapists, psychiatrists, and the like will usually trust the model or approach they first trained and practised in. There are many understandable reasons why practitioners may not wish to learn a different model, so, in my view, SF supervision, as other models, should be freely chosen by the supervisee.

Nevertheless, a great strength of the SF approach is its pragmatic adaptability to, and interest in, the needs of the client or supervisee. SF supervisors take respect for, and curiosity about, the ideas, language, and practice of the person they are working with as a main tenet of the approach. We adapt our language to that of the supervisee. We use the simple elements of the model to collaborate with the supervisee to help them to work better; we "coax expertise", in Thomas's (1996) delightful phrase. The SF approach allows us to supervise any professional who wishes to work with us in this way, simply, supportively and safely.

References

Briggs, J. R., & Miller, G. (2005). Success enhancing supervision. In: T. S. Nelson (Ed.), *Education and Training in Solution-Focused Brief Therapy* (pp. 199–222). New York: Haworth.

Hawkins, P., & Shohet, R. (2006). *Supervision in the Helping Professions*. Maidenhead: Open University Press.

MacDonald, A. (2007). *Solution-Focused Therapy: Theory, Research & Practice*. Los Angeles: Sage.

O'Connell, B. (1998). *Solution-focused Therapy*. London: Sage.

Pichot, T. (2005). Thoughts from a solution-focused supervisor. In: T. S. Nelson (Ed.), *Education and Training in Solution-Focused Brief Therapy* (pp. 277–280). New York: Haworth.

Thomas, F. (1996). Solution-focused supervision: the coaxing of expertise. In: S. D. Miller, M. A. Hubble, & B. L. Duncan (Eds.), *Handbook of Solution Focused Brief Therapy* (pp. 128–151). San Francisco, CA: Jossey-Bass.

Trenhaile, J. D. (2005). Solution-focused supervision: returning the focus. In: T. S. Nelson (Ed.), *Education and Training in Solution-Focused Brief Therapy* (pp. 223–228). New York: Haworth.

CHAPTER EIGHTEEN

Training for supervising transpersonal therapists and others

Suzanne Dennis

Over ten years, the Psychosynthesis and Education Trust has developed and delivered annual supervision training for therapists of any orientation who wish to supervise counselling and psychotherapy work using a transpersonal and integrative approach.

Transpersonal psychology is concerned with psycho-spiritual development.

An integrative approach is embedded in psychosynthesis. The founder of psychosynthesis, Roberto Assagioli (1888–1974), stated, "The position assumed by Psychosynthesis is a 'synthetic' one. It thus appreciates and weighs the merits of all therapies, all methods and techniques of treatment, without preconceived preferences" (Assagioli, 1967).

Assagioli was a pioneer of his time. He endorsed Freud's thinking, but also pointed out the limitations he saw in psychoanalysis. He was one of the founders of humanistic and transpersonal psychology, writing and teaching about his concept of the human psyche well before Maslow. He drew inspiration from eastern, as well as western, spiritual and scientific traditions. Psychosynthesis, therefore, sees itself as an open, non-dogmatic approach suited to training supervisors to work across orientations.

Evolution of the training

The supervision training has changed and lengthened in order to provide a robust training that meets the needs of supervisors in today's counselling and psychotherapy profession. Competent supervisors require a sophisticated grasp of relevant maps, a highly trained awareness of what is going on in the supervisory relationship, as well as a good ability to think systematically and ethically. The craft of supervision requires new skills. The training has evolved into a packed twenty-day course that, combined with study and practice hours, has been validated at postgraduate level.

Individual learning goals

This training requires students to identify personal learning needs depending on their previous training and experience. For those not previously trained in the transpersonal approach, time has to be allowed to read and reflect on this, and to increase familiarity with ideas about integration and eclecticism. Reading research on what works in therapy (Hubble, Duncan, & Miller, 1999; Miller, Hubble, & Duncan, 2008), can loosen fixed ideas about the rightness of a particular approach, and promotes open-minded enquiry, as can studying a case from different therapeutic orientations (Corey, 2001).

Supervision of supervision

Learning to supervise is challenging; not everyone is suited to this role. Containing anxiety, (both the supervisor's and the supervisee's), is demanding. Beginning supervisors may often resort to too much focus on teaching and structure, unconsciously distancing themselves from supervisees, or fall back on identifying with previous supervisors. For this reason, we require trainees to be apprenticed to an experienced (and trained), supervisor for supervision of supervision. Here, some of the challenges of supervising in practice, such as using authority and power wisely, systemic problems, and group dynamics can be given the space they deserve.

Supervision of supervision also provides cutting edge learning for the trainee supervisor through listening to and discussing recordings of their supervision sessions. This promotes awareness of unconscious processes, and enables reflection on the choice, style, and impact of a supervisory intervention on a supervisee.

The value of supervision of supervision is highlighted in an article by Packwood (2008), who recently completed a supervision training. It is titled "Gandalf's apprentice—the magic of supervision":

> To be the Wise One, Gandalf the white carries a great responsibility ... This ability does not come merely with age, with a short course or a bit of practice. ... This seems a much-neglected area both in the training and in the continuing development of supervisors ... We seem to overemphasise the "love" of theory and neglect the spiritual life of the supervisee ... We therefore need a developmental pathway that acknowledges more of the spiritual side of the supervisory process. An imitation or mentorship under the eye of an acknowledged wise supervisor is not widely seen as essential to a supervisee's development. [p. 36]

It is essential to explore the shadow motivations for supervising in order to assist the trainee supervisor to cultivate the capacities of presence, openness, and responsiveness. Supervisors might be motivated, for instance, by the desire for power, the wish for admiration, or the desire to keep up a defence that it is others who need help.

Presence

The ability to be open and to stay with the unknown is a key feature of the transpersonal approach:

> Whatever our theoretical framework and whether we are with a trainee, developing or experienced supervisee, while we hold

> authority it is important not to place the supervisee under psychic or actual pressure for specific outcomes. However much we know we must be able to let go, we must be involved but not attached to preconceptions of what ought to occur. [Dennis & O'Reilly, 2003, p. 38]

In psychosynthesis, the human psyche includes the spiritual, as well as the primitive, unconscious. The spiritual unconscious is where our sense of purpose and potential lie. If we repress the spiritual unconscious it can cause suffering and prevent growth and individuation, just as much as when we repress the primitive unconscious. Life offers us obstacles and challenges and we are each on an unfolding path. While the past has its influence, it is not an explanation of the present. Psychosynthesis works with both the primitive and the spiritual unconscious to evoke the self (best understood as the spiritual heart of a person), our potential. This transpersonal context holds awareness of the bigger picture of which we are a part.

Opening doors

Another working assumption of transpersonal supervision is that the supervisee "knows more than they know", that is, they know more about the client and the process of healing than they can access through the mind. Psychosynthesis supervision offers creative methods conducive to the transpersonal that allow the supervisory couple or group to transcend the structures of the cognitive mind. Guided imagery can dissolve a seemingly otherwise insoluble therapeutic block. Here, the supervisee is guided to identify and dialogue with an internal image or symbol representing the block, gaining insight and resolution. Drawing, mime, the use of symbolic objects, setting up constellations in individual or group supervision, provide penetrating ways to access the supervisee's wisdom, compassion, and the truth lying in the unconscious. The choice of pieces in sand tray work and the way we place them reveals new dimensions. Creative role-play, where the supervisee role-plays the client and the supervisor role-plays the supervisee, gives the supervisee a vivid experiential sense of what it is like to be the client. The supervisor can reflect on what it is like to be therapist with this client. A role-play is part of a dynamic supervisory process that allows the experience of being separate consciousnesses to dissolve and insight to emerge.

Intuition

The transpersonal supervisor needs to have ability to both play with and respect the unconscious, to use intuition, and to be able to support and hold the supervisee in the powerful feelings that can be evoked. They also need to facilitate considered reflection and interpretation by the supervisory dyad or group of what has emerged. As psychosynthesis therapist Rachel Charles' (2004), research showed, intuition is often accompanied by the sense of being right. We need to be wary, and at the same time to be able to treat intuition with respect. At best, these techniques bring tremendous insight and movement in the therapeutic process; at worst, they release energy that loosens up the interactive field in the supervisory and therapeutic systems.

Giving soul a voice in supervision

From the transpersonal meta-perspective, "supervision is a form of retreat", says Whitmore (1999). Supervisees communicate with their inner voice, images, and symbols, not only to uncover the meaningfulness of the countertransference, but also the subtle latent potential of the spiritual unconscious. The supervisor holds the space for the retreat, the holding for the retreat, and the transpersonal context for the retreat.

Why is it important to give the transpersonal space in supervision? Clarkson and Angelo's (2000) research found that the soul of supervision is as important as its body. Supervisees were asked to select and write about a significant supervision experience in order to find out more about what competences supervisees looked for in a supervisor. Various dynamic transpersonal qualities, such as "insight", "creativity", and "integrity", were just as important as "sound theory", "listening", "support", and "diverse knowledge".

Theory

Theoretically speaking, as far as models go (though the map is not the territory), we find it useful to draw on Hawkins and Shohet's process model of supervision which they call the "seven-eyed" model, where they see seven processes that are fruitful to explore in supervision (2006, p. 82). Just as Inskipp and Proctor (1995) added a seventh focus to Hawkins and Shohet's original six-foci model we have added an eighth all encompassing transpersonal focus.

Why choose to concentrate on Hawkins' and Shohet's model rather than other models which are described as integrative? (See Gilbert and Evan's integrative relational model [2000], or the models described in Part I of Carroll and Tholstrup [2001].) We find this model is useful in practice for practitioners from most psychotherapeutic orientations, from cognitive–behavioural to person-centred original trainings. It draws on systemic, psychodynamic, intersubjective, cognitive, behavioural, and humanistic approaches. It equips supervisors to adapt their system of supervision to suit the supervisee and increases their ability to work with a greater range of difference, especially trans-culturally.

The seventh focus that looks at the contextual systemic field is of a different order, as Hawkins and Shohet have realized as they have developed their thinking in this area (2006). Similarly, we would argue that the transpersonal context of the eighth eye is of a different order. While it could be argued that there is no need for a seventh or eighth eye as they permeate the other foci, it is essential to keep them on the map because, as Hawkins and Shohet say of the seventh eye, without it we "would lose the constant challenge that nearly all of us need: regularly to move our attention from what is naturally in our field of vision, to the wider domain in which we are operating" (2006, p. 102).

Indeed, often the spiritual is repressed, we shy away from the things that make us truly moved for fear of being overwhelmed, or because we defend against uncertainty, or fear being judged. Being on the edge, in a liminal space, seems too frightening, as can happen in an experience of spiritual emergence. Therefore, we need this challenge to remind us to take the risk to look at meaning and purpose, suffering, and the potential for growth in our lives, and allow the spiritual unconscious to have a voice. Here, we can be open to the mysterious sense that often we get the clients we need, to synchronicity, to archetypal patterns. We can be inspired by courage, integrity, humour, and love, as well as stay with, and accept, our helplessness in the face of suffering.

Transpersonal therapy or supervision should not be seen as the exclusive domain of transpersonal therapists and supervisors who have reached the "subtle" or "causal" levels of psychospiritual development, as John Rowan (2006) implies. The transpersonal is not up there or out there; it exists in consciousness, not outside it. In psychosynthesis, the transpersonal is seen as immanent: it is already there. There are a variety of ways in which the sacred can be cultivated and embodied; there is not one way. Evidence of this can be seen in other therapeutic orientations (see O'Hanlon, 2006), and in supervision (see Cameron, 2004; Shohet, 2008).

Supervisors do need to know enough about psychopathology to be able to guide supervisees to assess risk, and distinguish between spiritual emergence, spiritual emergency, and situations where psychiatric advice is indicated. They also need to know something about the distortions caused by the ego and narcissism that can accompany the psychospiritual journey.

Harnessing the power of groups

Group supervision can be particularly fertile ground for the transpersonal. In psychosynthesis theory, the stages of group dynamics are governed by the archetypes of love and will. Skilled handling of their interplay in group process results in more ability to think in symbols and imagery and access intuitive insights There can be a sense of trusting the process gained through travelling through the shadow of the group (which often involves attachment and rivalry about differing orientations) to the darker side of ourselves, discovering immanence as well as transcendence. We connect again to our common humanity. Sometimes we can feel the hair on the backs of our necks prickle in the presence of the group's soul. Or we may connect with the hidden purpose of coming together, which may be the conscious task or not.

Groups like this can enhance the supervisory experience of all the members and facilitate exploration of the unconscious to greater depth than individual supervision. Creative group experiential exercises are often used; these can be extremely rewarding especially in groups where there are different theoretical orientations.

Shadow

The breadth and openness of psychosynthesis, and its attitude of holding theory lightly, lends itself to supervising across orientations. However, the shadow side of inclusivity could be omnipotence. It is, therefore, imperative that, wherever appropriate, the supervisor has the humility to state that they know very little about the supervisee's orientation, that they are willing to learn more, and to think about the implications of this for the effectiveness of supervision and the supervisory relationship. Key to this is the initial contracting and regular reviewing. The supervisor has to determine whether they are willing to learn more about their supervisee's orientation and how to do so. It could be that it would not be wise to work together; it might not be what the supervisee needs, especially if s/he is a novice. Or it may be that the supervisor does not wish to spend time learning about that orientation and work on adapting their style.

The importance of developing the ability of supervisors to be aware of the implications of power imbalances, especially where the supervisor has an assessing role, and the ability to work with difference and diversity, cannot be over emphasized. Supervisors need to be able to work with difference, whether it is cultural, religious, gender, sexuality, age, disability, or difference in orientations. Where there is a power imbalance, such as being in the role of gatekeeper to the profession, we need to be open hearted.

Becoming a supervisor is an opportunity for tremendous growth. We are prompted to look back on our own training as therapists, on our own experience of supervision, and to take a more active role in being part of our profession. Engaging with the transpersonal and integrative approach is an exciting and rewarding challenge, which does not end with the training, but is instrumental in bringing strands together which carry us forward in a creative, ever-changing weave.

References

Assagioli, R. (1967). Psychosomatic medicine and bio-psycho synthesis. *Psychosynthesis Research Foundation, 21*.

Cameron, R. (2004). Shaking the spirit. Subtle energy awareness in supervision. In: K. Tudor & M. Worrall (Eds.), *Freedom to Practise: Person-Centred Approaches to Supervision* (pp. 171–188). Ross-on-Wye: PCCS Books.

Carroll, M. (2001). The spirituality of supervision. In: M. Carroll & M. Tholstrup (Eds.), *Integrative Approaches to Supervision* (pp. 76–89). London: Jessica Kingsley.

Carroll, M., & Tholstrup, M. (Eds.) (2001). *Integrative Approaches to Supervision, Part I* (pp. 11–89). London: Jessica Kingsley.

Charles, R. (2004). *Intuition in Psychotherapy and Counselling*. London: Whurr.

Clarkson, P., & Angelo, M. (2000). In search of supervision's soul: competencies for integrative supervision in action. *Counselling Psychology Review, 17*(4).

Corey, G. (2001). *Case Approach to Counselling and Therapy* (5th edn). Pacific Grove, CA: Brooks/Cole.

Dennis, S., & O'Reilly, J. (2003). The transpersonal in supervision. *Therapy Today*, August: 38–39.

Gilbert, M., & Evans, K. (2000). *Psychotherapy Supervision*. Buckingham: Open University Press.

Hubble, M. A., Duncan, B. L., & Miller, S. D. (1999). *The Heart and Soul of Change: What Works in Therapy*. Washington, DC: American Psychological Association.

Hawkins, P., & Shohet, R. (2006). *Supervision in the Helping Professions* (3rd edn). Maidenhead: McGraw-Hill.

Inskipp, F., & Proctor, B. (1995). *The Art, Craft and Tasks of Counselling Supervision*. Twickenham: Cascade.

Miller, S. D., Hubble, M. A., & Duncan, B. L. (2008). Supershrinks. *Therapy Today, 19*(3): 4–9.

O'Hanlon, B. (2006). *Pathways to Spirituality*. New York: Norton.

Packwood, D. (2008). Gandalf's apprentice—the magic of supervision. *Therapy Today*, July: 36–38.

Rowan, J. (2006). Transpersonal supervision. *Journal of Transpersonal Psychology, 10*: 14–24.

Shohet, R. (Ed.) (2008). *Passionate Supervision*. London: Jessica Kingsley.

Whitmore, D. (1999). *Handout from Supervision Training at Psychosynthesis and Education Trust*, London.

Epilogue

Penny Henderson

The range of ideas and approaches about supervision and supervision training represented in this volume is considerable, although it does not begin to represent all options available. I hope the references and different approaches will seed more cross-theoretical interest among trainers.

There *are* shared themes. Most authors concur, or imply, that teaching experienced practitioners calls for methodologies that capitalize on experience, enable deep reflection with more self-aware reflexive practice, and embody values congruent with the processes of supervision itself.

Most indicate the essentially contractual nature of a supervisory relationship. Learning to take authority, offer developmental feedback, be trans-culturally aware, and promote the development of ethical awareness is very important. Headlines are agreed, such as the importance of appropriate boundaries and an agreed focus within supervision

Our differences are also striking. All the last six authors were invited to say whether their approaches could usefully be generalized to offer supervision to supervisees who are not trained within their particular approach, and all are confident that they can. Yet, their particular ideas differ in crucial ways. The same implication is embedded in the earlier chapters, and readers will notice differing theoretical assumptions here, too. Some comparative research studies are badly needed.

The issues between these approaches that I think may be worthy of further research are as follows.

1. Is it essential that a supervisee bring live or recorded examples of their work for supervision to overcome omissions in disclosure of difficulties?
2. How far can training be adequate without some focus on organizational contexts of supervision?
3. Some approaches emphasize educational functions of supervision and do not emphasize the restorative functions or the containing power of the supervisory relationship. How does effectiveness of supervision vary as a result?
4. If transpersonal approaches can be applied within most theoretical frames, why are they not more included in supervision training?
5. What is the effect of not attending to unconscious process, and parallel process in particular, in supervision?

I think that more space to encourage reflective and reflexive practice about the social, political, global, and organizational contexts of the work is timely. We have always explored power in supervision in relation to difference and oppression. Yet, it is important also to weave into our approach to this topic a sense of our selves as embodied beings living within aging bodies. We have connections and responsibilities within personal and professional networks, and we are also a product of our own personal history and culture. For some people, spiritual matters, or the state of the economy or the planet, will frame or focus their study of how to be as a supervisor.

Most centrally, I want egalitarian and collegial values to be combined with a rigorous attitude to assessment from a position that notices, encourages, and celebrates development and life-long learning. Learning beyond the course will come from habits of reflection about experience, from feedback, and from time for creativity and self-care.

So, I end much as I began. I believe that courses must be connected to practice, and to current and foreseeable political and professional developments. Courageous leadership is important. Just as counsellors do not learn all they need to know in their initial training, so supervisors need many opportunities to develop within and beyond initial training. I hope this book will contribute to that.

APPENDIX 1

Professional organizations with some involvement in supervision

ABC	awarding body, www.abcawards.co.uk
BACP	British Association for Counselling and Psychotherapy www.bacp.co.uk
BABCP	British Association for Behavioural and Cognitive Psychotherapies www.babcp.co.uk
BAPCA	British Association for the Person Centred Approach www.bapca.co.uk
BAPPs	British Association for Psychoanalytic and Psychodynamic supervision (For psychodynamically focused supervisors) www.adbapps.freeserve.co.uk
COSCA	Counselling & Psychotherapy in Scotland www.cosca.org.uk
CPCAB	Counselling & Psychotherapy Central Awarding Body www.cpcab.co.uk
EAS	European Association for Supervision www.supervision-eas.org
EATA	The European Association of Transactional Analysis (for TA supervision and training), www.eatanews.org
HPC	(Health Professions Council) www.hpc-uk.org
NOS	National Occupational Standards www.ukstandards.org

UKCP United Kingdom Council for Psychotherapy www.psychotherapy.org.uk

UKRC United Kingdom Register of Counsellors www.ukrconline.org.uk

INDEX